The Streetsmart Guide to

Timing the
Stock Market

The Streetsmart Guide to

Timing the
Stock Market

When to Buy, Sell, and Sell Short

Colin Alexander

Second Edition

McGraw-Hill

New York   Chicago   San Francisco   Lisbon   London
Madrid   Mexico City   Milan   New Delhi   San Juan
Seoul   Singapore   Sydney   Toronto

3 4 5 6 7 8 9 0 DOC/DOC 0 9 8 7 6

ISBN 0-07-146105-1

This publication is designed to provide accurate and authoritative information in regard to the subject matter covered. It is sold with the understanding that neither the author nor the publisher is engaged in rendering legal, accounting, futures/securities trading, or other professional service. If legal advice or other expert assistance is required, the services of a competent professional person should be sought.

—From a Declaration of Principles jointly adopted by a Committee of the American Bar Association and a Committee of Publishers.

McGraw-Hill books are available at special quantity discounts to use as premiums and sales promotions, or for use in corporate training programs. For more information, please write to the Director of Special Sales, McGraw-Hill Professional, Two Penn Plaza, New York, NY 10121-2298. Or contact your local bookstore.

This book is printed on recycled, acid-free paper containing a minimum of 50% recycled de-inked fiber.

Library of Congress Cataloging-in-Publication Data

Alexander, Colin
    Streetsmart guide to timing the stock market : when to buy, sell, and sell short / by Colin Alexander.— 2nd ed.
      p. cm.
    Includes indexes.
    ISBN 0-07-146105-1 (pbk. : alk. paper)
    1. Futures. 2. Stocks. 3. Investment analysis. I. Title: Timing the stock market. II. Title.
HG6024.A3A45   2005

   332.63'228—dc22   2005012263

Contents

Preface to the Second Edition

How many times have you heard the statement, *Stocks have historically been a good investment for the long term,* and then thought, *Which stocks? When is the right time to buy them? Can I really hold some stocks forever?*

This book shows how to get the answers right sufficiently often to make investing in stocks really worthwhile. While these questions sound very basic, even many professionals don't always address them effectively. This was shown conclusively during the 2000–2002 bear market, which the first edition of this book forecast—it described, in detail and in advance, how to identify a trend reversal as it is developing, from bull market to bear market and back again. This book is therefore for all investors, from novices to professional money managers. It is based on technical analysis. *Technical* in this context does not mean complicated, but it does mean methodical. Technical analysis tells you when to buy or sell a stock on the basis of what its price action says about it. You can supplement technical analysis with fundamental analysis, which suggests which stocks to buy on the basis of companies' financial statements and assumptions about their business prospects. In fact, when technical analysis and fundamental analysis support the same conclusions, the results are likely to be spectacular.

This book describes step-by-step techniques for buying and selling stocks. It discards what you don't need to know, for there are few areas of greater information overload than the stock market. As an active trader in futures markets, I developed these methods for my own trading and described them in my book, *Five Star Futures Trades*. With appropriate modifications and additions, I have applied these methods to the stock market.

Soon after publication of the first edition of this book in mid-1999, the great bull market of the 1990s crested. Only technical analysis would have kept you in stocks for the last two highly profitable years. And only technical analysis told you when it was time to sell out—not at the absolute top but extremely close, in September 2000. Value analysis, as set out by Benjamin Graham and David Dodd in their great book, *Security Analysis,* would have had you out of most stocks from about 1997, when values were becoming extremely stretched according to historical benchmarks.

This second edition includes a substantial rewrite of the original material with some expansion of the concepts; it also includes new charts to illustrate the text and the use of technical indicators. The effectiveness of the methods described in this book is readily apparent from the updated examples that illustrate use of the indicators.

I hope this book helps you to invest in stocks successfully.

Acknowledgments

To Ruth Rodger, I owe an immense debt of gratitude. Her perceptive insights and constructive criticism were invaluable in developing a profitable system for trading futures. I have now carried these concepts forward, with substantial additions and modifications in some areas, for use in the stock market. I am also grateful to her for many valuable comments, and for the contribution of her writing and editorial skills to some parts of this book.

I am grateful to Peter Worden and the technicians at Worden Brothers, Inc., for the outstanding quality of their support for their *TeleChart* program, and for allowing its use to illustrate this book.

I am also grateful to Kimball Hansen and the staff at Ensign Software for permission to use one of their charts.

The Streetsmart Guide to

Timing the
Stock Market

CHAPTER 1

The Case for Timing

What to Buy and When to Buy and Sell

Market timing is the discipline that tells you *when it is timely* to buy a stock, or to sell one. Or to sell one short. Or to do nothing. Contrary to what some people say, timing the market in this sense is not about finding absolute tops and bottoms. That cannot be done with acceptable consistency. Instead, evidence from the action of the market itself answers the questions: *Is the stock (or the market generally, as represented by an index) going up, down or sideways? Is that pattern likely to continue? How can you tell when a significant move, up or down, may be starting to unfold?* Or *could this last surge be sufficiently overdone to set up a retracement?*

In one form or another, the discipline of timing the purchase and sale of individual stocks by means of technical analysis has always been used by successful futures traders, and by those successful hedge fund managers who have made a name for themselves. In most market conditions except for a roaring bull market—when you can buy pretty much anything—it is an absolute necessity given the unreliability of conventional security analysis. A former member of the Financial Accounting Standards Board of the Security and Exchange Commission, Walter P. Schuetze, is quoted as saying this: "Today's financial statements and reports are so complex and arcane as to be incomprehensible . . . Financial statements are not *fit for their intended use.*"[1] Fortunately, there are relatively few companies that engage in fraudulent accounting as perpetrated by the likes of Enron. However, *performance-enhancing* accounting is practiced almost universally, even by such stalwarts as AIG, Coca-Cola, General Electric, and Kellog. Sometimes, the booking of a loss or crediting back of a previous charge is a legitimate if discretionary exercise in smoothing the trend of earnings, although that exercise may be completely unexplained and it may also be extremely misleading.

This book shows you when it is timely to buy and sell stocks such as eBay and Johnson & Johnson (JNJ). It also shows how you can and, indeed, must avoid getting caught in a serious bear market for stocks generally or get caught in an individual stock that is going down the drain.

Looking for Great Stocks

Take eBay, for example (Fig. 1-1). This is obviously not a stock to mortgage the farm for. It is a relatively young company, and the stock has always been expensive, even when it made its retracement low in 2001. However, eBay has some of the characteristics that Microsoft had in 1989 when that stock was trading at 30 cents. The company is the overwhelming market leader in Internet auctions—everyone knows that. But the stock? Let's take a look.

In November 2002, eBay stock started moving out of an 18-month consolidation, and this was happening at about the time there was clear evidence that the major stock indexes were showing signs of making an important low. Sure enough, the stock started moving up from the $12 level, and over the next two years it didn't falter until it had reached almost $60.

A conservative investor—and all investors looking for a core portfolio of quality investments—could be looking for stocks such as JNJ (Fig. 1-2). Here is a stock that is in a perpetual uptrend on the monthly chart, interrupted by setbacks that are small, although sometimes of frustratingly long duration. It appears, however, to be as close as you are likely to get to a stock of the buy-and-hold variety for the very long term. If you bought

[1] *Barron's,* July 25, 2005, p. M10

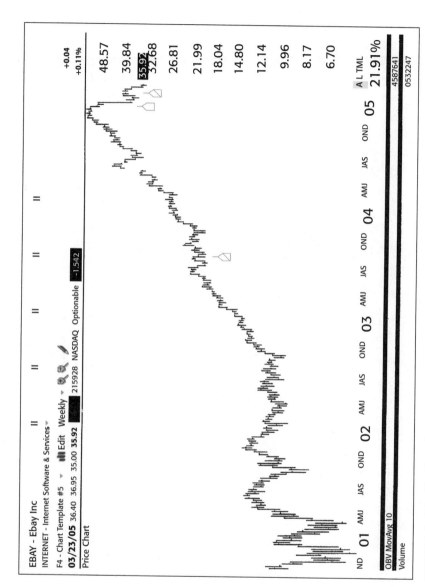

FIGURE 1-1 Weekly Chart for eBay.

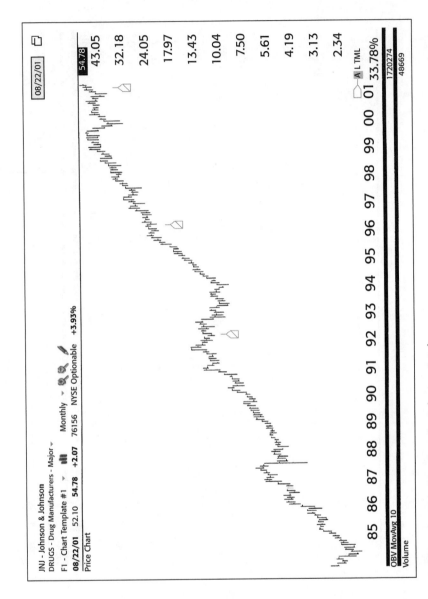

FIGURE 1-2 Monthly Chart for Johnson & Johnson.

JNJ at the absolute high for the move in January 1992, you paid $14.67. At the market bottom in August 1993, the stock made a low at $8.91. Assuming that you stayed in the stock, having failed to act on a sell signal, the decline of almost 40 percent would have been very uncomfortable to live through. However, you can readily see that this decline was not out of proportion to the gains in the stock during the 1980s. By August 1999, JNJ had climbed to a high of $52.94. At that price, it was almost four times what you paid for it in 1992 and more than five times its price at the 1993 low.

If JNJ is the kind of core-holding stock to look for, even conservative investors should keep an eye out for stocks like eBay that combine a unique franchise and, at certain times, a superb chart pattern. eBay achieved as much in two years as JNJ did in ten years!

Avoid Stocks Going Nowhere!

On the other hand, the kind of stock you need to avoid like the plague is General Motors (Fig. 1-3). In the 1920s, GM stock was the equivalent of Microsoft, and it multiplied in price by 150 times. Since then, things have changed for the company that was once an icon of U.S. business. After fluctuating wildly for several years, there was a reasonable, if not particularly convincing, buy signal at the $45 level in January 1996. At one point in May 2000 the stock made it to $94.63, at which point you would have doubled your money. Even so, compared with shares in other great companies, it was hard work owning this stock during the biggest bull market of all time. With alarm bells sounding for the overall market, including GM, you should have been out of the stock at or above the $65 level.

You might have bought GM in the mid-40s, and after holding it for the six years when it was actually doing something, you would have made a return of just 50 percent on your money. If you failed to get out, you could have held the stock for a round trip back through your purchase price and on below $30, where it had traded at the bottom in December 1994. Not a good experience!

The point of these examples is that it pays to look for companies whose shares have strong chart patterns. They are the ones most likely to continue to do well and, most important, are the least likely to set back severely. JNJ may be something of a tortoise compared with "whiz" stocks like eBay, but with its record of consistency going back many decades, it is most unlikely that the company will run into serious

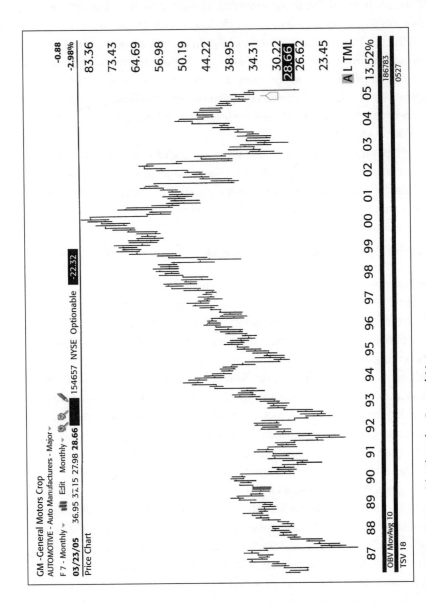

FIGURE 1-3 Monthly Chart for General Motors.

6

difficulties or that owning its shares will be hurtful to your portfolio. However, there is still a place for stocks like eBay in most portfolios, for a small holding, when charts show that it is timely to buy them.

Fundamental analysis does the job of looking at a company's financial statements and its business prospects. On its own, this does not necessarily lead you to stocks where the action is. A great-name blue-chip stock might look wonderful on the basis of its fundamentals, but in the real world people may not be interested in buying it. So the stock goes nowhere. On the other hand, when there are strong technical buy signals, it can be very rewarding to buy a stock like eBay that looks far too expensive or a stock about which you know little or nothing.

The point of this book is that you can tell from technical analysis when an individual stock or the market generally is in an uptrend or a downtrend or when the trend is sideways and ambiguous. Within this framework, the timing techniques described in this book tell you when the balance of evidence favors buying, holding a stock, selling, selling short, or doing nothing. In simple terms, this means buying a stock already showing, by going up, that it can continue to move up and vice versa when selling or selling short in a bear market.

As long as the technical indicators remain favorable, you can let profits run for a long time, occasionally for many years. When the balance of technical evidence turns against a stock, it is time to bank a profit or to prevent a loss from getting bigger. Over the years, you may buy and sell a stock several times. Since you can never tell beforehand how far down a stock might go once it starts going down, you must also be prepared to sell as well as buy. As was demonstrated in the recent bear market, even the greatest stock can fade and, in extreme cases, go down to nothing.

It is enough that the market-timing approaches presented in this book should deliver extremely good profits some of the time and that you should avoid devastating losses at any time. It is certain that you will sometimes misinterpret signals. Remarkably, you might think, you have to be right less than 50 percent of the time. When you are really right, you may succeed in buying a stock that goes up by 10 times or more. This, in essence, is the secret of timing.

The Great Reality Check

The broad generalization is correct that you must buy stocks for the long run. Otherwise, in 24 years, with inflation at just 3 percent, you halve both the real capital value and the purchasing power of the income delivered by fixed-interest securities. Inflation at 6 percent halves the value of money in 12 years. On the other hand, a company earning 10 percent on its equity and paying out 5 percent in dividends keeps half its earnings to reinvest in the business. Assuming profitable investment of the retained earnings, both the capital and the dividend should increase over the long term by approximately 5 percent annually, compounded.

However, along with the myth that you cannot time the market, market action between 1999 and 2005 showed that you cannot even hold onto a well-chosen portfolio of blue-chip stocks through thick and thin, as supposedly recommended by Graham and Dodd. That, in any case, is not what Graham and Dodd actually said. This is what they said in the first edition of *Security Analysis*, published in 1934, in the aftermath of the bear market that took the Dow Jones Industrial Average down from 386 in 1929 to 41 in 1932:

> Not many years ago "permanent investment" was one of the stock phrases of finance. It was applied to the typical purchase by a conservative investor, and may be said to have embraced three constituent ideas: (1) intention to hold for an indefinite period; (2) interest solely in annual income; and (3) freedom from concern over future developments affecting the company. A sound investment was by definition one that could be bought, put away, and forgotten except on coupon and dividend dates.
>
> The traditional view of high-grade investments was first seriously called into question by the unsatisfactory experiences of the 1920–1922 depression. Large losses were taken on securities which their owners had considered safe beyond the need of examination. . . . Even before the market collapse of 1929, the danger ensuing from neglect of investments previously made, and the need for the periodic scrutiny of all holdings, had been recognized as a new canon in Wall Street. The principle, directly opposed to the former practice, is frequently summed up by the dictum, "There are no permanent investments."[2]

[2] Benjamin Graham and David Dodd, *Security Analysis, The Classic 1934 Edition.* New York: McGraw-Hill, p. 228

The point is resoundingly valid, as it always has been, that no stock, no mutual fund, and no security of any kind can be regarded as a permanent investment beyond the need for review.

Sometimes You Should Sell Stocks and Buy Bonds

During the 1990s, there was a near-universal popularization among the mutual-fund-selling community of the case for investing in stocks for the long term and holding them through bull and bear markets, through thick and thin, until death shall you part. The corollary was that inflation was the death of capital if you invested in bonds and that only stocks would enhance wealth at a compound rate of at least 10 percent and, if recent trends were to continue, at a rate of 20 percent or more. Almost no one said that there were times to rotate investments out of stocks and into bonds. Allocating money into bonds was suggested, if at all, only as lip service to real diversification and as an almost superfluous insurance against the stock-fund sellers' unlikely misconceptions. In the event, between December 31, 1999 and December 31 2002, the assets of all U.S. stock mutual funds declined by 34 percent despite reinvestment of dividends. During that period, the rock-solid 20-year U.S. Treasuries rose by 24 percent without dividends, plus about another 18 percentage points in interest before tax. Many junior bonds did far better.

There really are times to buy and sell different asset classes. In a serious bear market for stocks, you *must* sell stocks. Depending on the economic and financial circumstances, as well as the technical indicators, you can buy bonds and hold them very profitably for a time but probably not for that perpetual long term and forever.

For the record, there have been many extreme and reciprocal swings in the market price of stocks and bonds. One was during the immense bear market in stocks between 1929 and 1932, and another was during the bear market in Japanese stocks between 1989 and 2002. In 1932, at the bottom of the Great Depression, long-term Treasury Bond yields fell almost to 2 percent although, because of the impact of the Depression on profits, yields on corporate debt not in default were much higher. Sometimes, stocks and bonds go in the opposite direction and sometimes both stocks and bonds can advance erratically in parallel, as they did in the United States from 1981. Twenty-year Treasuries almost exactly tripled between their ultimate bear market low in 1981 and 2005, but that increase in capital value did not significantly surpass the impact of inflation.

Indexes Comprise Good, Bad, and Indifferent

There is a real irony about those who say you should buy and hold stocks for the long term. They also say that it is reasonable to use an index representative of one's goals as a benchmark for judging the adequacy of performance. The Standard & Poor's (S&P) 500 might, therefore be said to be a reasonable benchmark for the adequacy of an individual or a money manager investing in a balanced portfolio of good stocks.

Consider the components of the S&P 500, as was done in 2005 by UBS equity strategist Tom Doerflinger and as reported in *Barron's*.[3] With heavy deal-making during the frenetic years 1999–2000, and with stocks leaving the index in consequence, 103 stocks had to be brought into the index at that time. In many cases, therefore, their inclusion occurred during the market's final frothing and with scant regard for underlying value. From a date a month before their inclusion, 21 of these 103 had declined by 75 percent or more by early 2005 despite the big gains from the 2002 lows. A surprising 134 of the stocks currently in the S&P 500 index would not qualify for inclusion in 2005 based on the parameters for selecting new components. Most of these laggards would fall short on market capitalization (minimum $4 billion), profitability (four consecutive quarters of profits as defined by generally accepted accounting principles, or GAAP), and a large enough public float.

In sum, although the history of markets tells us that investing in stocks is essential for the long run, there really are times to buy, times to hold, and times to sell. Technical analysis does not attempt to tell you when there are absolute tops and absolute bottoms, but it does tell you when there are signals to act—when the balance of evidence falls into place.

[3] *Barron's*, March 28, 2005, p. MW4

Six Primary Objectives

This book shows how to

1. *Buy the stocks most likely to have above-average performance, whether in established trends or just starting a potential long-term move.* The big winners, the ones with the potential to double or better, make investing worthwhile. At any given time, no more than 10 or 20 percent of all stocks are normally worth considering. With so many stocks to choose from, there is no need to compromise on quality. It is almost always better to buy on the basis of high-quality technical signals than to rely exclusively on fundamental analysis, which says nothing about timeliness or the overall direction of the stock.

2. *Run your profits, and cut your losses.* This book gives objective guidelines that show how to run profits and cut losses. Although you may sometimes stay in a great stock for many years, some stocks never get going. Then you lose three times. First, there is the loss in the stock trading below what you paid for it. Second, and often worse in the long run, is the opportunity cost resulting from not reinvesting the money in a better stock. Third, you may have to pay more tax than you should. Most people need to use their losses to offset capital gains tax after they bank the profits from their winning stocks.

3. *Sell when a stock or the market generally runs out of steam and before you get caught in a bear market.* Every buy-and-hold investor, by definition, makes a commitment to ride a bear market to the bottom—whether in a single stock, a mutual fund, or a portfolio that appears to be diversified but that comprises most of the same risks. This book shows how to avoid this disaster. Regardless of profit or loss, the foremost requirement is to protect your capital.

   You must not make the mistake of thinking that your stocks will buck the trend in a bear market. In a general bear market, 90 percent of all stocks go down. In the recent bear market, you could buy stocks that benefited from interest rates that were force-fed lower or from the declining U.S. dollar, which fell in response to those lower interest rates. Stocks that bucked the trend included metals and home-building stocks, and after an initial hesitation, the petroleum stocks joined them. Most stocks in the general list went down, and of course, those stocks that had gone up the most in the technology sector declined precipitously, with quite a number of once highly regarded stocks going to zero.

In a general bear market, you lose twice. You lose when your stocks go down, and you lose by not having the money available to buy bargains when the next bull market starts.

4. *Look after the risks, and let the rewards look after themselves.* A chapter on capital management discusses how to manage your money.

5. *Sell stocks short in a bear market.* This book discusses what all investors need to know about selling short. Even if you have no personal inclination to do so, you must know how to avoid riding a stock down while short-sellers profit at your expense.

6. *Take personal responsibility for your investments.* Owning stocks is like owning a business. You can employ a manager, or you can do the job yourself. Few businesses do as well as they should when an absentee owner farms out management.

Some people think of professionals in any field as people you can trust implicitly. Every profession includes charlatans and incompetents. The less you know, the more likely it is that your investments will be handled badly or for the benefit of the managers and salespeople rather than for your benefit. Ironically, there is a rough rule of thumb that the more prestigious the organization looking after your money, the more difficult it will be to recover losses if the organization lets you down. You can never rely on the regulators to help you—or the courts— assuming that you have money enough left to sue the financial manager that has abused you.

What You Need

This book, a computer with charting software, and a source of end-of-day stock prices provide the tools you need to be successful—if you don't already have a market feed, you may be surprised at the reasonable cost and how easy it is to use. You also need to make a commitment to set aside a moderate amount of time for homework to review your current investments and potential new ones. Investing should be stimulating and rewarding in every sense, although it has to be approached responsibly and in an organized manner, as you would approach any business.

For illustration, this book uses stock charts generated by the Worden Brothers' TeleChart software. There are other sources of data and several good software programs, but it is hard to beat TeleChart for cost and data management.

The TeleChart software includes two excellent technical indicators not discussed in this book. They are the *cumulative money stream* and *balance of power*. Developed by Don Worden, one of the pioneers of volume and money-flow analysis, these indicators show buying and selling pressure. The software comes with a booklet explaining these indicators. This book uses, in new ways, the similar On Balance Volume indicator, which can also be used with other software.

CHAPTER 2

Defining a Bull Market

Upward Zigzags

As a farmer has to know when the season is favorable for planting crops, so an investor has to know when conditions are favorable for buying stocks. This means buying stocks when they are going up in a bull market and not when they are going down or sideways.

It follows that in order to buy stocks when the season is favorable, you need a definition of a bull market, whether for the market generally as represented by the stock indexes or for an individual stock. It also follows that you will not go far wrong if you restrict the purchase of shares, and continuing to own them, to times when a bull market definition is in force. The good news is that a bull market, once established, may last for a very long time and often for a number of years and even for a decade or so. As a rule, really successful companies go on being successful, and their shares ratchet erratically higher in reflection of the increase in their underlying value.

A *bull market* or an *uptrend in a stock* occurs when the price action shows a succession of higher highs and higher lows on its monthly price chart. This pattern produces an upward zigzag (Fig. 2-1). As a general rule, the more tenacious and regular that upward zigzag, and the fewer erratic lunges upward or downward, the more likely it is to continue.

FIGURE 2-1 Bull Market Zigzag.

From a practical standpoint, it is enough to know what is actually happening—whether a market is in fact going up, down, or sideways. Many logical people, especially those new to markets, say that they would like to know what causes underlying patterns of supply and demand, and they are concerned by the frequent conflict between what they think ought to happen and what is actually happening. It is a truism, of course, that for every buyer there has to be a seller, and vice versa, and therefore one might be tempted to conclude that there is a standoff. Not so! What is important, and what is revealed by technical analysis and the approaches discussed in this book, is the relative aggressiveness and persistence of buying or selling. An aggressive buyer will take all the shares that are offered, say, at $10, and then will see what can be bought for $10.50 or less, and then at $11 or less, and so on. The number of shares traded at each price is there to see because the buyer leaves tracks that can be observed by others.

The opposite occurs when it is the seller who has to make the concessions—the price goes down. Of course, it practically never happens that any market goes nonstop in one direction. A large buyer's aggressiveness generally is tempered by patience. A determined buyer, such as a pension fund, wanting to establish a big position will buy some shares up to a certain price and then back off to see how much the higher price draws out sellers. Therefore, the price eases back a bit, and the pension fund comes back for more when the activity has died down, and the price has settled. When the desire to own the stock is strong, buyers will come back before the price falls below a recent low. And again, vice versa, when selling pressure is dominant. This is how the underlying forces of supply and demand create the pattern that appears on a chart as a zigzag.

Use a Line Chart

The monthly bar chart for General Electric (GE) shows that interpretation sometimes can be difficult, particularly when a market is going sideways, as this stock was in 1988 and 1989 and in 1994 and 1995 (Fig. 2-2).

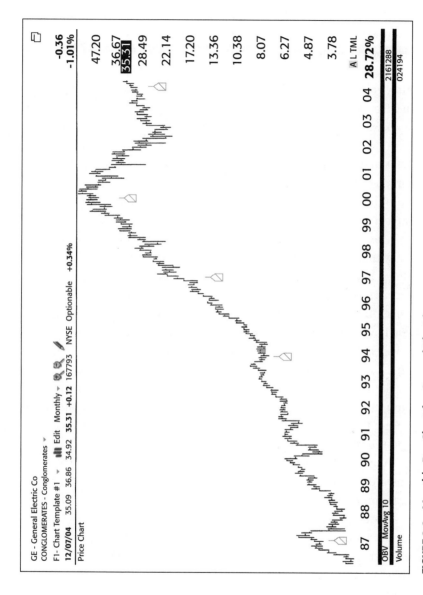

GE - General Electric Co
CONGLOMERATES - Conglomerates ▾

F1- Chart Template #1 ▾ ▮▮ Edit Monthly ▾ 🔍 🔍 ▱
12/07/04   35.09 36.86 34.92 **35.31** +0.12 167793   NYSE Optionable **+0.34%**

Price Chart

                                                                    -0.36
                                                                    -1.01%

47.20

36.67
35.31
28.49

22.14

17.20

13.36

10.38

8.07

6.27

4.87

3.78

A L TML

87 88 89 90 91 92 93 94 95 96 97 98 99 00 01 02 03 04 **28.72%**

OBV MovAvg 10   2161288
Volume   024194

FIGURE 2-2 Monthly Bar Chart for General Electric.

17

Although you may have a general idea that the next thrust out of sideways consolidation will be upward, the general idea lacks focus.

The remedy is to use a monthly line chart, which joins closes on the last trading day of each month (Fig. 2-3). The market-timing theory of zigzags will not tell you when price will hit the bottom, but it will show you by turning up as soon as the low is likely to have been completed. After going down and sideways for almost two years, the basing action in GE ended with a noticeably higher second low in early 1989, and the stock was on its way, with a powerful move up over the next 15 months. Although one almost certainly would have sold the stock in August 1990 and bought it back again later, for reasons described later, it turned out that for the next 11 years there were no serious aberrations from the uptrend. GE went from $3.75 to an eventual top at $60.75 in August 2000.

Most charting software can be set to produce a line chart automatically that connects the closing price for each time period. Thus, if GE closes at $50 at the end of June and at $51 at the end of July, the line moves forward one space and up $1 on the monthly chart regardless of price fluctuations during the month. (With some charting programs, you have to get the line chart by roundabout means. You can hide the price bars and retain the various studies, of which moving averages are one. A moving average set at 1 is the same thing as a line chart.)

Sometimes market action is so strongly bullish that you can identify an uptrend at a glance. There was no questioning the strength of GE during 1995 and 1996. Retracements stopped well above previous lows, and the stock was constantly reaching for new highs. In the strongest bull markets, which generally are also the safest ones in which to trade, upward market action shows persistence without either major surges or major plunges.

Reduced to its most basic terms, you can see that there is a low-risk new buy point each time the line turns up after correcting downward when there is, in addition, a clearly identifiable upward zigzag. This criterion, using an upturn in the monthly line chart on its own, constitutes a practical working tool for buying stocks.

Ideally, there should be other confirming indicators, and of course, if you wait until the end of the month, you may find yourself sitting on your hands while the market is running away from you—not a comfortable feeling! Since trends in stock prices tend to last a long time,

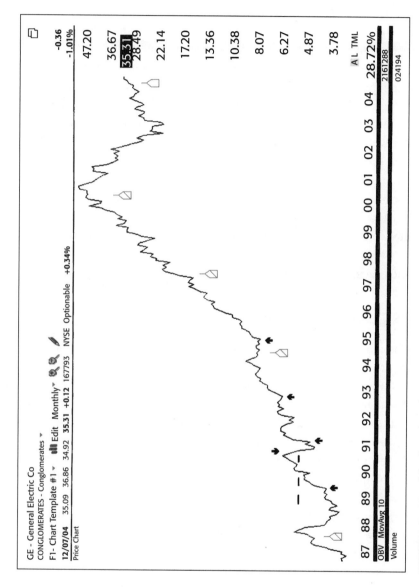

FIGURE 2-3 Monthly Line Chart for General Electric.

19

you generally don't go far wrong if you simply buy shares in a company such as GE when there is a strongly established uptrend and when you have the money on hand to do so.

In practice, even a strong bull market has aberrations, particularly when a bullish trend has been in force for some time. It can be all too tempting to sell a stock when it appears to be faltering, but it may be doing no more than digesting its earlier gains before continuing the uptrend. As noted earlier, aggressive buyers may be taking a rest. This means that some investors want to take profits in the stock, so the price sags a little. When the stock goes down further, additional investors want to lock in their profits. Some recent buyers may want to make sure that their small profit does not turn into a loss, and they sell too. After a time, selling decreases, and buying pressure again dominates as investors wanting to buy low on the retracement become more aggressive than the fearful investors baling out. Then the stock begins to move higher again.

Therefore, you have to distinguish between a normal retracement and one that may signify the start of a more substantial decline.

Be Confident in the Trend!

It is a matter of common sense, as well as prudent capital management, to retain confidence in a stock that violates an upward zigzag by an amount that is insignificant and probably aberrational. Accordingly, it is generally valid to continue a bull market designation when the price decline does not exceed the previous low by more than about 5 percent. A little more or less than 5 percent may be appropriate where there is an identifiable round number just above or below the 5 percent calculation. There is often a cluster of open orders, placed in advance by big-money investors such as pension funds, to buy just above a round number and a cluster of open orders to sell just below one. On balance over the long term, it pays to follow the money. As a very general rule, if the psychological support level of a round number attracts new money, most likely the stock is strong, and the uptrend will resume. If this psychological level is violated, then the overall desire to sell may be more pressing than any willingness to buy.

Look at GE in August and September 1990, when there were good reasons to expect weakness in the general market. GE had made a high at $6.29 and then began sliding. Given the low of $5.67 in February, one might have got out at about $5.30, or about 5 percent under that low. The stock subsequently declined to $4.70, where, with the wisdom of hindsight, you can see that it was a buy, not a sell. But you would not have known that until later, and in the meantime, the stock might have continued falling. The important thing was to be out of GE before losing money became painful. Never mind! You could get back in at $5.40 in November as a new zigzag was starting, in the form of a W, described below. Paying up for a small difference or even a somewhat bigger one is insignificant when you are looking for gains of 50 and 100 percent from a stock.

The buy signal in September 1995 came some time after the initial surge to a new high, which occurred the previous December and which, along with other confirming indicators—but not this one—could have justified a purchase at that time. In a sense, however, the delayed entry reinforces rather than detracts from the principle that a monthly upturn in a bull market that follows a monthly downturn results in an entry signal with a high probability of immediate success. It is a given that not all signals will be successful and also that some significant moves, both potentially profitable ones and potentially unprofitable ones, will occur without developing good signals.

The following is a summary of the profits and losses during the bull phases in GE stock from 1989 to November 2004:

Buy Date	Price	Sell Date	Price	Profit/Loss
May 1989	$ 3.75	October 1990	$ 5.15	$ 1.40
November 1992	$ 6.90	June 1994	$ 7.89	$ 0.99
September 1995	$10.72	January 2001	$47.50	$36.78
November 2003	$28.91	March 2005	$35.50	$ 6.59*
Total net profit				$45.76

*Still owned at that date.

The total net profit per share over the period of the chart, from May 1989 to November 2004, came in at $45.76, or 12.2 times the original purchase cost in 1989. The profit from a buy-and-hold strategy was $31.75, based on a last price of $35.50 minus the starting price of $3.75. You would have made $14.01 more by holding GE only during designated bull markets and selling the stock when market action negated a bullish phase. The result: More profit and far less grief!

It by no means always works this way—often you can indeed make more money with a buy-and-hold strategy, but just as important, if not more so, is risk management. However, if you don't keep an eye on the exit, you can get hurt, and if you are a latecomer to the party, the injuries can be life-threatening. However much faith you might have in GE, and regardless of the fact that things did turn around in the end, no one intentionally would want to ride with even such a blue-chip GE from $60 to its eventual bottom at under $30.

You would have been out of the stock at the following times, including almost all the general bear market from 2000 to 2003:

Time out of the market	Months
October 1990–October 1992	23
June 1994–October 1995	15
January 2001–December 2003	35
Total	73

There was bull market designation for just 58 percent of this 15-year period, which encompassed, of course, most of a major bull market and all of a major bear market. A timely sale in 2001, even if you didn't get the timing precisely right, protected a massive profit and averted a serious and long-lasting setback during the bear market. When out of the stock, you could have parked your money in Treasury bills or the money market, or you could have used it to buy stocks with stronger charts, which did exist but in entirely different areas of the board.

W Formations: The Start of a Bull Market

A bull market starts with a zigzag in the form of a W on the monthly line chart (Fig. 2-4). Of course, there are many more W formations than there are valid new bull markets. You have to consider these formations in conjunction with other technical indicators described in later chapters. Also, the reliability of an emerging bull market often is proportional to the length of time taken to develop it. The longer a stock

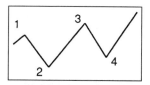

FIGURE 2-4 W Formation.

prepares for an upward move, the greater the probability of a valid W formation, and the farther the bull market is likely to go in due course.

Everyone loves to buy at the lowest possible price and to sell as high as possible. The reward is often greater and the risk is usually lower, however, when you buy into a strong bull market, such as GE between 1994 and 2000. Trying to get in on the ground floor of a possibly emerging bull market can be exciting when you get it right, so it is very much worth knowing what to look for.

The W formation that starts a bull market has an initial higher low that holds above the previous low. Although it may be psychologically more difficult to buy, a W formation is more bullish when the second low is significantly higher than the first one. When a market has been going down for some time, it may require more than one test of the initial low to finish shaking stock out of weak hands and to establish a springboard for higher prices. A successful third test down that holds above both the first and the second lows provides additional confirmation that the price may have stopped going down and the line of least resistance now may be up.

To identify a W formation on the line chart:

1. Look for a low at 4 on the chart that goes no lower than 2 and which ideally is somewhat above 2 so that there is no doubt that this low really is higher.

2. A monthly close above the close at 3 confirms the W.

After a stock has broken above 3 in the W formation, a retracement to the breakout level is so standard that you should not be concerned. This is normal price action. Some technicians suggest buying only on this expected retracement. However, the strongest stocks never retrace, and you can never tell in advance which these will be. The new upward zigzag remains in force as long as there is no new closing low beneath 2. In fact, a third test down that holds above 2 strengthens the interpretation that the stock has stopped going down and is holding what we call *support* (discussed later on).

The monthly line chart for GE shows a powerful buy signal in February 1991. On the principle that a market showing that it can move upward is likely to continue doing so, the fact that the second low was substantially higher than the first one enhances the probability that the ensuing move will be powerful.

As with all indicators, it is the concept that is even more important than the detail, and sometimes you may have to fudge the interpretation when other indicators confirm. The underlying philosophy is that you buy and sell on the basis of the balance of the evidence given that there are nearly always some minor conflicts even when there are very strong signals to act. Market action in GE shows slightly aberrational action on the monthly line chart in 1992. There is a good W, except for the fact that there is a wrinkled double top on the W at 3.

Similarly, there were actually four tests down in 1994, each one barely below the preceding one, before the price of GE stabilized, and the stock resumed its uptrend.

Then there is the V bottom in October 1998, from which the price surged upward without bothering to stop to confirm a zigzag until much later and at a much higher price. This aberration, however powerful, does not negate the principle that an upward zigzag comprising, by definition, a pattern of higher highs and higher lows is what a bull market is.

The chart for GE shows textbook bear market bottoms in the period 1987 to 1989 and a slightly imperfect one in 2002–2003. At that low, although there was a second lower monthly close, the second intramonth low held above the level of the first one. Note that there was not a single false W on the GE chart between the top and bottom of the recent bear market! The weekly and daily charts might have made you enthusiastic about attempting to get in early at a good price. However, as you can see clearly from the monthly line chart, the probabilities were against successfully buying low at a good price until the market itself showed basing action.

Zigzags Apply to All Indicators

The counterpart of a W at the start of a bull market is an M at the start of a bear market, discussed in the next chapter. The general principle of directional zigzags and Ws, and of M formations described in the next chapter, applies to charts of all durations: monthly, weekly, daily, and even intraday. There is a general principle that the reliability of Ms and Ws increases in proportion to the length of time they take to form. In practice, there are often very big M and W formations within which there are little bumps that signify nothing. The difference between a significant wrinkle and one that is not can generally be quantified on the monthly price-line chart by the 5 percent rule.

In addition to using Ms and Ws with price charts, the concept of Ms and Ws and directional zigzags applies to all indicators amenable to lineal plotting. These indicators include on-balance volume, moving-average convergence/divergence (MACD), and stochastics, which are discussed in later chapters.

Most people understand that you cannot expect any indicator to be right all the time, but many people look for the *magic bullet* that makes the most money most of the time. The upward zigzag on the monthly line chart comes close to being that magic bullet. It does not lead to success by any means all the time, but when it does, the rewards can come bountifully and almost effortlessly over many months and even years. The corresponding downward zigzag, discussed in Chapter 3, is less reliable for selling short because the stock market's major direction over the long term is upward, and markets spend approximately twice as much time in bull markets than they do in bear markets.

Defining a Bear Market

Conditions for a Bear Market

A bear market has the opposite characteristics of a bull market—a succession of lower highs and lower lows. However, there is one important difference in how it usually unfolds. The stock market tends to go sideways to upward about two-thirds of the time and down about one third of the time. However, a market often falls very much faster than it goes up. Sometimes a stock or the general market can drop like a rock, whereas a skyrocketing market is relatively unusual. It takes a constant flow of new money to make a stock go higher, but for a market to go down, all it requires is for the flow of new money to back off. A crash occurs when there is a vacuum under the market—a complete absence of buyers. Once there is a big enough decline under way, fear can lead to a crash as panicking sellers dump stocks at any price they can get.

The 2000–2002 bear market never saw general panics like the ones in 1929 and 1987. This one took on more of the character of relentless selling that alternated with rallies that stopped short of the latest highs. Stocks ratcheted down, but memories of the previous bull market induced enough investors to believe, wrongly for the most part, that declines provided opportunities to buy more stock at a good price. This is how bear markets work.

A Bull Market Dies Hard

It generally happens that bull markets make their eventual high, and bear markets begin, when valuations are stretched and optimism is high. Then, at some point, buying pressure starts to fall off, sellers become more aggressive than buyers, and the price fails to continue the pattern of making higher highs and higher lows. It can happen, although it seldom does, that a market simply stops going up and then collapses after making an upside-down V top. It almost invariably happens that there is another run at the top that fails to surpass the previous high, and there may be multiple runs at the top that fail. When in doubt during a strong bull market, you can generally live by the futures trader's saying: *A bull market dies hard!*

Nevertheless, bull markets always end, if only to go sideways, and there always will be bear markets eventually. The trend reversal as the bull market of the 1990s ended came in textbook fashion, with topping action that was drawn out over about a year. Eventually, the supply of new stock on the market, from initial public offerings (IPOs) and from those who had bought shares earlier at lower prices, overwhelmed the willingness of buyers to absorb what was offered for sale. All the factors reversed that had caused the bull market to feed on itself.

The fact that optimism continued to live on, discussed later as a contrary indicator, combined with the fact that there never was a full-scale panic, suggests, of itself, the possibility that the bear market may yet resume some time in 2005 or 2006.

Downward Zigzags and M Formations: The Start of a Bear Market

Reversing the pattern for a bull market zigzag, the monthly price chart for a stock shows a succession of lower highs and lower lows in a downward zigzag (Fig. 3-1).

FIGURE 3-1   Bear Market Zigzag.

You may not be interested in selling stocks short. However, the recent bear market has shown clearly and, for many investors, painfully that you must know what a bear market looks like and what establishes the technical conditions for short-sellers to start betting on a declining market. No doubt you have bought a stock only to find that it goes down instead of up, as you had hoped. As described in Chapter 22, it is possible to reverse the process by selling first and buying back later. If the stock has gone down, the short-seller makes money, and in effect, it could be the money that you lost.

Bear markets start with a downward zigzag in the form of an M on the monthly line chart (Fig. 3-2). Then a pattern of successively lower highs and lower lows gets under way. Rallies are caused by those wanting, mistakenly, to buy low and by short-sellers banking profits.

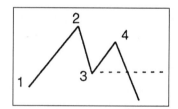

FIGURE 3-2   M Formation.

To identify an M on the line chart:

1. Look for a downturn at 4 on the chart that goes below the one at 2.
2. When there is a close below the one at 3, an M formation is confirmed.

Reversing the pattern of an emerging bull market, there may be an upward retracement back to the breakdown level before a more sustained decline gets under way. Until there is a new bull market designation, don't be fooled into thinking that a retracement means that the stock is now resuming its uptrend. There may be a retracement all the way back to the right-hand high of the M without violating its validity. In a confirmed bear market, the price stops at that level, and in a very weak market, it stops much below that level.

As you can see from the chart for General Electric (GE) in Chapter 2, the bull market in that stock did end, and its decline from top to bottom was 64 percent. The chart for GE formed a huge M over a period of about a year, with a big plunge to the middle of the M before the price staggered back to make the lower right-hand high. The length of time it took to form this big M accords with the principle that the longer a pattern takes to form, the greater is its significance.

Nortel in a Bear Market

As is now generally known, weaker companies than the mighty GE did far, far worse during the bear market, with many disappearing altogether. The formerly great Nortel Networks (NT) was once at the top of the market, as fine a blue chip as could be found on the board. Prestige, however, does not necessarily mean that the underlying value is sound or that things cannot go wrong (Fig. 3-3). The monthly line chart for NT shows that the stock was in a powerful, if erratic, bull market during the 1990s. It went from a low of $1.78 in April 1989 to a high of $89 in July 2000. The final maniacal acceleration took the price to its eventual high in less than two years from a low of just $6.70 in October 1998.

Once NT made its decisively lower high in January 2001, it was "game over" for this stock. At that level, there were, no doubt, those who thought that it was cheap simply because it had come down so far from the high. But the new trend was unmistakably down. Never mind that this was a price just half what it had been at its high; you had to look where it had come from over the preceding two years. By that measure, the stock was still high.

Once the stock went through the monthly low in 1998, from which it began its final ballistic flight, its bull market had its back completely broken. During this decline, it was remarkable how many people close to the high-tech industry were oblivious of the fragility of the company's fortunes. Even for many close to the company it was "holy writ" that this one-time hundred-billion-dollar company, once rivaling Microsoft and GE in market capitalization, was as solid as the Rock of Gibraltar. It eluded them that even without the accounting problems that were to come to light subsequently, NT had very serious problems.

The technical picture showed that when NT turned down in February 2001, it was even then by no means too late to sell. In the event, it was never too late to sell. Once the stock turned down there, it continued its sickening slide all the way to a mere 43 cents in November 2002.

The chart for NT illustrates both sides of the futures trader's adages: *There is no price so high that it cannot go higher still,* and *There*

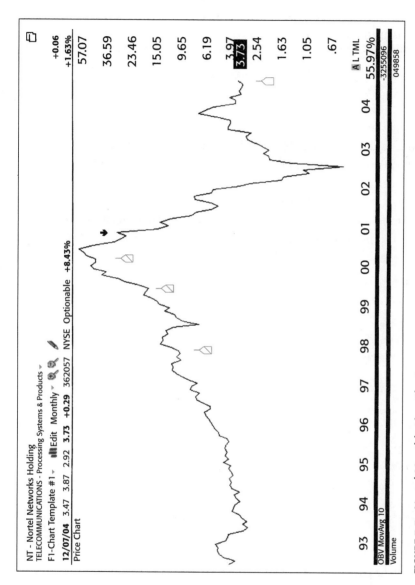

NT - Nortel Networks Holding
TELECOMMUNICATIONS - Processing Systems & Products ▾
F1-Chart Template #1 ▾   ▥ Edit Monthly ▾ 🖉 🖉
12/07/04 3.47 3.87 2.92 3.73 +0.29 362057 NYSE Optionable +8.43%
Price Chart

+0.06
+1.63%

57.07

36.59

23.46

15.05

9.65

6.19

3.97
3.73

2.54

1.63

1.05

.67

Ⓐ L TML
55.97%

OBV MovAvg 10   -3255096
Volume   049858

93   94   95   96   97   98   99   00   01   02   03   04

FIGURE 3-3 Nortel Monthly Line Chart.

31

is no price so low that it cannot go even lower. Regardless of what the future may hold for NT, market action favored more strongly a short sale at the end of 2004 than it suggested any reasonable prospect of making money by buying it.

Some Stocks Don't Come Back

In its own feeble way and at least for now, NT has survived. However, even the strongest of blue chips may not merely be humbled as NT has been. They may crumble to nothing, as did many technology stocks in the 2000–2002 bear market. Until after the event, you can never know for certain which stocks will or will not pull around or at what price level. Once you get locked into a real disaster like Enron, a longtime component of the Dow Jones Utility Index and once regarded as a solid and stable blue chip, you may find yourself riding a stock to a decline all the way to zero.

CHAPTER 4

Sideways Markets

Endless Chop

You are in the stock market for one reason—to make money. Therefore, it is as important to know about *sideways,* or *trading-range, markets* as about bull and bear markets. It is a truism that you can't make any worthwhile money in a stock that is stuck in a trading range. You may want to be patient with a stock that has done well for you, but you don't want to put new money into a stock going sideways, at least until it shows that it may be ready to start a new move up. Otherwise, the only justification for holding a stock going sideways is if you get a decent dividend. For most serious investors, this is not what makes the investment worth the trouble. Worse, you are almost certainly tying up money that could otherwise be invested in real winners. Figure 4-1 shows a sideways, or trading-range, pattern.

FIGURE 4-1 A Sideways or Trading-Range Pattern.

Conditions for a Trading Range

There are intermittent uptrends and downtrends, but they never seem to last. Often the stock stops going up somewhere around the level of the previous highs and stops going down somewhere around the level of a previous low. In other words, it seems to chop around endlessly without really going anywhere.

You must understand and internalize the fact that most of the time the majority of stocks are not worth owning. Sideways action, ambiguity, and perversity represent normality in the stock market. Even in the strongest bull market, as few as 10 to 20 percent of all stocks show really good technical action. In a bear market, the percentage of stocks in a confirmed downtrend may be higher than 80 to 90 percent because a general decline is more comprehensive than a general bull market.

Wal-Mart in a Trading Range

A major problem for many investors is that a stock going sideways may appear to have substantial underlying value that the investor hopes the market will recognize eventually. However, a stock is almost certainly going sideways because of a lack of interest in either buying it or selling it, for whatever reason.

Wal-Mart (WMT) is a company that has performed wonders both for consumers and for shareholders (Fig. 4-2). You could have bought WMT at $3.97 on the buy signal in January 1989 and held onto it until December 2004, when it was worth $52.50, which is a very satisfactory return. However, this stock exemplifies the adage that most investments tend to make money in surges. Year in and year out, Wal-Mart continues to increase sales and profits and to enhance shareholder value. Better yet, it pays a dividend that has been increasing steadily and at a rate of increase of almost 17 percent over the five years to 2004. At that rate, the rule of 72 suggests that its dividend yield of just 1 percent will double every four years or so.[1] The trouble is, of course, that WMT is such a great stock that its price tends to get ahead of its

---

[1] The rule of 72 states that a money will double in the number of years equal to 72 divided by the rate of interest. Thus, at 8 percent interest, compounded annually, money will double in (almost exactly) 9 years (or 8 years at 9 percent interest).

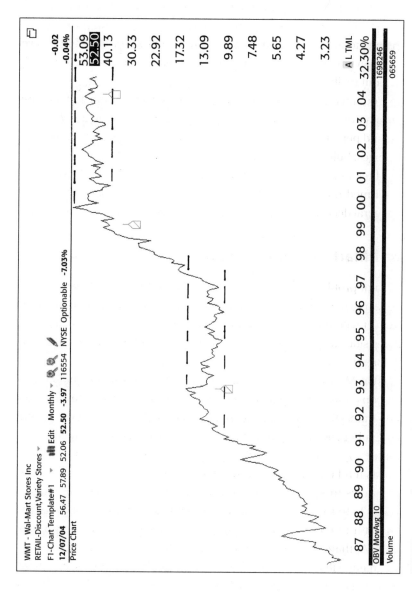

FIGURE 4-2 Wal-Mart Monthly Line Chart.

underlying value. Even if the dividend continues to double every four years, it will still yield only 4 percent in 2012.

After WMT had reached the $12 range in September 1991, it then got stuck in a seemingly interminable trading range until the breakout above the 1993 high of $17 in 1996, six long years later. Then, of course, the stock went on climbing to an eventual high of $70.

Even a company as solid as Wal-Mart was not immune to the ravages of the ensuing bear market, which took the price down to a low of $41.44 in October 2000, for a decline of 40 percent. However, the mere fact that WMT stopped going down did not mean that the stock was going to go up. Instead, a period of seemingless endless chopping began, which was still very much in progress in December 2004. WMT began trading in a broad sideways range between the 2000 high and the 2001 low, and there were no signs of it ending, except that it seemed to be more likely to test the low of the range before testing the high, possibly repeating the chart pattern between 1991 and 1996.

Although this is obviously a fantastic company, there is little good about it that is not well known and represented in the price of the shares already. At the end of 2004, the stock was trading at 22 times its expected earnings for that year, whereas the company's earnings growth rate for the preceding five years was just 13 percent. Using the criterion for valuing growth stocks that these two numbers should be approximately equal, it could take a further three or four years of consolidation before the next leg up starts. In the meantime, there were some known headwinds that might delay the next upward thrust. Interest rates were rising, making this stock's tiny yield less inviting. In addition, the decline of the U.S. dollar was almost certainly taking its toll on pricing as imports became more expensive.

There is little doubt that Wal-Mart will continue to be a sound investment over the very long term, particularly if it is able to export its business model successfully. Realistically, however, the chart for WMT in December 2004 strongly suggests that money would be better invested elsewhere and not put at risk until there are signs that the next upward surge may be getting under way.

Paradoxically, as we shall see in Chapter 11, trading-range markets often set the stage for some of the biggest moves. However, you don't know when, if ever, any worthwhile move might start until technical action shows that it might start. Paradoxically too, the longer a trading range lasts, the more substantial the eventual move might be.

CHAPTER 5

Volume and On-Balance Volume (OBV): Follow the Money

The Difference between Persistent and Random Market Action

When the buying is persistent, the chances are that an uptrend will continue, with fluctuations on the way as those intentionally buying low and selling high make their move within the intermediate fluctuations. In due course, the major trend may reverse—most likely when there is a general bear market—but it may take a long time before this happens and far longer than you might expect. When at last it is the selling that becomes persistent, the probabilities favor a downward extension and a major correction or a bear market, as we saw in Chapter 3.

This chapter shows how to interpret what is happening to the forces of supply and demand for stocks beyond the day-to-day noise-on-the-line fluctuations in stock prices. One day, one week, or a month when there is a surge in volume, this shows that if the price goes up, there is a bulge in demand. When the price goes down and there is a surge in volume, the selling pressure is heavier. You can see a surge in volume on a vertical volume bar displayed underneath the price chart.

Buyers take all the stock offered and keep moving their bids up and taking what sellers are prepared to offer at successively higher prices until they have succeeded in getting all the stock they want. It stands to reason that when you want to buy something but can't get it at your price, you have to increase the amount you are prepared to pay and then see if anyone wants to sell to you at the higher price. When buying is aggressive, you can expect an increase in both volume and price. Once a rising price trend can be seen to be under way, some potential sellers will be attracted to take advantage of the higher price. Others, in seeming contradiction of most people's understanding of the law of supply and demand, will refrain from selling in the expectation that the price will go higher still. Still others, seeing the rising price and the newfound aggressiveness of buyers, get on the bandwagon for the ride.

When, on the other hand, there is persistent selling, for whatever reason, and when that selling is less and less willingly absorbed by buyers, the price has to go down to find takers. Lower prices will certainly lead some investors to think that they are buying stock on sale, at a bargain price, but the declining price will lead others to sell precisely in order to protect themselves from the risk of the price going lower still.

There is constant ebbing and flowing in both price and volume, most of which occurs randomly. However, the general principle is valid in the stock market that you can detect persistence in buying pressure or selling pressure. By extension, therefore, it is better to buy a share that shows, by persistent buying pressure, that it is going up. Similarly, the general principle holds that persistent selling pressure is likely to precede more persistent selling that is likely to drive the price lower, and the price may go down a lot more.

Trading volume provides the raw data with which to analyze buying and selling pressure. The standard approach to interpreting trading volume is to assume that in bull markets there should be higher volume on days when the market goes up and lower volume on days when it declines. A bear market should have the reverse—higher volume on down days and lower volume on up days. Also, when there is a greater frequency of days when the price goes up, you can tell that it is the buyers who are more persistent, and vice versa when there are more days when the price declines.

Short Surges May Be Meaningless

A short-lived surge in trading activity may mean nothing. It could simply be that one or more large institutions are repositioning their holdings, with both the buyer and seller having their own reasons to trade. On the other hand, when buying or selling pressure becomes both pronounced and also persistent on one side of the market or the other, it may be that smart or big money (often but not necessarily the same thing) wants to build or liquidate a position with some degree of urgency. As a general rule, very big and smart money takes its time to build a position. If these investors want to buy 10 million shares and average daily volume is half a million shares, it may take several months to complete the purchase, by buying shares when they can, sometimes just 10,000 or 20,000, sometimes bigger lots, depending on what is offered at the price they are prepared to pay. If they bid for the entire 10 million shares all at once, the price would be jacked up in front of them: You don't intentionally make it a seller's market when you want to buy.

An immense bulge in volume may occur when there is a big announcement of news that changes everyone's perception of a stock. This may signal the start of a new thrust in price up or down. On the other hand, when volume is really immense, it may signify a buying or selling climax and then at least a temporary reversal of direction. Short-lived buying climaxes at tops occur relatively seldom, but climactic panic selling is a notable characteristic of market bottoms.

Volume Can Forecast Price

A reliable way to tell the difference between a short-lived surge in volume and the kind of persistence that may indicate a trend in both buying and price is to generate a cumulative tally of what volume is doing and to look at the net result of what is happening *on balance.*

To create the *on-balance volume* (OBV) indicator, each day's total trading volume is added to the cumulative sum when the closing price is higher than the close of the previous day. When the closing price is lower, the day's volume is subtracted. When there is no change in price, the volume goes the same way as it did the last time the price changed. When the cumulative sum is plotted on a chart, normally it should rise steadily when price is rising, and it should decline steadily when price is going down. In a rising market, there are more days when the price goes up rather than down. Also, total volume tends to be higher on those days when the price goes up. On days when the price goes down in a rising market, buyers take a rest, but sellers are not aggressive. Thus volume backs off. In a declining market, selling pressure predominates, and rallies are weak, with lower volume on the days price rises.

Joe Granville and Don Worden, working independently, noticed that when there is divergence between OBV and price, volume generally precedes price. This means that in a trading range, volume may give advance warning of the direction in which the price is likely to go eventually, when it breaks out of the range. When price appears to be going one way and OBV the other way, it may forecast a trend reversal, with OBV showing the way. OBV can sometimes start diverging from price quite a long time before the reversal in price occurs. The idea is that smart money starts to build a position, or to liquidate one, quietly and before the price of the stock responds.

Early warnings from OBV are particularly useful when a stock has been going sideways for some time. Price action alone may not tell you anything about which way the stock is going to break out or when. Much as a saucepan coming to the boil starts to put upward pressure on the lid, OBV may show that pressure to break out of the range is developing, especially when there is a pronounced increase in overall volume.

When price is strong and makes a new high, OBV should confirm it. If it doesn't, there is negative divergence, and it may be a sign that buying pressure lacks staying power. Similarly, failure to confirm in a bear market may mean that selling pressure is easing, and at least there may be a rally, if not necessarily a trend reversal.

New Applications for OBV

Granville originally used OBV on daily charts. But OBV is even more useful when used with monthly and weekly data, and there is no more powerful indicator of the potential for a major long-term trend to continue. Since most fluctuations in price occur within a major trend (whether up, down, or sideways), it is invaluable to confirm the direction and the structural soundness of that trend. As we saw in Chapter 2, the best stocks to own are ones in a long-term uptrend on the basis of zigzags on the monthly chart. OBV often confirms this price action for a very long time in a strongly trending market. When OBV remains positive during retracements, it can help you to maintain the confidence required to stay with a stock.

A refinement of Granville's use of OBV is to plot the OBV line (OBV 1) together with a 10-bar moving average of OBV (OBV 10). If possible, therefore, use software that can perform these functions. (With the Worden TeleChart software, you must superimpose a 10-month moving average of OBV 1 using the moving average command.)

Let's proceed now to a list of the principles for using OBV that are applicable to charts of all durations: monthly, weekly, and daily.

Interpreting OBV

The underlying principle is that a bullish market should have higher volume on days (or weeks, or months) when the price goes up and lower volume on days when the price declines. In addition, there should be more days over a period of time when the price goes up than when it goes down. And vice versa in a bearish market. Action is like the waves lapping toward the shore, with net progress toward land when the tide is coming in and still lapping toward the shore but with net outward progress when the tide is going out. These points apply to monthly, weekly, and daily charts:

1. The most bullish pattern occurs when OBV 1 has established an upward zigzag above a steadily rising OBV 10 on the monthly chart.

   There can be minor aberrations, particularly when the two lines remain close together and the deviation from the trend is barely perceptible. As when using the monthly price line to interpret the major trend, it is important to try to see the big picture and to avoid getting distracted by little bumps on the chart.

2. The most bearish pattern occurs when OBV 1 has established a downward zigzag below a steadily declining OBV 10.

3. OBV gives a buy signal when OBV 1 crosses the rising OBV 10. A downside crossover constitutes a sell signal when OBV 10 is pointing *down.*

4. OBV also gives a buy signal when OBV 1 has been above a rising OBV 10 and it makes a new upturn. We assume that both OBV and price should be starting the next leg of an upward zigzag. A corresponding downturn below a declining OBV 10 constitutes a sell signal.

5. The strongest and most reliable bull moves generally begin after the two OBV lines have started rounding upward for many months on the monthly chart. Rounding on a chart of any duration shows gathering momentum.

6. A bulge in OBV 1 far beyond OBV 10 may indicate a buying climax when it occurs to the upside, or it may indicate a selling climax when it occurs to the downside. A climax means that there has been a scramble to buy or sell. Such panic buying or selling often occurs prior to a significant retracement, which may turn into a trend reversal.

7. Many of the most extended market declines start with a pronounced weakening in the OBV line for many months. This pattern is a reflection of smart money liquidating stocks that probably have been bought at much lower prices a long time ago and possibly also of smart money entering new short positions.

8. When a stock makes a higher high in price that is not accompanied by a higher high in OBV 1, it is likely that buying pressure is fading. The next move in the stock may be down, not up. Smart money may be selling or even going short. Similarly, when OBV 1 fails to accompany price to a new low, it is probable that knowledgeable investors are starting to accumulate the stock.

9. When buying a stock, the weekly and daily OBV charts should normally both line up to confirm an OBV buy signal on the monthly chart. When selling short, they should both line up to confirm the OBV monthly sell signal.

OBV and Exxon Mobil

The monthly line chart shows how both the price of Exxon (XOM) and OBV began trending strongly upward in 1995 and continued trending strongly upward until the climactic surge in October 2000 (Fig. 5-1).

Price ran into resistance in July 2001 just below the high of the preceding October, but there was a very substantially lower high for OBV. When price and OBV turned down, the price of the stock began a significant decline in conjunction with the market generally, as represented by the major stock indexes. From top to bottom, XOM went from $47.72

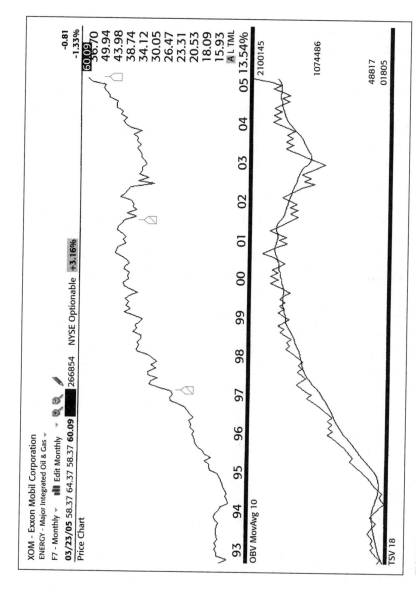

FIGURE 5-1 Monthly Line Chart for Exxon Mobil with OBV 1 and OBV 10.

to $29.75, with OBV and downward zigzags in price confirming all the way and with OBV 1 most particularly confirming until its final clmactic downward spike.

The four lows in OBV 1 in 2003 look like the coil of a spring, and indeed, futures traders use exactly that expression to describe a market winding up for a more powerful move up or down. If it had not been for OBV 10, you might have feared that XOM was running out of steam, but the moving average for OBV never wobbled even as both price and OBV 1 dipped in mid-2003. Sure enough, in April 2003, OBV broke out to the upside convincingly along with the price of XOM. Note that the monthly line chart for XOM continued to show a steady upward zigzag pattern into 2005, actually doing better than OBV. This is the kind of chart pattern to stay with, and not to get jostled out of, so as to allow for the possibility of XOM moving from the $60 range toward $100.

The weekly chart for XOM from 2002 until early 2004 showed such a bearish pattern for OBV that one would not want even to consider buying the stock until that changed (Fig. 5-2). Finally, toward the end of 2003, OBV 1 had established an erratic but essentially clear pattern of higher highs and higher lows, with OBV 10 generally confirming. The big bulge in OBV 1 in early 2005 suggested the possibility that there had been at least a temporary buying climax, but given the overall strength, there was no cause to consider selling.

The daily chart for XOM shows price going sideways with a barely perceptible upward bias toward the end of 2004, whereas OBV clearly has a downward bias (Fig. 5-3). Traditionally, followers of OBV would have called this action *negative divergence* and would have expected the apparent upward bias in the sideways pattern to fade and to be resolved with an eventual downturn in price. Sometimes, and in fact quite often, you have to avoid letting the daily chart make you impatient. Once price and OBV both broke strongly to the upside on the daily chart, XOM was on its way. The small upturn in OBV after crossing OBV 10 in January 2005 provided a signal, in accordance with this indicator, to buy the stock at $51.60. It was to move very rapidly above $60 within a few weeks. In view of the power of that move, the stock was entitled to a period of consolidation, which appeared to be occurring in March 2005.

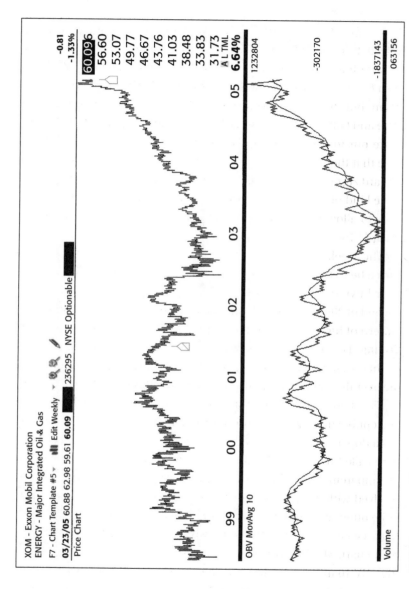

FIGURE 5-2 Weekly Bar Chart for Exxon Mobil with OBV 1 and OBV 10.

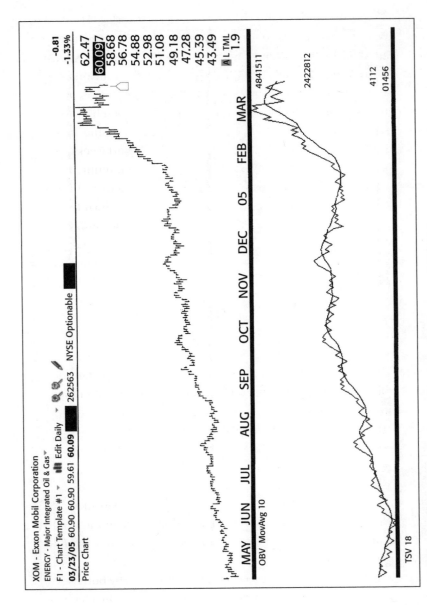

FIGURE 5-3 Daily Bar Chart for Exxon Mobil with OBV 1 and OBV 10.

OBV and Nortel

The monthly, weekly, and daily charts for Nortel Networks (NT) show how OBV was sounding the alarm when the stock was making its top and beginning the long plunge. On the monthly chart, the August 2000 high in price was substantially higher than the previous one (Fig. 5-4). In the meantime, however, OBV merely equaled its previous high. Once OBV 1 had crossed below OBV 10 in October, there was essentially no justification for continuing to own the stock. Although the stock was to halve in price within a few short weeks, you had to consider where the stock had come from. After multiplying in price so many times, a halving in price still left NT far above where it traded during most of 1999. The big bulge in volume, shown by the vertical bars in August, September, and October, was accompanied by faltering in both price and OBV. This might have suggested that there was a massive shift from profit-takers into the hands of emotionally driven late-comers who thought the sky might really be the limit. (The huge surge in volume in 2004 merely reflects the fact that $10,000 will buy a thousand shares of a $10 stock but only a hundred shares of a $100 stock.)

See too that there was a really clear-cut M in OBV 1 at the top in 2000 and that it was more clearly defined than the one for the price line: Ms and Ws occurring in the technical indicators are often more reliable than what you see from price action. Although it is extremely unlikely that one would have wanted either to buy or sell NT at the end of 2002, it is interesting to see that a small W was already forming in OBV 1 as price made its eventual low.

The weekly chart for NT showed OBV confirming the uptrend splendidly until the fall of 2000 (Fig. 5-5). Then it began to form a very ominous shape like an upside-down saucer. Although there was a single, short-lived bulge in early 2001, OBV on the weekly chart resolutely confirmed the downtrend.

The daily chart for NT shows a complete breakdown by both price and OBV when the $60 level for price gave way (Fig. 5-6). On a technical basis, from that point there was absolutely no justification whatsoever for anyone to own any of this stock. On the basis of both technicals and fundamentals, it was an exercise in negligence for any responsible investor to have continued to own it. Once a stock starts

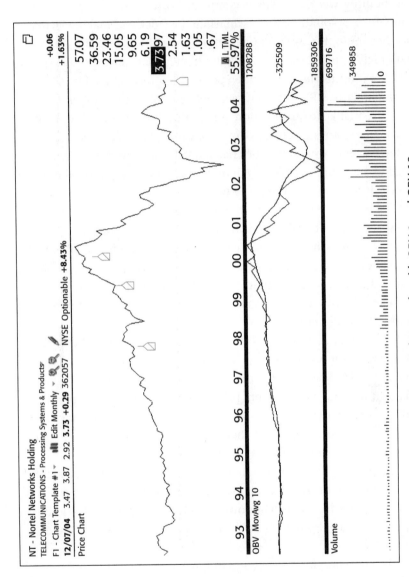

FIGURE 5-4 Monthly Line Chart for Nortel Networks with OBV 1 and OBV 10.

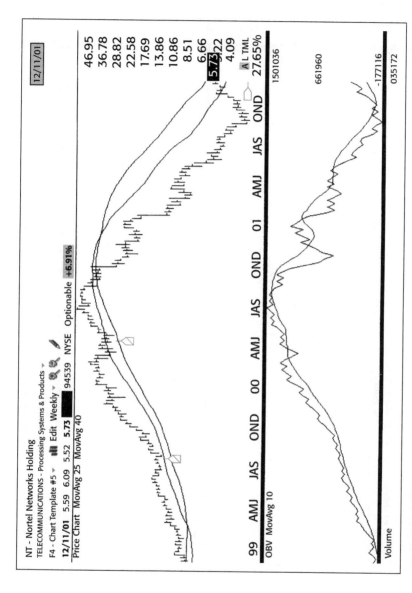

FIGURE 5-5 Weekly Bar Chart for Nortel Networks with OBV 1 and OBV 10.

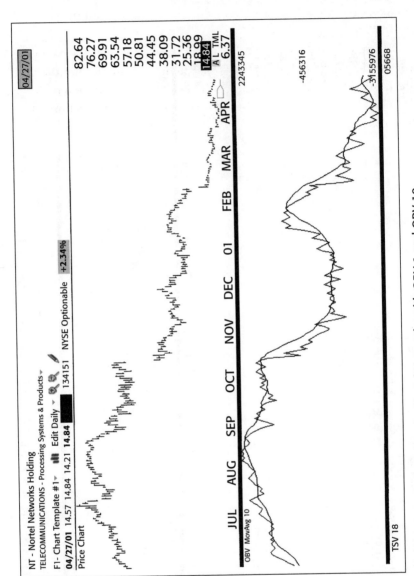

FIGURE 5-6 Daily Bar Chart for Nortel Networks with OBV 1 and OBV 10.

falling like a rock, as did NT, there is no knowing when it will hit bottom until there are definitive signs of it doing so that are confirmed by market action and corresponding technical indicators.

OBV is not an infallible indicator, but it is extremely reliable when it is used in conjunction with our other indicators on the monthly, weekly, and daily charts. Even when price dips, you can have a high level of confidence when OBV 1 is above OBV 10, and the direction of OBV 10 is upward.

CHAPTER 6

Moving-Average Convergence/Divergence (MACD)

Direction and Momentum

Moving-average convergence/divergence (MACD) is a broad-brush indicator for the big picture. It shows major longer-term shifts in momentum and is exceptionally useful for confirming the likelihood of a trend remaining in force. Its importance is outstanding because it shows differences that the eye doesn't see when looking at zigzags on the line chart for price that seem to keep on going more or less the same.

Although it is not necessary to know how MACD functions in order to use it, it may be helpful to have a general idea. It is a combination of three exponentially smoothed moving averages that are expressed as two lines. The MACD fast line (*fast MACD*) is an oscillator constructed by subtracting a shorter moving average from a longer one. The shorter moving average is constantly converging toward and diverging away from the longer one. Hence its name. The MACD slow line (*slow MACD*) is generated from an exponential moving average of the oscillator.

As with on-balance volume (OBV), turns in fast MACD are a signal for action, whereas turns in slow MACD indicate the probable major price trend.

MACD is a standard indicator available on all good charting software packages. The recommended setting (often the default setting) is 12, 26, 9. A decimal setting of 0.15, 0.075, 0.20, used on some software, produces an almost identical result.

Using MACD

The MACD fast and slow lines, as well as crossovers and zigzags, act much the same way as OBV 1 and OBV 10. MACD and OBV often produce remarkably similar results despite the fact that their data sources are totally different. This difference means that these two indicators are particularly powerful when in clear agreement. Conversely, these two indicators deliver a valuable warning when they diverge.

As a powerful but slow-moving indicator, MACD may lag at market turns, particularly when they occur quickly. Therefore, it is essential to use MACD in conjunction with other indicators, especially with price action. When other indicators are leading, you can often tell whether MACD's lagging performance is likely to follow.

MACD has the following uses, which are applicable to the monthly, weekly, and daily charts:

1. MACD delivers a buy signal when fast MACD crosses slow MACD and both lines are rising. When there is a fast turn in a stock, it may take a little longer for the direction of fast MACD to bring all three components of the signal together. The most reliable signals occur after fast MACD has had time to form its own W. The reverse applies for a sell signal.

   MACD is our slowest indicator to turn and the last to respond to changing circumstances, particularly on the monthly chart. Therefore, other indicators are likely to confirm a new trend on the monthly and weekly charts before MACD confirms the change in direction. On the other hand, it is a great indicator for showing the potential durability of a trend over the longer term.

2. MACD also gives a buy signal when fast MACD has been above a rising slow MACD and it makes a new upturn after turning down. You can assume that both MACD and price are starting the next leg of an upward zigzag. A corresponding downturn below a declining slow MACD constitutes a sell signal.

3. MACD can serve as a leading indicator for price by showing a shift in momentum—which is quite different from direction—that is not evident on the price chart. However, loss of momentum reflected by MACD may just mean that the stock needs time to consolidate its gains or, in a bear market, its losses.

4. When price makes a higher high but MACD makes a lower high, the stock is losing upward momentum, and vice versa when there is divergence in a declining market. Sometimes there can be a very big difference between price action and MACD that continues for a long time. The greater and longer-lasting the divergence, the greater is the likelihood of an eventual trend change in price.

5. An established uptrend is likely to remain in force when fast MACD is above slow MACD and both lines are rising. Similarly, MACD confirms an established downtrend when fast MACD is below slow MACD and both lines are falling.

   When MACD is strongly rising on the monthly and weekly charts, it is highly likely that the trend will continue. You can buy into corresponding long-term uptrends or sell short into corresponding long-term downtrends with relatively low risk by using signals generated by MACD and other indicators.

6. The zero baseline distinguishes between confirmed bull and confirmed bear markets. Unless there has been an M or a W, topping or basing action in MACD, crossing over the zero baseline seldom provides a useful trading signal because it generally occurs too late. Sometimes the zero baseline helps to interpret the momentum of MACD. A steep MACD suggests a powerful move, whereas a shallow one indicates a lack of power.

7. Fast MACD normally draws away from slow MACD when price momentum in the stock is accelerating. The most reliable price trends generally occur when the two lines establish and maintain a constant distance between each other. When there is an upward bulge in fast MACD after a stock has made an extended move up, it may indicate a buying climax. Although there may not be an impending trend change, it is likely that the stock will at least have to go sideways or down slightly for a while. A bulge in fast MACD is more likely to warn of an outright

trend reversal because the long-term major direction of stocks is upward; few stocks keep on going down forever, but many have major long-term secular uptrends.

8. In a strongly trending stock, on charts of shorter duration such as the weeklies and dailies, MACD can go flat or change direction without necessarily signaling a trend reversal. It may simply be showing that the momentum has gone out of the stock for the time being. The stock may just need to consolidate its previous gains in a bull market or its losses in a bear market. After a period of consolidation, the trend may resume.

9. The likelihood of an impending change in direction for a stock increases when MACD makes a double top or a double bottom or multiple declining tops or rising bottoms. It often traces out its own M or W zigzags a considerable time before price changes direction.

10. When there is a bulge either up or down in fast MACD that extends far beyond the previous range, far beyond slow MACD, and far beyond the zero baseline, the probability increases that price has gone too far and that there may be a significant retracement and possibly a trend reversal. When a big bulge at an apparent extremity starts rounding back toward the zero base line, MACD assumes some of the characteristics of a long-term stochastic, the overbought/oversold indicator described in Chapter 10.

11. The bottom of a bear market may be signaled when MACD has extended as far down on the monthly chart as it went up at the top of the preceding bull market. Ideally, there should be a clear upward rounding on slow MACD, as well as an upside crossover, before buying when MACD is far below the zero baseline.

12. Except when there is an extreme oversold condition and when there are other buy signals in force, it seldom pays to stay in a stock, let alone to buy it, when MACD is clearly trending down on the monthly and weekly charts and, in addition, when price on the monthly chart has violated its 5 percent allowance below the last low on the monthly line chart.

MACD and General Electric

On the monthly chart for General Electric (GE) there was a new buy
signal in early 1995 as fast MACD resolved its sideways action by
crossing above slow MACD, which was going sideways above the zero
baseline (Fig. 6-1). Note how the two MACD lines subsequently main-
tained a strong upward and evenly spaced trend while price moved
strongly upward.

MACD really came up trumps during the major upward thrust that
peaked in 2000. It told you to stay in the stock for the accelerating ride,
but the bulge at a very high level for fast MACD also suggested that it
was too good to last and that you should be watching for an exit from
the stock. You might have had the foresight to get out very close to the
top as fast MACD rolled over, and indeed, with hindsight you can see
that the bull market had ended. Failing that, the downside crossover
by fast MACD really showed that upside momentum had gone out of
the stock.

For the entire duration of the bear market, MACD showed that this
was a stock to avoid. Note, however, that it reached an extremity at the
bottom that was almost exactly equal and opposite of its amplitude at
the top. This fact alone suggested that the stock might not go down
much farther. Then note how fast MACD made a double bottom, or a
W, much as price was doing. In both cases, the right-hand low was
slightly below the left-hand low but barely perceptibly so for MACD.

MACD on the Weekly Chart

The weekly chart for MACD and GE shows two important things (Fig.
6-2). First, note how MACD made its high at the top in price at the end
of 1999. Although price appeared to rediscover its upward momentum,
this was not what MACD was saying. The third lower high in MACD
toward the end of 2000 was to show, correctly as it turned out, that all
was not well with the bull market in GE. The bulge in fast MACD on the
monthly chart was suggesting that the bull market had become too
good to be true.

Once MACD headed down and crossed below the zero baseline,
you could tell that the bear market was socked in for the duration. Yes,

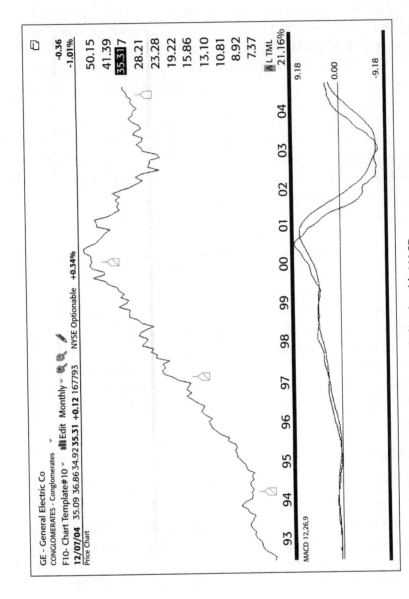

FIGURE 6-1 Monthly Line Chart for General Electric with MACD.

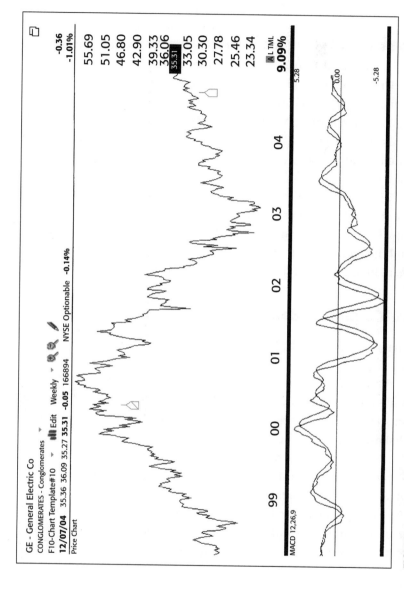

GE - General Electric Co
CONGLOMERATES - Conglomerates
F10-Chart Template#10   Edit   Weekly
12/07/04 35.36 36.09 35.27 **35.31** -0.05 166894   NYSE Optionable -0.14%
Price Chart

-0.36
-1.01%

55.69
51.05
46.80
42.90
39.33
36.06
35.31
33.05
30.30
27.78
25.46
23.34

L TML
9.09%

MACD 12,26,9

5.28

0.00

-5.28

99   00   01   02   03   04

FIGURE 6-2   Weekly Line Chart for General Electric with MACD.

there was an upward lunge in mid-2001 that occurred in conjunction with a strong rally in the stock and with MACD crossing above the zero baseline. Coming as it did out of a V bottom rather than a W, there was no base to support an upward move in price or MACD. When fast MACD turned down again at a level below the previous highs, there was an opportunity to sell, not an invitation to buy.

On the other hand, there was good solid rounding out by MACD from mid-2002, which was something of the equal and opposite of what had occurred at the top in 2000. Looking at the price chart on its own, it would have been hard to tell that the bear market was approaching its end. But MACD was showing that momentum was going out of the decline.

In the event, neither MACD nor price was to do all that much with the move out of the low, and in the event there were better stocks to buy. However, GE is an important bellwether for the overall market, and the basing action in the stock provided considerable encouragement for an interpretation that one could be looking for stocks to buy.

MACD and CR Bard

The monthly chart for CR Bard (BCR) was not as strong as GE's during the big bull market of the 1990s, but it surpassed GE's after the top in the general market (Fig. 6-3). During the 1990s, both MACD and price wandered sideways with a slight upward bias. Most of the time, MACD was holding above the zero baseline, and dips below it were shallow and brief. The chart for BCR illustrates the point that it is worth keeping an eye out for better stocks to buy than the ones you own or think you want to own. Notwithstanding that GE is as solid a blue chip as exists on the basis of its long-term track record, as well as reasonably good action by MACD on the monthly chart, it was not difficult to find stocks with better charts after 2000. BCR, the maker of medical instruments and supplies, provides an example of a strong chart where, in 2003–2004, the ratio of reward to risk was much better than for GE.

BCR made its high for the bull market early, in March 1999, at $29.94. It then made its bear market low ahead of the market generally, at $17.50, as early as April 2000. Once MACD crossed above the zero baseline in early 2001, after dipping remarkably little below, you could

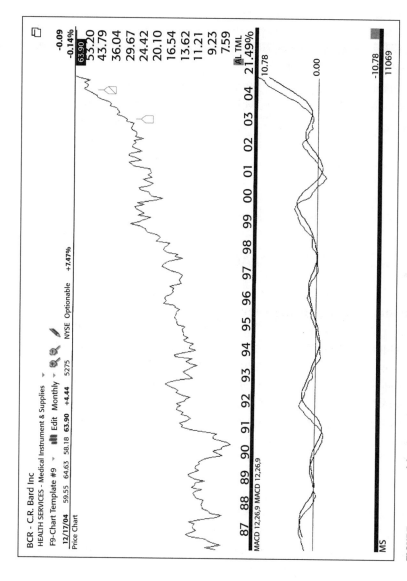

FIGURE 6-3 Monthly Line Chart for CR Bard with MACD.

put this stock on a watch list to buy as and when the general outlook became less bearish. When fast MACD turned up for the second time in early 2003 and crossed above slow MACD after consolidating above the zero baseline, this constituted a powerful buy signal. Sure enough, it led to an almost trouble-free doubling in the share price over the next year or so.

The weekly chart for BCR shows choppy action in MACD between 1999 and mid-2002, even as MACD on the monthly chart was starting to strengthen (Fig. 6-4). Then in 2002 began a textbook series of higher lows in fast MACD and a cross above the zero baseline with a third low after consolidating above it. The upward move in BCR was on its way. On two occasions upward momentum flagged, and MACD headed down toward the zero baseline but stayed above it. More ominous is the potential double top in early 2005.

Learn to Believe in MACD

When MACD is acting well and a stock is moving higher on the monthly chart, believe in this indicator. The probabilities strongly favor a continuation of the trend until MACD and price action show real fatigue. MACD helps you to maintain confidence in the underlying principle of markets that a trend in force is likely to remain in force until something more serious comes along to stop it. Even then, the probabilities tend to favor a consolidation rather than a trend reversal unless MACD really shows signs of faltering, as illustrated in this chapter.

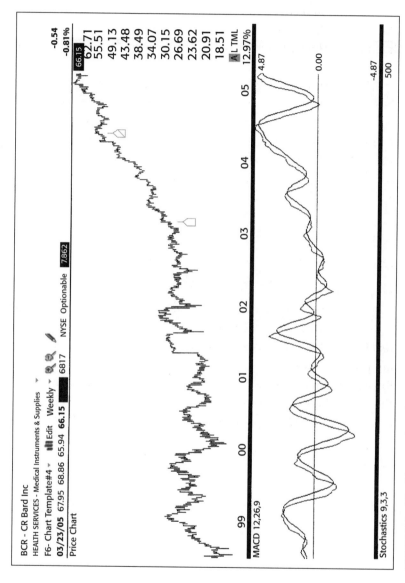

FIGURE 6-4 Weekly Bar Chart for CR Bard with MACD.

CHAPTER 7

The Building Blocks for Charts

Price Bar Action

This chapter takes a break from discussing technically generated indicators in order to look at individual price bar action. Even a single bar may show whether there is greater buying or selling pressure for that particular time period. Several bars taken together and put in the context of the larger picture may indicate the kind of momentum that leads to a more significant move in price. For readers unfamiliar with the terminology of bar charts, this is the most basic evidence that technical analysts look at.

The *basic bar* is the building block for all bar charts. It represents the range of trading for a certain period—a day, a week, or a month—on its respective bar chart (Fig. 7-1).

FIGURE 7-1   The Basic Bar.

The bar is set against a scale for calibration and has a notch on the right-hand side to indicate the *final price* at the end of the period. When there is a notch on the left side of the bar, it denotes the *opening price* for the bar.

The *closing price* is particularly significant, depending on whether it occurs at the top, bottom, or middle of the bar (Fig. 7-2).

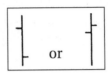

FIGURE 7-2   The Closing Price.

If the close is at the top, it suggests greater buying pressure. If the close is at the bottom, it suggests greater selling pressure. A close in the middle is neutral, but we assume that it has the same message as the previous bar's close.

Smart professional money tends to trade toward the end of any given period, whether a day, a week or a month, once it can be seen which way the wind is blowing. On the other hand, more speculative money and, obviously, day-trading money trades on or near the open. If price opens at or near its high for the period and closes near the low, speculative money is likely to bank the loss while the loss is small and manageable, and smart money will stand aside.

Stocks tend to go up at the beginning of the week, the month, and especially also at the beginning of the year, as new money coming into the hands of money managers is put to work and as individual investors respond to recommendations they have received. The upward tendency is so pronounced in early January that there is almost always a substantial anticipatory year-end rally. The test of the soundness of a January rally is what happens for the rest of the year!

An *inside bar* is one where trading is confined within the high and low prices of the previous bar (Fig. 7-3). If traders cannot push out either the high or the low of the previous bar, assume that the heavy money is taking a rest.

An *outside bar* is one where price exceeds both the high and the low of the preceding bar (Fig. 7-4). An outside bar is particularly significant

FIGURE 7-3 An Inside Bar.

if the close is at the extremity of its range or if it occurs on monthly or weekly charts. It suggests that weak short-term traders, those having a perspective no longer than the duration represented by a few bars, have been forced out of the market. Now the stock may continue in the direction of the strong close. If the range has been unusually great compared with the range of recent bars, the indication of direction from a strong close is additionally significant.

FIGURE 7-4 An Outside Bar.

A *closing-price reversal* occurs when price exceeds the previous bar's high and closes below the close of the previous bar. It also occurs when price exceeds the low of the previous bar and closes above the close of the previous bar.

A *downside reversal* (Fig. 7-5) is the term for this reversal when it moves from a high toward the downside (the new indicated direction).

FIGURE 7-5 A Downside Closing Price Reversal.

An *upside reversal* (Fig. 7-6) occurs when price moves from a low toward the upside (the new indicated direction).

The closing-price reversal is important. It suggests the possibility that the stock may be setting up for a worthwhile move. However, there are many more reversals than important changes in direction, so

FIGURE 7-6   An Upside Closing Price Reversal.

you must consider one in conjunction with other indicators. It should not be used indiscriminately.

A *key reversal* is a combination of a closing-price reversal and an outside bar. Price exceeds both the high and the low of the preceding bar, and the close is beyond the preceding high or low (Fig. 7-7).

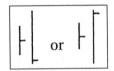

FIGURE 7-7   A Key Reversal.

A *high/low reversal* occurs when price closes at one extremity of the trading range on one bar and at the opposite extremity on the next bar (Fig. 7-8). Although sometimes omitted from textbooks, the high/low reversal is particularly significant when followed by another high/low reversal or when one occurs shortly before or after a closing-price reversal.

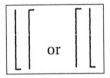

FIGURE 7-8   High/Low Reversals.

An *accumulation pattern* consists of a pattern of bars, each having successively higher lows and, ideally, also higher highs (Fig. 7-9). During accumulation, persistent buying pressure finds buyers unable to buy as low as they could before, resulting in successively higher lows. It is likely that price can continue to move higher.

An accumulation pattern can be significant regardless of the closing price for the bar. It is valid on all charts but increasingly more so on weekly and monthly charts.

FIGURE 7-9   An Accumulation Pattern.

A *distribution pattern* is the reverse of an accumulation pattern (Fig. 7-10). Sellers are able to sell only at successively lower prices as buyers become steadily less aggressive about how much they are prepared to pay, or as buying dries up.

FIGURE 7-10   A Distribution Pattern.

A *consolidation* or *congestion area* occurs when price moves sideways. A wider band of equilibrium is often called a *trading range*.

A *gap* often occurs on daily charts. It is a blank space on a chart with no direct connection to the preceding bar or group of bars because no trading has occurred at the intervening prices. As a rule, the bigger the gap, the more significant it is likely to be. All gaps show a surge in buying pressure when the gap is upward or in selling pressure when it is downward. Gaps often occur after news announcements that significantly change investors' views of a stock and set its price on a new course. They are particularly significant on the weekly chart when there is a change of perception between the close on Friday and the opening of the market on Monday morning.

We also consider that a gap occurs when the opening price gaps away from the previous close and never comes back to the previous close, even if there is not a complete separation between the bars. This is not a standard technical interpretation of a gap, but it is useful.

When a stock has gapped up from a previous close, the gap is *filled* when there is a close at or below the price from which it gapped. A gap is *tested* when a stock returns into the gap and even beyond the close from which the stock gapped but does not fill it on a closing basis. The same applies in reverse when there has been a gap down.

Gaps represent levels of support or resistance, as discussed in Chapter 11. A stock often retraces and tests into a gap after the initial surge of buying or selling pressure abates. If the surge leading to opening of the gap is well founded, the gap should remain open. After a stock has gapped up, new buying should come back for a stock as it settles back.

A *common gap* can occur at any time. It has little significance by itself, but it is used in price rules, described in Chapter 8. Often occurring within a congestion area, a common gap is generally filled within a few days by price moving back to establish a connection with the other bars on the chart. Of course, you never know until after the event whether this will happen or whether you are looking at the start of a breakout to a new price level.

A *breakaway gap* occurs when price breaks away from a congestion area and never looks back. It is a reliable indicator of important buying or selling power. It suggests that a major move may be just starting. Although it can be alarming to see how far price has moved on the first day of a breakout, the rule of thumb is that the more powerful the breakout, the further price is likely to go and the more reliable the breakout is likely to be. Consequently, there is unlikely to be another chance to trade at a more favorable price and with a more manageable risk than there is by trading right away.

A *runaway gap* occurs in a stock that is continuing to tear away in a major run. These gaps occur when a stock starts to go straight up or collapses downward. They are sometimes called *midpoint gaps* or *measuring gaps*. The idea is that they tend to show up around the midpoint of an apparently nonstop move. Nevertheless, this is only a rough rule of thumb for estimating how far a runaway move might go before it stops for breath.

An *exhaustion gap* occurs at the end of a substantial move. You can never be certain until after the event whether a runaway gap is actually an exhaustion gap. An exhaustion gap occurs either when price gaps back the other way, leaving an island (the next definition), or when the gap is filled by price closing below the bottom of the gap when the market is going up or above the top of a gap when the market is going down. The expression *exhaustion gap* comes from the concept that the immediate buying or selling pressure is exhausted. These gaps often occur as a result of panic buying or selling. When the panic ends, the price can go the other way very fast. Sometimes you may be able to make an intelligent guess to identify an exhaustion gap when it occurs under circumstances where other indicators suggest the possibility that a top or bottom is being formed.

An *island* consists of one or more days of trading where there is a gap on the chart in both directions. It is often the ultimate manifestation of exhaustion at the end of a major move. It assumes greater significance when it comprises several bars. Then it signifies that the greedy or the desperate have truly finished doing the wrong thing.

Five consecutive closes in the same direction constitute a pattern of unusually persistent buying or selling and suggest that it is likely to continue. When this bar formation is wrong, it may be because it signifies exhaustion at the end of a major move or a major correction.

Always Follow the Footprints

You need to look closely at a market's strength or weakness by examining its price action. Close inspection of individual bars and groups of bars often gives vital clues that confirm a direction or warn of a possible change in direction.

A strongly rising market tends to have the majority of closes at the upper end of the range. It also tends to have a higher number of closes up than down. When the direction is up, individual advances are usually larger than individual declines.

A rising market that is tiring may show aberrational behavior despite its ability to make gains in closing prices. For example, one downside reversal bar is likely to be a random aberration, especially if it has a small range. Several downside reversals suggest that sellers are asserting themselves. Gains early in the period are being consistently knocked down by sellers later on. Consequently, there is a high probability of at least a short-term correction, if not necessarily a change in the major trend. This interpretation is reversed when a declining market starts to show signs of buying pressure.

Gaps constitute one of the most obvious indicators of pent-up buying or selling pressure. One small gap within a consolidation area may mean nothing. They occur frequently and are likely to be filled soon—hence their designation as *common gaps*. There is an informal rule that a gap remaining unfilled for three days on a closing basis is likely to remain unfilled, with price most likely continuing in the direction of the gapping. The incidence of several gaps up indicates the release of pent-up buying power, suggesting a stock to own.

When there are several daily gaps down in a stock, it is highly likely that the stock will soon take a more substantial tumble. Downward gapping that leaves behind an island above the market is highly likely to signify exhaustion of the uptrend, at least for the intermediate term.

Chapter 8 looks at how groups of bullish bars develop a buy signal and how groups of bearish bars develop a sell signal.

CHAPTER 8

Price Rules

When to Pull the Trigger

The essence of timing is knowing when to place the order to buy or sell a stock or when to sell one short. This chapter describes price patterns or rules that call for action when other indicators confirm their buy or sell signal.

It is easy to look at a chart and get a general idea that you might like to own a stock. But should you buy it now or wait? Or should you have done it last week? All too often you can be overtaken by emotions. You want to see whether anything is going to happen before you make a move. But once the stock does move, is it then too late to buy? If you do buy, what is the risk of doing so just as a significant retracement begins? In the worst case, you may buy into a buying climax just as a major bull move comes to an end. Alternatively, you may buy a stock, expecting it to go up, but it never moves. On the other hand, you may own a stock that appears to be falling out of bed. Should you sell it today, or should you have sold it last week? Or should you hold it? It is all too easy to be driven by fear of losing a profit or of taking a bad loss and to sell out at the worst possible time.

Perfection in timing is unachievable. Nonetheless, the eight price rules described in this chapter come as close as possible to achieving

timely entries and exits. They apply to charts for all time periods—
monthly, weekly, and daily, as well as for the very short-term trader,
intraday. Although developed independently, they follow the same
general principles as the ancient Japanese candlestick price bar patterns. Neither price rules nor candlesticks should be used as stand-
alone indicators (although some people try to use candlesticks on their
own). Both these approaches help in deciding when to buy or sell, provided they are related to the bigger picture.

It is worthwhile to grasp the underlying principles of the price rules
before looking at them in detail. Both buy and sell signals are illustrated because it is just as important to know when to sell a stock or
when to sell short as when to buy. The rules themselves are not cast in
bronze, and they can be stretched occasionally if other indicators suggest that such a move would be a reasonable course of action. The
most important thing is to understand what they are about.

Price Rule Principles

1. When random buying or selling occurs in the ordinary course of
   business, price charts show random patterns. When there is a
   persistent weighting of pressure toward either buying or selling,
   price charts also reflect this fact. One footprint in the sand says
   nothing. When a pattern of footprints starts to point the way,
   start looking for evidence that the trail may continue. Put
   another way, you want to buy strength and to sell weakness, but
   only when the probabilities favor continuation of either the
   strength or the weakness.

2. A close at the extremity of a bar's range suggests that the stock is
   likely to continue in the direction of the strong close. This is particularly so when there are several consecutive strong closes in
   the same direction.

3. Ideally, a price rule signal should be in force on the monthly and
   the weekly chart before buying or selling a stock.

4. A price rule signal must occur on the daily chart to buy or sell a
   stock. Completion of a price rule on the monthly or weekly chart
   delivers a signal in its own right, but this signal must be confirmed by a price rule signal on the daily chart.

5. It is important to act on a price rule signal as soon as it occurs. The best signals lead to price following through immediately. By waiting for more confirmation, you increase the risk of a retracement as the stock moves away from a price rule signal. Confirming the balance of evidence can sometimes be too much of a good thing once a stock starts moving.

6. After completion of a buy signal, there may nevertheless be a retracement that would permit you to buy at a lower price. However, the signals that let you do so are often the ones that fail. The best signals often lead to a profit right away. In the long run, it pays to act as soon as a strong price rule occurs. Price rules occur on daily, weekly, and monthly charts, as well as on intraday charts, with each bar representing, say, five minutes or an hour. The most powerful expression of a potentially strong move occurs in conjunction with a signal on the monthly chart as a manifestation of the potential for a major long-term move. Shorter-term charts deliver the signal for pulling the trigger. It often happens that there are signals occurring simultaneously on monthly, weekly, and daily charts. When this happens, there is a very high probability of a worthwhile move starting right away.

7. Occasionally, but only very occasionally and when the major trend is very strong, you might intentionally buy low or sell high before a price rule develops. Should you be inclined to jump the gun on a signal, there is an informal but remarkably consistent rule that the big-money funds move in three-day spurts, whether to buy or to sell. Therefore, the risk is reduced considerably when buying into a strong trend (or selling in a declining market) on the third consecutive day of a retracement. If the trend is really strong and you wait for a three-day retracement, it may never come. The probabilities favor buying into strength when manifested by good buy signals, and successful investment is an exercise in playing the probabilities.

Conditions for All Price Rules

1. To complete a price rule, the final bar has to close in the *top 25 percent* of the bar's range for a buy signal or in the *bottom 25 percent* for a sell signal.

2. A price rule may take longer to complete than the minimum specified time. Thus it could take four or five bars, rather than three, to complete a three-bar close rule (rule 1, shown below). It could also take until the fourth or fifth bar to obtain a close in the top or bottom 25 percent of the bar's range, thereby completing the signal.

3. When price closes in the middle of the range, the result is neutral. Assume the same closing designation as for the previous bar.

4. When an emerging pattern is violated, start counting again at the beginning of the formation with a new bar 1.

5. When a price signal is completed (and other indicators confirm the action), buy or sell right away. If you miss the signal, don't chase the stock. Wait for a new signal.

Price Rules

1. The Three-Bar Closes Rule

A buy signal occurs on completion of two consecutive bars in which price closes in the upper half of the range and the next bar closes in the top 25 percent of its range. A sell signal is the reverse (Fig. 8-1).

Buy Signal   Sell Signal

FIGURE 8-1   The Three-Bar Close Rule.

2. The Reversal Rule

Shorten the proving time from three bars to two when either of the two bars is a reversal—closing price, key, or high/low reversal (Fig. 8-2).

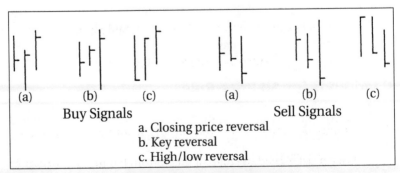

(a)   (b)   (c)   (a)   (b)   (c)
      Buy Signals   Sell Signals
                   a. Closing price reversal
                   b. Key reversal
                   c. High/low reversal

FIGURE 8-2   The Reversal Rule.

3. The Gap Rule

Shorten the proving time from three bars to two when a gap occurs (Fig. 8-3).

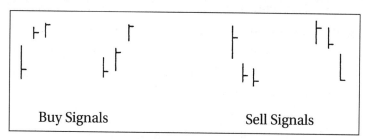

Buy Signals   Sell Signals

FIGURE 8-3 The Gap Rule.

4. The Island Rule

Shorten the proving time to one bar when an island occurs. It is not necessary for closing price(s) within an island to be in the top or bottom of the range. An island may consist of one bar or many. However, the more time taken to form an island and the more symmetrical the gapping, the more likely it is that price has reached an important turning point and will continue in the direction of the new gapping. Islands often indicate absolute exhaustion of the previous trend (Fig. 8-4).

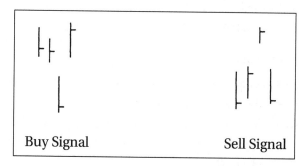

Buy Signal   Sell Signal

FIGURE 8-4 The Island Rule.

5a. The Lindahl Buy Rule

Within *nine* bars from the bar of the *low* for the formation (Fig. 8-5*a*):

1. Price must exceed the high of the bottom bar for the formation: *b* must take out the high of *a*.

2. Price must then take out the low of the preceding bar: *d* must take out the low of *c*.

3. To buy, price must take out the high of the preceding bar and close above the preceding bar's close and the current bar's opening price (*e*).

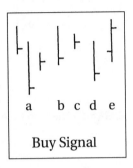

FIGURE 8-5A   The Lindahl Buy Rule.

This formation may be completed in as few as three bars or as many as nine, depending on the number of intervening bars that do not contribute to development of the formation. Put another way, it is not significant when price exceeds previous highs and lows. There may be several neutral bars in between.

5b. The Lindahl Sell Rule

Within *eight* bars from the bar of the *high* for the formation (Fig. 8-5*b*):

1. Price must exceed the low of the top bar for the formation: *b* must take out the low of *a*.

2. Price must then take out the high of the preceding bar: *d* must take out the high of *c*.

3. To sell, price must take out the low of the preceding bar and close below the preceding bar's close and the current bar's opening price (*e*).

This formation may be completed in as few as three bars or as many as eight, depending on the number of intervening bars that do not contribute to development of the formation.

Commodity futures researcher Walter Bressert, our source for Lindahl signals, found that valid buy signals may require one more bar

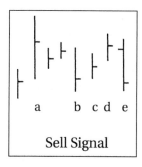

FIGURE 8-5B The Lindahl Sell Rule.

than is required to complete a valid sell signal. Some people find it difficult to grasp the detail of Lindahl signals. It may take time, but it is worth the effort. Lindahl signals are very reliable when other indicators indicate a turn in price. They also occur very frequently on stock charts of all durations. If you have difficulty learning to recognize Lindahl signals, think of them as looking like a miniature M or W formed by just a few bars. A Lindahl signal on a monthly chart tends to be very reliable because it takes so long to form.

6. The Trend Continuation Rule

Shorten the proving time to one bar when there is a single reversal bar in the direction of an established and unmistakable trend. A clear and unmistakable trend requires the 25- and 40-bar moving averages to confirm the direction on the monthly, weekly, and daily charts (Fig. 8-6).

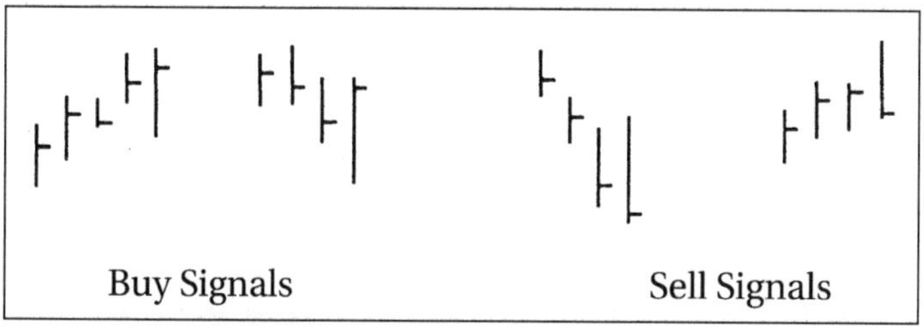

Buy Signals   Sell Signals

FIGURE 8-6 The Trend Continuation Rule.

It is psychologically difficult to chase a rapidly moving stock. This price rule provides the mechanism for buying with both a manageable stop loss and a high probability of making a profit right away. (The stop is just beyond the extremity of the price range of the entry bar, as discussed in Chapter 16.)

This price rule may also be used when other indicators suggest that a consolidation within a clearly established trend is ending.

7. The Trend Reversal Rule

Trade with the direction of a single, very big reversal bar, even though the trend appears to be in the opposite direction—hence the name *trend reversal* (Fig. 8-7).

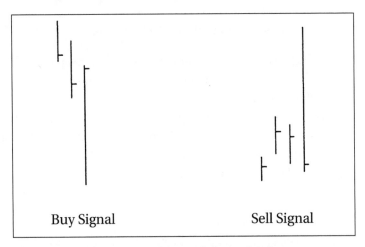

Buy Signal   Sell Signal

FIGURE 8-7   The Trend Reversal Rule.

This rule is useful for selling an existing position after a buying climax. The probabilities seldom favor using it to buy against the direction of an established trend.

8. The Double Reversal Rule

Trade on completion of a second reversal bar in the same direction within a period of six bars or fewer, whether closing price reversals, high/low reversals, or a combination. Both reversal bars should close in the top or bottom 25 percent, as appropriate, of the bars' ranges (Fig. 8-8).

As suggested by the name *double reversal,* this rule is a double trend continuation (rule 6). Double reversals occur often and are very reliable. They also occur frequently in Lindahl formations (rule 5).

When buying, the signal is much stronger if the second low is higher, and when selling, if the second high is lower—unless the sec-

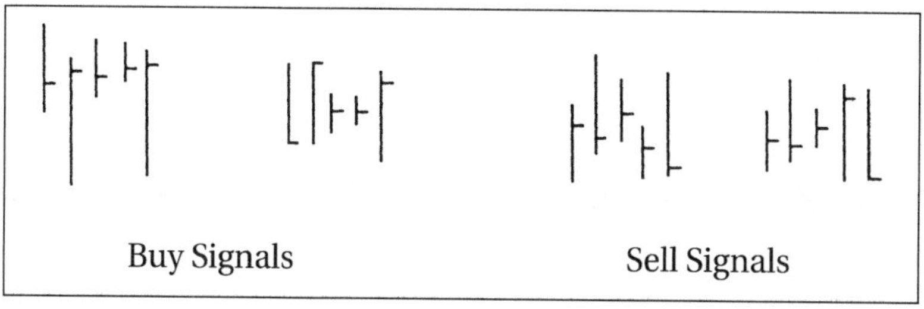

Buy Signals   Sell Signals

FIGURE 8-8   The Double Reversal Rule.

ond reversal is exceptionally powerful. The same goes for closes. Ideally, the second one should be higher when buying and lower when selling. Occasionally, this rule can be completed in as few as two bars. It is very powerful when the second bar completes a double reversal and is also a key reversal bar.

Illustrating the Price Rules

All the buy-signal price rules except rules 7 and 8 are shown on the daily chart for Qualcomm (Fig. 8-9). The double reversal rule (rule 8) is illustrated by a strong sell signal, and the trend-reversal rule (rule 7) is illustrated with a less than completely conclusive single bar. With its outside-day range, however, the signal is powerful, and indeed, price action was to follow through quite strongly over the next few days. Since, of course, Qualcomm was in a bull market, the correction signaled by these sell signals was brief, and the uptrend soon resumed. Note, of course, that sometimes more than one signal can be completed on the same day, with double reversals and Lindahl signals quite often occurring simultaneously.

Chapter 9 shows how using price rules and moving averages together can lead to identifying stocks with a high probability of immediate profit and a low risk of loss.

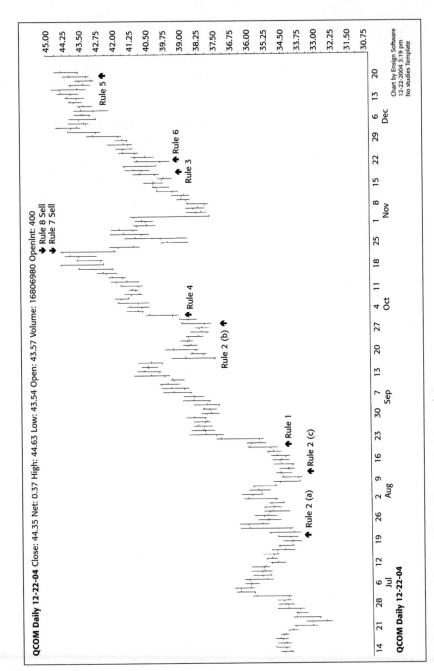

FIGURE 8-9 Qualcomm Daily Chart with Price Rules.

Moving Averages: Use with Price Rules

A moving average provides another way to identify the direction of a trend. When the direction is up, the trend is upward, and vice versa when the direction is down. A moving average is a curved version of a trendline or a smoothed version of many price bars. It consists of the average of the closing prices for a designated number of preceding months, weeks, or days.

As such, a moving average serves a purpose like looking in a rear-view mirror: If the land behind is falling away, you know you are going uphill—or not, as the case may be. As with a rear-view mirror, you can, of course, only tell where you are going now. A rear-view mirror doesn't tell you when the road suddenly comes to an end and falls off a cliff, and a moving average may give little or no warning of an imminent disaster that suddenly halves the value of a stock. However, relatively few roads come to such an abrupt end, and relatively few stocks—especially those of major corporations—collapse suddenly. Although that is no guarantee that the trend will continue, the probabilities strongly favor the expectation that the trend in force will keep on going.

Confirming the Direction

Confirmation of the validity of the *direction* occurs when price is above a rising moving average or below a declining moving average. The point is that for a rising moving average to keep on going up, the price has to keep moving ahead of the averages, and vice versa when it is going down. A crossover does not, of itself, suggest a signal, but it serves as a warning of flagging momentum—at least for the immediate future.

Ideally, for a new purchase with an immediate prospect of gain and a small risk of loss, the price should cross above a rising moving average and then consolidate there for a time, as if it were cradled by the moving average. There should be a consolidation comprising fairly gradual upward rounding of lows made by the bottoms of price bars and a succession of somewhat higher highs. Under the best of circumstances, which does not occur very often, there will be a simultaneous conjunction of market action on the monthly, weekly, and daily charts.

Subject, therefore, to the reservation that moving averages are a lagging indicator, monthly moving averages serve extremely well to indicate the major direction of a stock. Sometimes a stock's monthly moving averages maintain a direction for many years. This long-term persistence generally occurs in stocks of companies operating in areas of the economy that are growing steadily and benefiting from a steady stream of innovation. They often occur in such areas as health care, which is always innovating and growing with improvement in the human condition. The trends of stocks in cyclical industries, by definition, tend not to last so long, although stocks in any industry can move far enough or long enough to be worth owning. Cyclical stocks may be exceptionally attractive at certain times because they tend to go to extremities of profitability or losses. Therefore, there may be a huge upward move when investors perceive that a period of hard times may be ending.

In sum, when monthly, weekly, and daily moving averages for a specific stock show the same direction, the probabilities favor continuation of the major trend. When a stock trades at or near the rising moving averages, the time may be very favorable to buy (or to sell in a bear market). The risk is low relative to the potential reward.

When looking for a new upturn in a stock, it seldom pays to act until the confirming pieces fall into place. What you give up in terms of a better price, you gain back in evidence confirming the probability of being right. Therefore, it is generally better to wait until both price and the moving averages show signs of developing an upward rounding pattern. Getting in on the ground floor is a mug's game. Too many elevators remain interminably stuck at the ground floor or, worse, fall to the basement. An upward rounding pattern generally allows plenty of time to climb on board.

Settings for Moving Averages

Most effective for standard use are simple moving averages with settings of 25 and 40 days, as well as the 200-day moving average on daily charts, which closely corresponds to the 40-week moving average.

Simple moving averages provide a slightly longer-term perspective than weighted or exponential moving averages, which give more weight to nearby market action. Many technical analysts use the 25- and 40-day settings, so their effectiveness for potential support or resistance tends to be self-fulfilling.

Using two moving averages of different time periods makes it easier to interpret what is happening. Usually, but not always, the one of shorter duration turns before the longer one. Often the longer-term one resolutely maintains its direction while the shorter one wobbles. When there is a conflict, it generally pays to heed the longer moving average. Some people use moving average crossovers as a signal for action, but the statistical reliability of this use is unsatisfactory.

Using Moving Averages

1. As we saw in Chapters 2 and 3 when looking at the principle of upward or downward zigzags, the monthly chart shows the big picture. In a strong bull market, the price of the stock should be above the uptrending 25-month moving average, and the 25-month moving average should be above the upward inclining 40-month average. A very strong stock may remain above these moving averages for many years. The probabilities favor the engineer's rule that a trend in force is likely to continue.

2. In a strong bull market, a stock should move upward and away from its monthly averages for a time, and then inevitably, at

some time, price and the moving averages will converge again. This may be accomplished either by the stock settling back, by the moving average catching up, or by a combination of these two market actions.

3. This valuable and simple principle means that a stock that has moved significantly above its rising moving averages may be regarded as somewhat *ahead of itself,* as well as ahead of its underlying rate of climb, and may be technically *overextended* or *overbought.* Therefore, there is a risk of convergence by way of price retracement rather than simply by consolidating and waiting for the moving averages to catch up with price. This risk means that it is seldom timely to buy a stock that has moved significantly beyond the moving averages.

    Emotionally, many people find it difficult to resist the temptation to chase a stock that is moving fast and far beyond its moving averages. A rough rule of thumb is that the risk of an early retracement increases the farther price has moved away from the moving averages, and the more days of powerful action have elapsed. Therefore, you want to try to jump into a stock on the first or second day of powerful market action, not the fifth or sixth. This is not to say that you cannot be successful when entering later, but you have to be prepared to live through a significant retracement. A conservative long-term investor is wary of chasing an overbought market. Such an investor waits patiently for prime opportunities to buy, when the relationship between price and the moving averages suggests that the ratio of a probable early gain is favorable relative to the risk foreseeable in the near term.

4. The corollary of point 3 is, of course, that a stock on or close to a rising moving average is positioned right at its rate of climb (or its rate of descent when going down). Upward progress in price is therefore likely to resume shortly. Obviously too, there is less risk in buying a stock when the price level is not overextended.

5. There may be a prime low-risk opportunity to buy for the long term when price is at or near steadily climbing 25- and 40- *month* moving averages—an opportunity that may occur seldom in the shares of a company with a record of outstanding corporate performance year after year.

6. Following on from points 4 and 5, there are two variants of the moving average touch, or convergence, when price and the moving average come back to meet each other:

   a. The moving averages are moving up at a steep angle, and there has been a sharp retracement in price. In this case, the retracement is likely to be short-lived, and you have to act fast so as not to miss the opportunity to buy at a good price before the stock starts zooming again.

   b. There has been a period of consolidation, and price has been hovering or cradling above the moving averages.

7. In the latter case, the longer the consolidation lasts without the stock falling away, the more worthwhile the next move up is likely to be when it starts moving up again.

8. Since convergence of the monthly moving averages may occur several years apart, the 25- and 40-*week* moving averages do the job of offering the next-best intermediate opportunity to buy when the prospect of an early gain is good and the risk of a hurtful loss is low.

9. The 40-week moving average corresponds almost exactly to the 200-day moving average that is widely regarded as the most important pivotal average to define a bull or a bear market, both for market indexes and for an individual stock.[1]

10. The 25- and 40-day moving averages show the direction of the near-term trend, and there may well be a low-risk entry point on a retracement that converges with these averages.

---

[1] It has been suggested that this single indicator proves the effectiveness of technical analysis, and disproves the so-called, and inane, random-walk theory. According to random-walk theory, you cannot predict the future of stock prices by any known methodology, technical or fundamental. If random-walk theory held good in any aspect of life such as accounting, a banker would not, for example, be able to differentiate between a good credit risk and a poor one by looking at the credit record. Similarly, a stock analyst would be unable to say whether to prefer a stock like Johnson & Johnson or General Motors. This is clearly nonsense. A 200-day moving average crossover works fine in a confirmed bull market, much as you know that the sun is shining when you can see that it is. During any kind of choppy market conditions such as those in the 1970s or between 1999 and 2001, it was hopeless for many stocks and for indexes like the S&P 500, with many random crossovers following one after the other. The 200-day moving average crossover, on its own and without even considering its direction, is not useful.

Walgreen Co. and the Monthly Moving Averages

On the basis of the monthly chart, you can readily see that Walgreen Co. (WAG), was always a stock to buy during the 1990s (Fig. 9-1). WAG has truly been an investor's dream for a very long time, and market action in 2004–2005 suggests that this happy condition will continue.

The company started in 1901 and operates the Walgreens chain of pharmacies, as well as providing prescriptions ordered over the Internet. There is no obvious reason to fear that the company might experience operational difficulties or that its inexorable upward progress will seriously falter. The one obvious cause for concern is that the shares are almost always extremely expensive according to standard valuation criteria. Although quality is almost always expensive compared with junk, in the long run it almost always pays to buy quality in the stock market, as elsewhere.

Buy Off the Monthly Chart

In the early 1990s, between 1991 and the end of 1994, WAG was essentially dead money as the price fluctuated within a range between about $4 and $5 (adjusted for splits). While this might seem like an agony if you bought at the upper end of the range, you have to remember that this is how markets work. It is impossible to be a successful investor without being prepared to withstand periods of harassment while a stock consolidates. Another way of looking at what is happening is to think in terms of the fundamentals—the company's profits and dividends—having to catch up with the share price.

In mid-1994, there was a rule 1 buy signal in conjunction with a rule 2 buy signal with an upside key reversal. Then there were two further strong monthly closes and an upside breakout above the trading range, and the stock was on its way for the rest of the decade.

There was no subsequent touch or convergence of price and the monthly moving averages until 1999, when first a near-convergence and then a penetration and rebound both suggested two opportunities to buy. The second of them paid off smartly after a huge tumble and a massive upside reversal in March 2000. The month's range was from a low of $21.94 to a high of $28.44, which shows that you sometimes

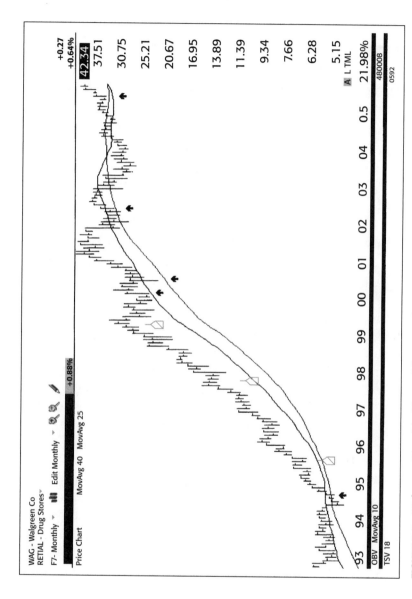

FIGURE 9-1 Walgreen Monthly Chart with 25- and 40-Month Moving Averages.

need fortitude stay in a good stock. Given how far WAG had moved up during the 1990s, this fluctuation did no damage to the case for owning the stock, uncomfortable as that retracement was to live through.

Evidently, from March 2000 until the end of the year, many investors saw WAG as a defensive stock. However, from a high of $45.75 in October 2000, the stock joined in the general weakness and fell to an eventual low of $26.90 in February 2003, for a decline of 41 percent. In the context of the fact that the stock still had multiplied by five times over the preceding 10 years, this was not too hard to live with, except for those who had bought it near the high.

Toward the end of 2004, market action delivered a new buy signal, as in point 6(b) above, as a result of extended sideways trading and the price of the stock having been cradled above the monthly moving averages. There may well be some fits and starts, as there were from 1992 to 1993, and the buy signal may yet abort. However, it is still a good signal.

Buy Walgreen Off the Weekly Chart

The weekly chart for WAG shows how this stock was really laboring at the end of 2000 and early 2001, during the time when the general market was experiencing so much difficulty (Fig. 9-2). It was hardly surprising that the stock was to join in the decline, although one would not necessarily have predicted that it would fall so precipitously from the $42 level to a price just under $29. This tumble illustrates the point that there really are times to sell all stocks. Once a bear market becomes entrenched, there is a high risk of unpleasant downside surprises, and the probability of bullish upside ones is very small.

The weekly chart begins to show a sea change in 2003–2044, with a strong case for buying the stock when it settled back to the now-rising 25- and 40-week moving averages in early 2004. From there, the stock was on its way, with a further opportunity to buy on the convergence toward the end of 2004.

Buy Walgreen Off the Daily Chart

The daily chart for WAG during 2004 shows the stock breaking below the 25- and 40-day moving averages (Fig. 9-3). However, you can

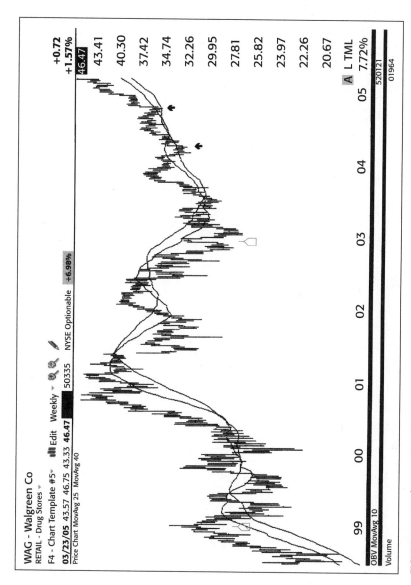

FIGURE 9-2 Walgreen Weekly Chart with 25- and 40-Week Moving Averages.

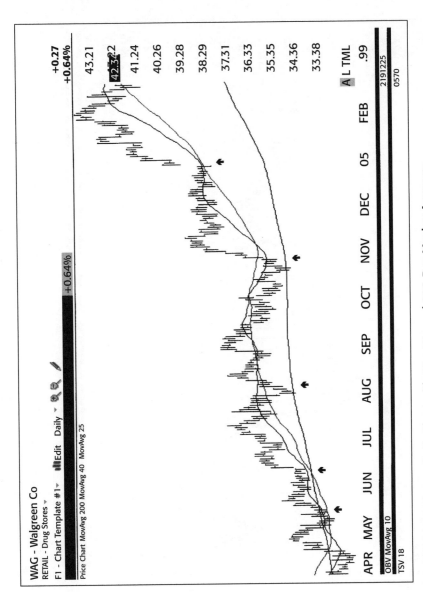

FIGURE 9-3 Walgreen Daily Chart with 25-, 40-, and 200-Day Moving Averages.

readily see the magic of the 200-day moving average doing its job, as, of course, happened with its counterpart, the 40-week moving average on the weekly chart.

When You Should Wait to Buy

The search for ground-floor opportunities is always enticing. The challenge is to differentiate between those opportunities potentially worth the risk and going with stocks in an already established trend. Walgreen shows how a stock may go sideways for what seems like an interminable time—often for many months, sometimes for many years. Find a stock like Walgreen that you think you would want to own, and then watch and wait until the pieces fall into place. It's one thing to sit on a great stock that you already own, but you want to avoid the frustration of wondering whether you made a mistake. If you just go out and buy a stock, however wonderful the company, you can find yourself married to what is, in effect, dead money.

Chapter 10 brings moving averages together with stochastics. This indicator shows how to measure an overbought or an oversold condition, when to buy in a bull market at the end of a downward retracement, and when to sell short when a bear market rally is cresting.

Stochastics—
Overbought/Oversold Indicator:
Use with Moving Averages in a
Trending Market

When to Buy Low and Sell High

One technical indicator, *stochastics,* helps to achieve that elusive goal that many investors dream of—of buying low and selling high. Of course, it is not quite as simple as that, but the idea is nevertheless sound.

When a stock has gone up powerfully, stochastics show a very high or *overbought* reading, and vice versa when a stock has fallen sharply and stochastics reach an *oversold* level. Emotions invite some people to chase a surging market and to despair of one that is collapsing. Others are never satisfied unless they buy as near as possible to an absolute bottom and sell as near as possible to an absolute top. Stochastics do the job of suggesting when price might reach a top or a bottom, and, when they turn, stochastics suggest that price may turn too.

There are often wonderful buying opportunities when a stock has sold off sharply but remains, in the big picture, in an uptrend. Similarly, there are often prime opportunities to get out of a stock that you own or to sell short when a major bear market rally crests prior to resumption of the major downtrend.

However, you do not use stochastics, on their own, to anticipate a trend reversal: Markets can go much farther than you might expect, in both directions, and you don't stand in front of the proverbial freight train. It is worth repeating yet again the axiom: *A trend in force is likely to remain in force—until market action shows, decisively, that there may be a trend reversal.* Stochastics, therefore, seldom help to identify tops in a stock that is in a major uptrend or bottoms in a stock in a major downtrend. An extreme reading may serve only to indicate the power of the trend, not that the stock is likely to make an imminent trend reversal. Stochastics can go to an overbought or an oversold reading and stay there for a very long time.

Settings for Stochastics

For the technically minded, stochastics show the relationship between the most recent close and the high-low range for a given period. They are similar to the *relative strength index* (RSI). Since RSI is based only on closing prices for a given period, it does not reflect the full range of price action. That information is useful in our core overbought/oversold indicator because we attribute so much importance to the range for a given bar. When there is a very powerful reversal, stochastics may show a turn that is not evident in the RSI.

As with moving-average convergence/divergence (MACD), stochastics are plotted as a fast line %K and a slow one %D. The fast line shows immediate responsiveness to price action; the slow line shows a more deliberate response. There is quite a wide range of settings that accomplish essentially the same results, although the main thing is to get used to working with what you see.

It is hard to improve on a setting in widespread use, and that often is a default setting, of 9, 3, 3*S*. Most software does not require the final *S* because the fast variant is not in common use.

The setting expresses the following: %K, the fast line, is based on 9, the number of bars included in the calculations; %D is a three-day moving average of %K. The final 3 smoothes both %K and %D to produce the slow stochastics. The following section presents the parameters for using stochastics.

How to Use Stochastics

Stochastics are used in the same way on the monthly, weekly, and daily charts. This is not a stand-alone indicator. It must be used in conjunction with other indicators. The following are the specific applications:

1. A turn in %K, the fast line, is a signal to buy or sell at whatever level it occurs.

2. A new turn establishing a zigzag, at any level, reinforces the likelihood of price also continuing in the direction of the turn.

3. When %K is below 20, an important buy signal may be developing. %K moving above 20 triggers a buy signal.

4. When %K is above 80, a sell signal may be developing. A move back under 80 generates a sell signal. (%K crossing 20 or 80 should not be confused with %K crossing %D, the slow stochastic. Although in general these crossovers confirm what is happening, they occur too randomly to help with timing.)

5. An overbought %K above 80 counts as a negating indicator on the entry checklist to buy (described in Chapter 18). An oversold %K below 20 counts as a negating indicator on the entry checklist to sell short (described in Chapter 22).

6. An overbought or oversold level indicates that a stock may be vulnerable to a retracement. It is particularly important to heed overbought or oversold readings on the monthly chart. Buying a stock with an overbought %K or selling one short when it is oversold may involve above-average risk, particularly when the stock is pressing against previous levels of support or resistance (discussed in Chapter 11).

7. An overbought or oversold reading does not mean that you cannot buy or sell a stock at all—just that there is a powerful amber light flashing, and you have to pay special attention. Extreme readings may be an expression of powerful buying or selling, particularly when a stock first breaks out of a consolidation or a trading range. %K almost always will show a high reading when the price of a stock first moves to a new 52-week high and a low reading at a 52-week low. Then, despite extended stochastics readings, there may be a prime opportunity to buy or sell, as long as you do it right away.

8. Ms and multiple tops in %K developing at a level above 80 may be particularly significant, especially when occuring on longer-term charts and especially when price has been able to make little or no further upward progress. They suggest that buying has really been running out of fire power and that sellers have become more willing. Similarly, Ws and multiple bottoms developing at a level below 20 may suggest exhaustion of selling pressure, so the line of least resistance for price now may be upward. This point proceeds from the concept that is fundamental to our overall approach, namely, that persistence indicates what is likely to happen, and a second signal is more than twice as likely to succeed as the first one.

9. Stochastics and price should more or less work together. When they don't, there is what technicians call *negative divergence*. When there is a lower high in stochastics but a higher high in price, stochastics are more likely than price to indicate the underlying strength of the market, and vice versa in a declining market.

10. Stochastics often work extremely well when used in conjunction with moving averages in *an already designated bull or bear market*. When there is a very low stochastics reading and price turns up at or near the rising moving averages, there is often a prime buying opportunity. When there is a very high stochastics reading and a price turns down at or near the declining moving averages, there is often a prime opportunity to sell short (or a prime opportunity to sell a stock that you should no longer own).

Stochastics and the
Dow Jones Industrials

Stochastics work most successfully as an independent indicator only in markets that you seldom want to invest in! Sometimes you can identify a trading range within which the market goes from the bottom of the box to the top and then back again. When the %K fast stochastic goes below 20 and then turns up and, in addition, price is at the bottom of the box, it may be time to buy. When %K goes above 80 and then turns down and, in addition, price has reached the top of the box, it may be time to sell.

The monthly chart for the Dow Jones Industrial Average during the years 1965 to 1983 shows how this concept works in a broad trading-range market (Fig. 10-1). This example may prove to be particularly useful in the next decade or so. The 25- and 40-month moving averages wandered approximately through the middle of the range, serving roughly as a median and not succeeding in showing the direction until the end of 1982, when stocks broke out of their huge trading range and the big bull market began.

This chart demonstrates the special effectiveness of point 8 above, about Ms and Ws occurring in the indicators as well as price. There is more than twice the chance of success on a second signal occurring at an overbought or an oversold level than there is on just one. Price and, as shown by arrows on the chart, stochastics made a double bottom after going below 20 in 1970, 1974, 1978, and 1982, and the ensuing upward thrusts were very substantial, sometimes taking stochastics right up to the 80 level and the Dow went a very long way, if not always to the top of the range. Double tops occurred only in 1972 and 1976, but they preceded major declines.

The problem with reliance on stochastics on their own is shown by the blast-out in 1983, when the Dow was to skyrocket by 300 points, or 30 percent above the top of the range, before running out of steam. In this case, stochastics merely expressed a very powerfully moving market.

Note that the period from 1965 to 1983 was absolutely not by any means the wasteland for astute investors that you might expect from looking at the chart for the Dow Jones Industrials. Throughout this period, there were many opportunities to buy great shares at a very good price. However, it had to be done very selectively. It was during this period that many fortunes were made, by finding great individual stocks. It was during this period that Warren Buffett and his conglomerate Berkshire Hathaway really got under way—and not just in the bull market that took off in the early 1980s.

Stochastics and Apache Corporation

The monthly chart for Apache Corporation (APA), the independent oil and gas producer, shows stochastics in practice in various market conditions (Fig. 10-2).

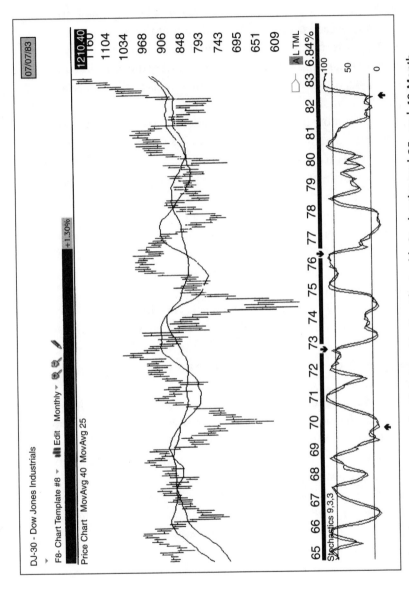

FIGURE 10-1 Dow Jones Industrials Monthly Bar Chart with Stochastics and 25- and 40-Month Moving Averages.

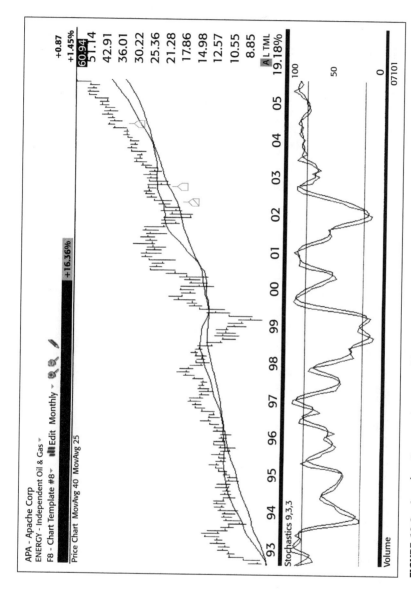

FIGURE 10-2 Apache Corporation Monthly Chart with Stochastics and 25- and 40-Month Moving Averages.

Stochastics formed a double top in 1993 ahead of the decline from the $14.50 level to the $9 level—a decline that looks small on this chart but which was, of course, significant.

For the next four years of sideways market action, stochastics on the monthly chart had nothing to say until the significantly lower second high occurred in mid-1997, when the price was at a new high. In accordance with point 9 above, the significantly lower high in stochastics, in conjunction with a higher high in price, shows negative divergence. This sets off a warning that the stochastics rather than price are more likely to be signifying the underlying strength of the market. Given that the stock had not been exceptionally strong, there was a distinct possibility of it setting back more seriously than just for a routine retracement.

The washout in 1999 occurred in conjunction with a bottom in the price of crude oil just above $10. There was no reason even to consider buying APA on the basis of the 25- and 40-month moving averages. However, there was a superb W in stochastics, with both lows under 20. If you suspected that the price of oil was not going to zero, and if you were aware that APA was a well-financed, well-managed, and strong company in the petroleum business, you might have been inclined to heed the double bottom in stochastics in 1999 despite the paucity of other confirming indicators. When the second upturn occurred, it showed that the downside momentum had totally gone out of the stock and that there was now a reasonable probability that everyone wanting to sell the stock had already done so. Stochastics provided one of the few ways of knowing that this was a stock to consider buying and specifically *when*—namely, on completion of the second stochastics upturn from below 20 in conjunction with a very strong monthly reversal bar.

Much the same occurred at the low in 2001, but with a significant difference. This time there was just a single upturn in stochastics from a deeply oversold reading. However, in this instance, the 45-month moving average was still inclining strongly upward, and price had held at this average with just a temporary penetration.

After the upturn in 2001, APA was on its way and never seriously faltered. The monthly chart shows two further prime buying opportunities in 2002 on the basis of price rules and convergence with the monthly moving averages. Stochastics confirmed the second one, with a W occurring in the middle of the range between 20 and 80.

Now we come to another really important point about stochastics that eludes many investors. In a really strong bull market, stochastics go to an overbought condition and jam there. A ripple below the 80 percent line most likely means nothing. The fact that there is an extremely overbought condition doesn't necessarily mean that you can't buy it, but you should at least look for an entry when there is a correction on the weekly or daily chart.

Buy Apache from the Weekly and Daily Charts

The weekly chart for APA shows numerous opportunities to buy the stock on completion of small corrections that were not perceptible on the monthly chart (Fig. 10-3). Time after time the stock came back to the 25- and 40-week moving averages and notably to the 40-week moving average that equates to the 200-day moving average. Stochastics did not by any means always come close to reaching an oversold reading below 20, but new upturns always coincided with a new upturn in price.

The daily chart for APA shows much the same thing as the weekly chart (Fig. 10-4). If you looked only at the daily chart, you might have been very nervous during the apparent plunge from the high in April 2004 from the $46 level to the $38.50 level, which was 16 percent below the high.

It is essential, however, to remember the point that a stock bought when the time is right and the indicators first deliver a confirming signal is one that you can allow room to fluctuate without becoming anxious. It is mostly when you chase an already overbought stock that has moved far away from its moving averages that you may have to live through an uncomfortable retracement. If you bought when stochastics were coming out of a low and when price appeared to bouncing off the moving averages, you would know that selling was likely to be close to running its course. A mental stop of just 10 percent or so below such an entry would be easy to live with compared with what happened on the retracement from the April 2004 high. Then, as it turned out, you would have had to allow the stock the full 16 percent room to fluctuate that it actually took, plus a further 10 percentage points or so. Not so good!

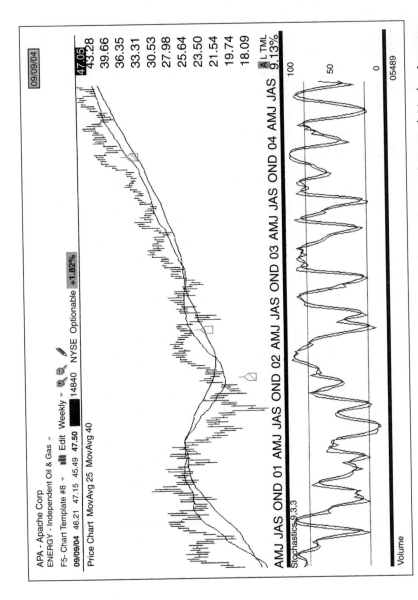

FIGURE 10-3 Apache Corporation Weekly Chart with Stochastics and 25- and 40-Week Moving Averages.

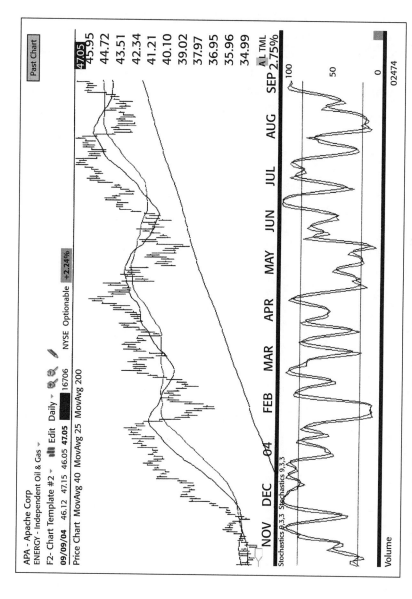

FIGURE 10-4 Apache Corporation Daily Chart with Stochastics and 25-, 40- and 200-Day Moving Averages.

Many people find stochastics the hardest of all indicators to believe and to act on. However, it is from this disbelief that the best opportunities for entry often develop. There is a saying that the best trades are the hardest ones to take and that the easy ones are the ones most likely to blow up in your face. Yes, it is hard to buy rather than sell when there are retracements in a bull market. As you can see from the chart for APA, however, the probabilities are favorable when you do.

CHAPTER 11

Support and Resistance: Trendlines, Channel Lines, and Linear Retracement

Drawing a Trendline

Trendlines, along with channel lines, which are their counterpart, stand the test of time. Since many investors use them, their effectiveness becomes self-fulfilling.

A trendline connects lows in a rising market and highs in a declining market. You can draw a tentative trendline when two prominent highs or lows become established. The validity of a trendline is confirmed only when price returns to the assumed trendline for a third time or more and again turns there. It is often tempting to assume that a trendline is developing on the appearance of every small blip in price action. However, most good trendlines require a significant length of time between highs and lows. By extension, the longer a trendline remains in force, the more validity it has.

Many software packages and chart services provide a choice between arithmetic and logarithmic chart scaling, and their respective impact on trendlines is significant. Arithmetic scaling treats all price action the same, regardless of the percentage of fluctuations. Logarithmic scaling produces charts that adjust for the proportion, or the percentage, of price fluctuations. Arithmetic charts are useful when there is no more than about a doubling in price from the low point on the chart to the high. Logarithmic charts are useful when larger moves are involved. Logarithmic charts therefore generally are more useful when drawing trendlines and channel lines for stocks. However, arithmetic charts are better for Treasury bonds and commodity futures markets.

Drawing a Channel Line

After finding or assuming a trendline in a rising market, find the most distant point above the trendline, ideally the one found between the two lows that mark the contact points for the trendline, and draw a line parallel to it. There is then an upper channel line and a lower trendline between which the stock should fluctuate. In a declining market, draw the trendline by joining highs in price and then draw a channel line parallel to it from the most distant point below the trendline.

The idea behind trendlines and channel lines is that price typically zigzags backward and forward between the trendline and the channel line. In a steadily trending market, price moves backward and forward while maintaining a steady overall direction. It is similar to the way a sailing boat tacks backward and forward while maintaining an overall direction between the two tacks—hence the term *linear retracement*. A trendline is, in a sense, a form of moving average (discussed in Chapter 9), for it shows both direction and speed.

In both a rising market and a declining market, you may want to draw a channel line that fits best the overall strength (or weakness) and direction of the market, rather than at an absolute extremity—channel lines are less consistent than trendlines, with more susceptibility to overshoots and undershoots. Failure to reach all the way to a channel line may signify impending weakness in the overall strength of the trend. However, for a strongly moving stock, it is also worth drawing one or more additional lines parallel to the channel line and at the same distance from it as the distance between the original trendline and the first channel line. If the stock goes through a channel line, it is likely to fluctuate within a new range bounded by the original channel line and the next parallel and equidistant channel line. The original channel line becomes support and, in effect, the new trendline.

When a stock declines through an uptrend line in a bull market, the probabilities favor a downward extension, and it seldom pays to hold a stock once it has decisively penetrated a clearly upward trendline on the monthly chart. In the event that there is a false breakdown, sometimes known as a *bear trap*, you can always buy the stock back. However, the best stocks to own rarely violate major trendlines. Even a breakdown that appears to be an aberration may be a harbinger of trouble ahead. Similarly, it seldom pays to continue holding a stock short once it has gone up through a major downtrend line.

The Standard & Poor's (S&P) 500 and Linear Retracement on the Monthly Chart

Since the stock market crash in 1987, trendlines and channel lines have worked for the S&P 500 index almost like dancing (Fig. 11-1).

The first potential trendline on the monthly chart for the S&P can be drawn from the October 1987 low at *A* to *B*, after the market showed that it had stopped going down and had drawn away from there. At the same time, a potential channel line can be extended from the preceding high at *D*, parallel to the assumed trendline. Four years later, the S&P 500 retraced to the assumed trendline at *C* and turned exactly there. The assumed channel line briefly stopped the new move up at *E*, but the market resumed its uptrend with renewed strength after a brief pullback.

Once the S&P 500 made a new high, one could assume a new and steeper upward trendline marked from *F* that has its starting point at *C* and goes on to *G* and *H* before failing at *I*. The sharp decline from 1190 to 923, or 22 percent, stopped with uncanny exactitude at *H*, right on that upward trendline.

A first channel line that might have been drawn parallel to this upward trendline off the high at *E* produced the only assumption that failed, but it failed only because the market was too strong and went beyond it. However, the channel line drawn off the high at *J*, after the stopping point at *H* had been found to be good, served as the upper boundary for the rest of the bull market.

Note that the S&P 500 made an unsuccessful attempt to reach the channel line before it fell through the upward trendline at *I*. Once the trendline was broken, the bull market ended, decisively, and the bear

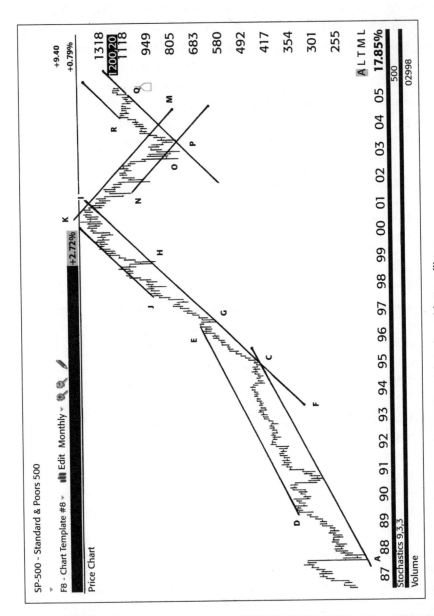

FIGURE 11-1 Standard & Poor's 500 Monthly Index with Trendlines.

market began. It might have come as a surprise to those unfamiliar with the long-term history of markets that such a severe bear market was to unfold. However, it should not have been any surprise at all that the bull market did come to its eventual end. This much is generally known—that all markets eventually end.

Once the new bear market began, one major rally stopped at a new downward trendline from K to L. Once this downward trendline was assumed, it was, of course, possible to assume a channel line parallel to it beginning at the low at N. In due course, there were to be two monthly closes just below this channel line and then a final test from which the S&P 500 rebounded and never looked back when the new bull market began. When the downward trendline from K to M had been crossed, the new bull market was confirmed.

Once an identifiable low could be confirmed at Q, one could assume a potential new bull market that was likely to have its upward thrusts contained by the channel line extending from the high at R. Should the S&P 500 seriously falter and fail to reach toward that channel line, it might turn out that the bull market was short-lived. It might prove to be no more than a huge rally in a secular bear market, like the rally that crested in January 1930 after rallying by 52 percent from the low of the crash the previous October.

Trendlines and Channel Lines on the S&P 500 Weekly Chart

The weekly chart for the S&P 500 index between 2000 and 2005 shows the same thing as the monthly chart but in more detail (Fig. 11-2).

On this chart, you can see better that it would be possible to assume, initially, a steeper downward trendline than the one drawn from A after the high at B stopped the big bear market rally. A tentative channel line parallel to the trendline and connecting the initial lows from D to E was to be significant in reflecting the speed and direction of the market. In accordance with channel-line theory, it was the low at F that signified the amplitude of this bear market's fluctuations.

You can see that the rally at C produced a double top, with the second high slightly above the downward trendline. Count this as an imperfection but not a serious one in view of the continuing decline of the 40-month moving average.

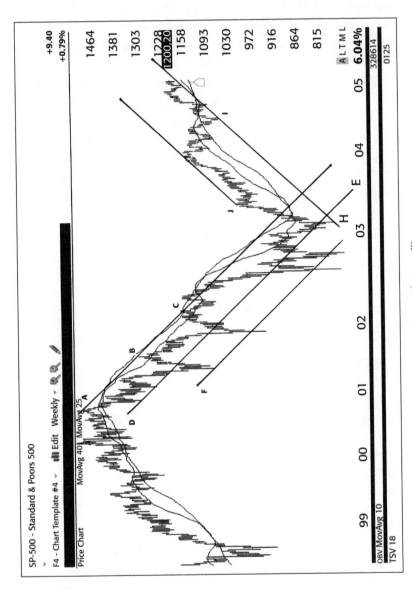

FIGURE 11-2 Standard & Poor's 500 Weekly Index with Trendlines.

Once the downward trendline had been penetrated decisively with the upside breakout in early 2003, the bear market could be declared ended. This might have been a brave thing to do except for several other confirming indicators. Market action at the bottom comprised a kind of double W, with three sharp declines to approximately the same level and with the third one delivering enough thrust to make the charge through the downward trendline. In addition, there was enough basing action between July of 2002 and March 2003 to make the 25-month moving average turn up by the time the breakout occurred, and the 40-month moving average turned up soon afterwards.

There is no doubt that the upward trendline *H-I* is drawn correctly, as well as the channel line extending from *J*, which already has achieved a second validation. The sell-off in January 2005 sorely tested this new upward trendline, and the market needed to get on its way in order to inspire confidence in the potential durability of this new bull market. A downside penetration of the upward trendline *H-I* could well signify that the entire rally is no more than an echo rally in a secular bear market.

Trendlines and linear retracement theory apply to all charts of all durations for all markets. Trendlines also can be used on technical indicators such as on-balance volume and momentum indicators. They do not by any means work all the time—no indicators do. When they work, though, the messages they send can result in spectacularly successful investments. The greater challenge is to have the confidence to believe the technical signals when they occur and to act on them when it is timely to do so.

Support and Resistance at Historic Highs and Lows

There is an important element of the psychology of buying and selling that has nothing to do with what you can learn about a company from analyzing its balance sheet. It is simply a question of where the price of a share has been before. When someone who is losing money in a share is disappointed, there is a strong temptation to hang on until it is possible to break even. Thus a share that has gone down from an identifiable high is likely to run into selling when it comes back to or close to that level.

Similarly, if buyers have stepped in to buy a share at a certain level that has previously contained a decline, people will come back if it returns to test that level again.

Once a share has broken above a previous resistance level, it is likely that retracements will hold at a level at or above that breakout level. Similarly, in a declining market, rallies are likely to run into trouble at the underside of the congestion area from which the price broke down. Note the principle that previous resistance, once decisively exceeded, becomes the first strong level of support for downward retracements. After a downward break, previous support, once decisively broken, becomes a strong potential lid for any subsequent rallies.

The monthly chart for Caterpillar, Inc. (CAT), shows how time and again the price heeded previous highs and lows (Fig. 11-3). Since each bar represents a month of trading activity, you also can see how long it can take for the market to pay attention to those levels—it has a memory because investors have a memory!

The bottom line on the chart begins at the level of the 1994 high and extends across to support the price in 1996, 2000, and 2002.

There is a short line at the 1995 high that shows how CAT had to consolidate for eight months before it was able to break out to a new high and move to what were to be new highs.

The ensuing climb to the 1997 high put in place a high that was to be exceeded just a tad in 1999, but essentially sellers came in at that level and knocked the price down again. Once the price finally went on to a new high in 2003, the previous resistance became support for the retracement in 2004.

Gaps as Support and Resistance

The daily chart for Amazon.com shows the price gapping all over the place (Fig. 11-4). Once price gaps, it should follow through. It can and often does come back to try to fill the gap, but if it does not do so soon, it may never happen. As a general rule, you want to beware of buying or holding a share that gaps against you and fails to get back soon to above the level of the gap.

The big gap down in October 2004 showed that there were aggressive sellers determined to get out of the stock at any price rather than see whether they could do better on a retracement. In the event, the gap proved to be a temporary selling climax, and the shares climbed back to the September high and even went a little higher. The upward surge at the end of December 2004 might have suggested, in isolation,

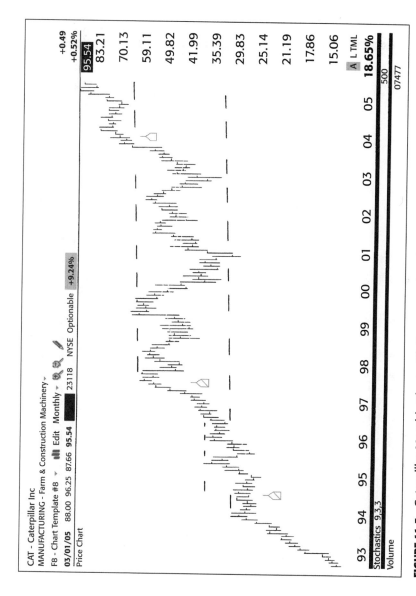

CAT - Caterpillar Inc
MANUFACTURING - Farm & Construction Machinery ▾
F8 - Chart Template #8 ▾ ▥ Edit Monthly ▾ ◔ ◕ ✎
03/01/05 88.00 96.25 87.66 95.54 ▮ 23118 NYSE Optionable +9.24%
Price Chart

+0.49
+0.52%

95.54
83.21
70.13
59.11
49.82
41.99
35.39
29.83
25.14
21.19
17.86
15.06

Stochastics 9,3,3
Volume

93 94 95 96 97 98 99 00 01 02 03 04 05

A L TML 18.65%
500
07477

FIGURE 11-3 Caterpillar Monthly Chart with Support and Resistance.

115

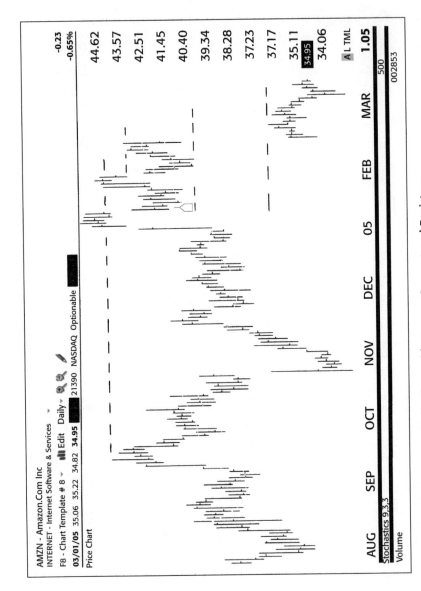

FIGURE 11-4 Amazon.com Daily Chart with Gaps as Support and Resistance.

that the stock was taking flight despite the shakedown in October. However, the monthly chart (not shown here) told a different story, and the surge was short-lived, stopping only a little beyond the September high, which proved to be the ultimate resistance level before the next break.

After the next gap down in January 2005, the shares were able to rally all the way into the gap plus a grand total of 6 cents, on the basis of the closing price, before falling away again.

The stock then gapped down again on February 4, jumping far beyond the support of the lows a few days earlier. When taken in conjunction with the hopelessly feeble attempts at holding, there was no reasonable expectation of the shares starting to climb again in the foreseeable future. For the time being, they were holding above the October low, but it was likely that that support level would soon give way.

There is an informal rule that a gap unfilled on a closing basis for three days may remain unfilled because buyers and sellers have established a new equilibrium bounded by the gap left behind. Gaps left behind when stochastics (discussed in Chapter 10) have been at an extreme level, beyond 10 or 80, increase the probability of the support or resistance holding in the future.

Curious as it may seem, support and resistance levels work! They do so for two reasons that are partly psychological and partly historical. First, investors remember where they previously bought or sold their shares or wanted to. Second, investors and market makers know this, and they know where the trendlines and the support and resistance levels are on the charts. All in all, therefore, investors make happen what they expect to happen, and they do so with sufficient reliability that one can know in advance what to expect, and one can trade accordingly.

CHAPTER 12

Chart Patterns That Work

The Long-Term Saucer Bottom

The single most reliable chart pattern may be the symmetrical saucer bottom with an upward incline on the right-hand side. When it develops over several years on the monthly chart and in addition the price has recently made a new all-time high, the likelihood of an upward extension is almost guaranteed. The development of this chart pattern is almost certain to occur in conjunction with strong price-rule buy signals on the monthly, weekly, and daily charts.

The chart for WAG in 2005 shows the stock in the process of completing this kind of saucer (Fig 12-1). The stock made a high in November 2000 at $45.75. In due course the price settled back to $28.65 in March 2003, when the major stock indexes also made their third and final low for the bear market. Compared with the more vigorous market action in many speculative or oversold stocks, WAG's advance from that eventual low was rather sedate. Nevertheless, the steady uptrend was to become tenacious, and it was also to gather momentum—an immensely positive sign.

There is a rough rule of thumb that the target price should be as far again as the amplitude of the range from which the stock breaks out. The longer the consolidation, and the more powerful the stock's history, the more likely the stock is to exceed that target. On this basis a reasonable minimum price target for WAG would be $62.85, up from a price of $48 in July 2005, by the end of 2006, and from there it could keep on going.

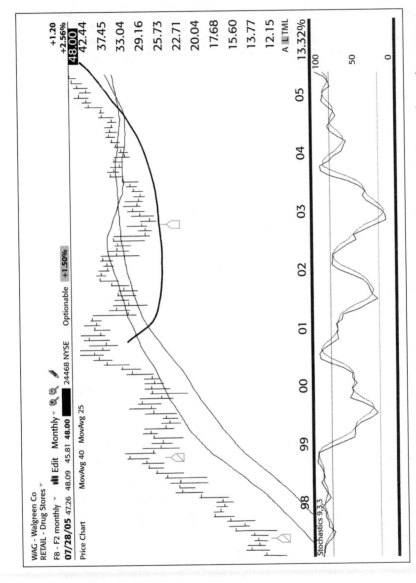

FIGURE 12-1 Walgreen Co. Monthly Bar Chart: Saucer Bottom with 25- and 40-month moving averages and upwardly zigzagging stochastics.

The amplitude of the retracement from top to bottom since the high in 2000 was $17.10, and this number is added to the 2000 high of $45.75.

Walgreens stores sell prescription and nonprescription drugs and general merchandise through its drugstore chain in the United States. In addition, the company provides pharmacy benefits management, mail service prescriptions, and other clinical services. The business model, with its immensely strong franchise, is likely to be good a line business as the population ages and spends more on all aspects of health care. At a price of $48, WAG had a price/earnings ratio of 31 and a dividend yield of just 0.6 percent. In 2005 the 5-year growth rate in earnings had been 15 percent, and the 5-year growth rate in dividends just 8 percent. Given that the stock was selling at a P/E twice its growth rate and its dividend was miniscule, WAG was expensive. Nevertheless, the chances of things going wrong were small. Technically, the long-term saucer bottom suggested that something might be going on in the company to justify not only its current price but a price that could be significantly higher in the foreseeable future.

The Short-Term Saucer Bottom

Granted that long-term saucer bottoms in great stocks are relatively few and far between, you can still find shorter term saucer bottoms occurring with reasonable frequency. The daily chart for SBC Communications (SBC) was developing just such a pattern in the summer of 2005, and it did so in conjunction with a leap over its 200-day moving average (Fig. 12-2). At a price of $24.73, SBC had a price/earnings ratio of 16 and a dividend yield of 5.4 percent. Better yet, it had a 5-year record of dividend increases approaching that of WAG, at 6 percent.

SBC is engaged in the highly competitive domestic telecom industry and the stock had been struggling off its low and was still more than 50 percent below its 2000 high. Nevertheless, this component of the Dow Jones Industrial index looked to be on its way to living successfully with its challenges in the marketplace.

The Trading-Range Breakout

A long sideways trading pattern may suggest great upside potential with low downside risk, and the prospect of getting in, if not necessarily on the ground floor, at least when the ratio of reward to risk is highly

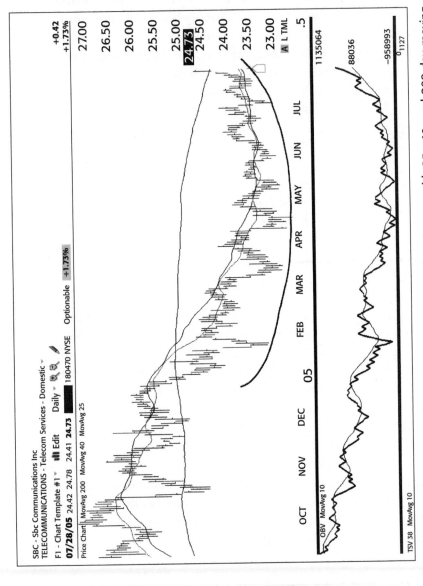

FIGURE 12-2 SBC Communications Daily Bar Chart: Saucer Bottom with 25-, 40- and 200-day moving averages, and OBV.

favorable. These situations develop during a period of consolidation, with chart patterns forming that suggest that there is no particular interest in buying or selling to move the stock strongly one way or the other.

It does not follow, of course, that all or even most sideways market action is a forerunner of a worthwhile move. Sometimes a stock can be becalmed for years on end, trading between a floor below and a ceiling above. The price of Bank of England stock went more or less sideways for 150 years, sometimes doubling, sometimes halving, but never going much farther either way. That agony ended with nationalization in 1946.

It may also be that a company's shares remain stuck in a trading range because its business is mature and its management has neither the desire nor the means to make the business grow. Worse, a company's shares may be trading sideways because its technology is obsolescent. Shares of a mining company, for example, may languish because its ore body is in sight of exhaustion. In such cases, the eventual resolution of sideways trading may be downward.

How Success Starts

This is how emerging corporate success starts and how the shares begin a significant move out of a trading range. At last, there is enough critical mass of corporate success, as well as enough critical mass of ownership by smart money. Then new buying pressure comes in to disturb the equilibrium of buyers and sellers. The stock appears on the list of actively traded stocks or on the list of stocks making a new 52-week high. This makes people start to pay attention and to try to find out if anything is happening. Closer examination leads to more widespread appreciation in the form of buyers putting real money into the stock, and being prepared to pay a progressively higher price to get in.

There is time enough to consider buying the stock now. If the company has laid good groundwork, its newfound success will not be a short-lived aberration. The stock may be the next Microsoft, McDonald's, or Wal-Mart. Investors climb on the bandwagon, and the stock begins to surge. Everyone likes to buy a great stock early. It may seem as if the stock has come a long way already. However, even buying early may mean buying after a double in the expectation that the price will go on to double and double again.

By no means do all breakouts follow through. Nevertheless, some of those that do go on to great things make buying breakouts really

worthwhile. The winners make huge money, whereas the losses are relatively small. If you double your money on half your purchases of breakout stocks and lose a quarter on the other half, on balance, you make
lots of money. Besides, you may well be able to improve on those ratios.
You can often tell at the time which are likely to be the best breakouts
by looking at other indicators, notably on-balance volume (OBV) and
moving-average convergence/divergence (MACD).

St. Jude Medical Comes to Life

When a stock is trading within a range, as St. Jude Medical (STJ) did
from 1990 to 2000, there is no prospect of making a big profit any time
soon (Fig. 12-3). This stock began a decade in the $7 range, and there is
exactly where it ended.

In 1995, STJ broke out of the trading range that had lasted for five
years. It did so by way of a big spurt from a level below the bottom of
the developing range as it then was. After more than doubling from its
low, it looked as if it might be taking flight. However, there was no long-
term record of gains in the price of the shares, as there had been at the
end of the 1980s, and this surge did not develop from a particularly good
base. The cradling above the 25- and 40-month moving averages was
relatively brief before the stock settled back down again. Although there
were good reasons to expect this breakout to succeed, it did not, so count
this as one that simply did not work. STJ was to settle back into its trading
range for a further five years.

Over the two-year period between 1998 and 2000, an impressive W
formed on the monthly chart. Despite the severity of the general bear
market, here was a stock that had made its low in 1998 and held well
above that low in February 2000. Better yet, market action kept on
improving for the stock even as the bear market was grinding lower for
the high flyers of the previous decade, as well as for most blue chips.
There were two obvious places to buy the stock. The first was on completion of a powerful monthly rule 5 buy signal when the breakout
occurred. As can be seen in hindsight, there followed six months of
sideways action, which might have seemed at the time to be hard to
live with. However good the concept of market timing may be, as long
as no damage is done to the chart pattern, you cannot escape from the
need to be patient when a good signal is in force and while a stock digests
a gain. As often occurs, STJ had to settle back briefly to the breakout

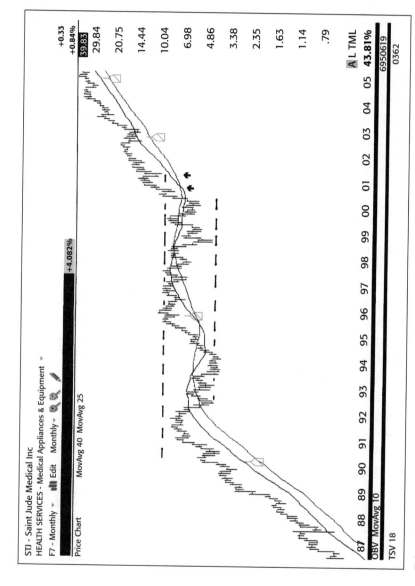

FIGURE 12-3 St. Jude Medical Monthly Chart: Sideways Pattern.

level before making a monthly upside reversal, from which the ensuing move up was to get under way.

It didn't hurt to know that STJ is in the medical appliances business, operating in an environment that has been very good for health care companies. Specifically, STJ's primary business is cardiovascular medical technology.

The recent bear market was unusual in that there were quite a lot of stocks on the general list that were managing to buck the trend. STJ illustrates the point that stocks that are already strong may be the ones to buy when the overall market shows signs of stabilizing. If you waited to buy STJ until October 2002, you would, of course, have had to pay about 50 percent more. Even so, you would have then proceeded to double your money over the next year or so.

The Head-and-Shoulders Top

The monthly chart for McDonald's for the period 1996–2002 illustrates a head-and-shoulders pattern, as well as a reverse head-and-shoulders pattern completed over the next four years (Fig. 12-4). The idea is that the stock surges strongly to a new high, making in the process the left shoulder. Then it settles back and surges again to a higher high, making the head, before settling back yet again. Next, it surges a third time to make the right shoulder. This time the stock fails to exceed the previous high before turning down again.

To signify a top with the greatest reliability, the pattern should take a significant time to form on the monthly chart, often a year or more. On the chart for McDonald's, each stage lasted for many months, with the shoulders taking over a year to form. Ideally, the formation should be as symmetrical as possible, and the right shoulder should be equal to or lower than the left one.

Confirmation of a head-and-shoulders formation occurs when the stock breaks below the so-called neckline, indicated here with a dashed line. Then you can expect the price to fall substantially more, and you can expect a decline equal to the distance from the bottom of the shoulder to the top of the head, and maybe more. Head-and-shoulders formations occur quite often when price is setting up for a significant decline. Although, obviously, they don't always follow through, it is generally better to get out of a stock early rather than late in case a serious decline does occur.

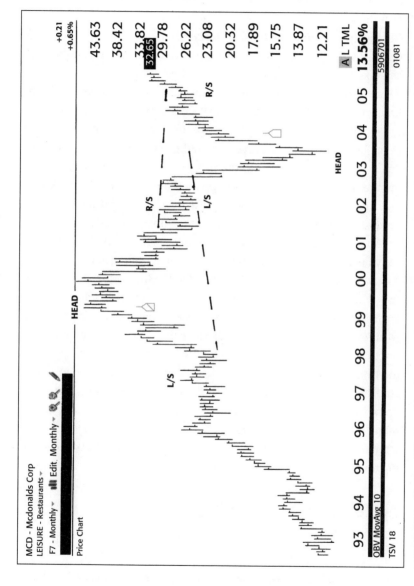

FIGURE 12-4 McDonald's Monthly Chart: Head-and-Shoulders Pattern, Reverse Head-and-Shoulders Pattern.

The Reverse Head-and-Shoulders Pattern

The reverse head-and-shoulders-pattern is, as the name implies, a head-and-shoulders pattern turned upside down. This, too, is a reliable pattern that suggests the possibility that a substantial move can develop. Obviously, few stocks go to zero and certainly not many shares of companies of the stature of McDonald's. On the other hand, a bull market can take the price of a share up by a multiple of several times.

Reversing what happens with a head-and-shoulders bearish formation, you can see that McDonald's (MCD) was trading sideways for some time in 2001–2002. Then it plunged at the end of 2002 and rebounded to the level where it was previously trading sideways. There it consolidated in a similar fashion to the previous sideways action before the plunge down to the low. If, as happened here, an upside breakout to new highs follows after completion of a big reverse head-and-shoulders pattern, the probabilities strongly favor a substantial advance.

A reverse head-and-shoulders pattern suggests that the stock has truly been through the wringer with climactic selling at the bottom, as surely occurred in McDonald's stock. On the first low, the stock tested the mettle of patient shareholders. Many of those buy-and-hold long-term investors still held onto the stock. Then a cathartic cleansing wrung out many of the last diehards who bought at a much higher price. They thought they were in for the long term, but the pressure of the final panic sell-off was too much. Now smart money could really start accumulating the stock with confidence. However, there is no point in trying to be smart too early. The best chart patterns can take many months and even years to develop, not just a few days or weeks after a selling climax. Buying too early may simply lock you into a trading range like the one we saw lasting for years in STJ.

Apple Computer Takes Flight

Sometimes advantageous chart patterns can be staring you in the face, but their interpretation is not immediately obvious. The monthly chart for Apple Computer (AAPL) shows rather an effective reverse head-and-shoulders pattern once you look at it closely (Fig. 12-5). The relatively low head and the much higher right shoulder than the left one constitute

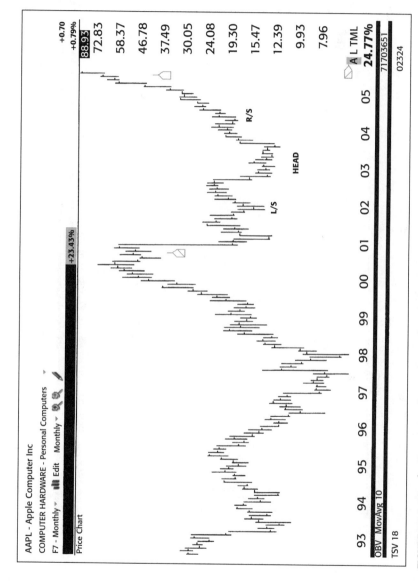

FIGURE 12-5 Apple Computer: Reverse Head-and-Shoulders Pattern.

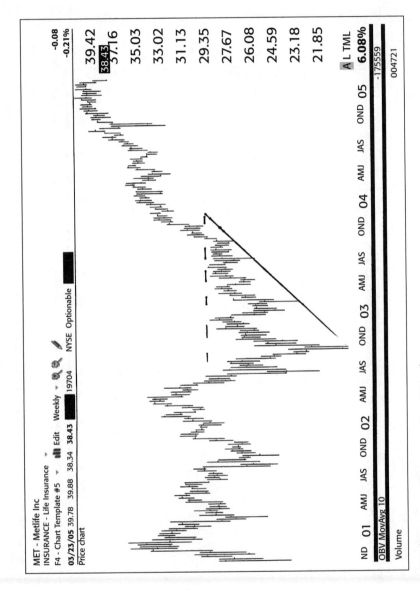

FIGURE 12-6 Metlife: Ascending Triangle.

a powerfully bullish pattern, and once the January 2002 high was taken out, the stock took off like what looks like a rocket on the monthly chart but what looks like an orderly and steady climb on the daily chart.

As background, at the low, the company was valued at not much more than its cash on hand, with the computer business and the research and development of the iPod valued at next to nothing. Then iPod hit the market, became an immediate success, and also went on to exceed all expectations.

The Ascending Triangle

The ascending triangle is also a very powerful chart pattern when other indicators confirm. It occurs as a consolidation during the course of a major move or as one is just starting. The idea is that you see a succession of higher lows, but there is a flat lid on top of the highs within the formation. Eventually, price approaches the apex of the triangle, and the passage of time compels it to break out one way or the other. Since it is evident that sellers became less aggressive each time the price tested downward, the probabilities favor an increase in the aggressiveness of buyers if the price breaks upward.

This is exactly what happened in Metlife (MET) toward the end of 2003 (Fig. 12-6). As with other consolidation patterns, an upward breakout suggests that price may reach upward toward an initial target by an amount equal to the vertical base of the triangle. In this case, the triangle has a base comprising approximately $6 in price, thereby setting up an initial target of about $36. On reaching $35.80 in February, the price went sideways for the next seven months until it swooped down into an October seasonal low and then went out to a new high.

CHAPTER 13

Major Market Turns

Establishing the Conditions

There are regularly recurring conditions—political, financial, demographic, and emotional—that are likely to establish important highs and lows on the charts. For example, an obvious financial condition influencing stock prices is the raising or lowering of interest rates, discussed in Chapter 23. Given the immense amplitude of stock market fluctuations, investors can profit munificently from an awareness of cyclical forces manifested with uncanny regularity. You may as well benefit when you have the wind behind you, and put out less sail to the wind, or none, when storms are more likely.

Looking for lows is particularly worthwhile because you can make so much money when you get in during the early stages of a new bull market or a new upward thrust within an ongoing bull market. Similarly, you need to protect profits and not to buy more stock when cyclical forces are within a time frame to crest ahead of a period of prolonged consolidation or, worse, new bear market. Mapping these cyclical forces helps you to avoid the tragic consequences that many investors have experienced during recurrent bear markets—notably but by no means exclusively the one between 2000 and 2002.

The Four-Year Presidential Cycle

Foremost among conditions for lows, and more erratically for highs, is the four-year presidential cycle for the stock market. There is a regular rhythm that sets up a pattern for a rising stock market during the year of a presidential election. Incumbents want to win if they are seeking reelection or in any case to secure a successor from their own party. This political imperative mandates delivering as much of the unpopular strong medicine as possible during the first year or two of the four-year term and as much good stuff as possible heading into the election.

Within the presidential cycle there is a semi-independent tendency for stocks to go up between October and May of any year regardless of the presidential cycle and to go sideways to down between May and October. Many of the most prominent lows have occurred in October, making that a prime time to buy when the technical conditions are right to do so. Within the four-year presidential cycle, you should be looking for market lows in October two years before the next presidential election. In order to finish the job of cleansing the market at the low, it has generally been safer to time an entry at the end of October rather than earlier in the month. You might get in at a better price earlier in the month, but the risk of a return to the low or of a new low is less by the end of the month. Less obvious as to the exactitude of timing, or even the need to do so, one should be prepared to sell in the first week of January after a presidential election.

Table 13-1 shows that market action in the Presidential cycle has had only one really big failure over a period of more than a century, namely at the time to buy in 1930. Otherwise, it has worked with sufficient reliability to constitute one of the most valuable big-picture indicators for market timing. The table shows that the net result for buy-and-hold versus buy-and-sell using the Presidential cycle is extremely similar for more than a century.

The table does not show the fact that the swings between tops and bottoms are considerably more extreme for buy-and-hold than for buy-and-sell, notably in the period between 1929 and 1933, but also between 2000 and 2005. Make a relatively small adjustment for the big loss booked as a result of the losing buy signal in 1930, and the buy-and-sell strategy handily beats the buy-and-hold strategy. Similarly, the setback in the NASDAQ 100 between its all-time high in March 2000 and the sell in January 2001 resulted in a huge drawdown which might have been lessened considerably by selling earlier on the basis of market timing indicators. Nevertheless, the point remains valid that selling captured a substantial gain and averted turning a big profit into a big loss.

Consider too the fact that the buy-and-sell strategy is in the market for just 26 months in every 48-month cycle, or just over half the time. Therefore the risk for the buy-and-hold strategy is significantly higher, particularly if you buy at or near a market top. Buy-and-hold tends to outperform buy-and-sell during strong bull markets, notably during the 1950s and the 1990s. Buy-and-sell tends to outperform at other times, and notably during the long-drawn-out sideways period in the 1960s and 1970s. Here are more explanatory comments to put the numbers in the table in their historical context:

1898–1901. A bull market had already been under way from a January low at 40—a number that was to have to be revisited many times over the next 30 years. The exit was about 10 percent off the top for the move.

1902–1905. The entry occurred during the course of a protracted bear market and just ahead of a breakdown that was to end at 42 in December the following year. From that seasonal low, the Dow was to move up very strongly to its eventual high at 103 in 1906, a full year after the programmed sell at 65. Therefore, both the entry and the exit should have shifted exactly one year later.

1906–1909. Here too, both the entry and the exit shifted exactly a year late. The actual range of the presidential bull market extended from 53 in December 1907 to 100 in January 1910.

1918–1921. The top came early, so strict application of the exit timing in January 1921 resulted in turning a substantial profit into a moderate loss. At the top there was a clear broken trendline and a marked head-and-shoulders pattern.

1925. The exit occurred exactly as the market was breaking out of its decades-long consolidation and meant missing a worthwhile leg of the powerful bull market. However, the re-entry in October 1926 captured a near doubling in the Dow by January 1929.

1929. The exit in January was early but not wrong. It averted the crash in October.

TABLE 13-1 The Presidential Cycle

The Presidential Cycle: When to Buy and Sell the Cycle

Parameters:

1. Buy the Dow Jones Industrial Average in the last week of October, two years before the next Presidential election.
2. Sell in the first week of January after the Presidential election.

The table shows the Dow Jones Industrial Average compared with the result using this Buy/Sell timing, with 1898 = 100 for both.

Buy Date	Buy Price	Sell Date	Sell Price	% Gain (Loss)	1898 = 100 Dow	Buy/Sell
1898	55	1901	70	27	127	127
1902	60	1905	65	8	118	137
1906	95	1909	85	(11)	154	122
1910	83	1913	83	-0-	151	122
1914	53	1917	96	81	174	221
1918	86	1921	74	(16)	135	185
1922	96	1925	121	26	220	233
1926	158	1929	304	94	552	452
1930	190	1933	59	(69)	107	140
1934	93	1937	182	97	330	276
1938	151	1941	133	(12)	242	242
1942	107	1945	154	44	280	349
1946	171	1949	175	2	318	355
1950	225	1953	292	29	536	459
1954	363	1957	499	37	907	629
1958	539	1961	622	15	1,130	723
1962	570	1965	869	52	1,580	1,099
1966	809	1969	925	14	1,681	1,252
1970	754	1973	1,031	37	1,875	1,716
1974	633	1977	978	54	1,778	2,642

TABLE 13-1   *(Continued)*

Buy Date	Buy Price	Sell Date	Sell Price	% Gain (Loss)	1898 = 100 Dow	Buy/Sell
1978	792	1981	980	24	1,781	3,276
1982	995	1985	1,189	19	2,162	3,898
1986	1,851	1989	2,131	15	3,874	4,483
1990	2,346	1993	3,268	39	6,231	5,942
1994	3,850	1997	6,567	71	11,940	10,655
1998	8,592	2001	10,662	24	19,385	13,212
2002	8,397	2005	10,608	26	19,287	16,647
NASDAQ 100, from the 1992 Presidential election: 1990 = 100						
1990	174	1993	355	104	100	100
1994	398	1997	853	114	228	490
1998	1,400	2001	2,267	61	367	1,302
2002	989	2005	1,564	58	580	898

1930. This buy constitutes the one major failure during the twentieth century. Perhaps it might have been handled with a stop loss, or one might have heeded the well-known market principle that the unfolding bear market could be expected to have something of an equal and opposite pattern in order to unwind the excesses of the roaring bull market that had ended in 1929. (This principle, however, failed to work between 2002 and 2005, when the presidential cycle worked munificently!) In any case, despite it being the time to buy in accordance with the four-year presidential cycle, all other indicators were powerfully bearish, and—not necessarily a bearish indicator, as such—the economy was flat on its back. Major bear markets average about two years or a little less. This one was to last 34 months from top to bottom.

1934–1937. This period was exceptional, and a timely buy captured most of the money to be made during the 1930s.

1938–1941. This small decline occurred as World War II was imminent.

1942–1945. Once the United States joined the war, it was an easy assumption that victory was only a matter of time, with the next cycle expressing the optimism for a future that proved, in due course, to be very profitable.

1946–1949. As occurred after World War I, it was to take some time for reconstruction to deliver results sufficient to propel stocks higher.

1950–1962. Once the postwar consolidation ended, a major bull market began. The buy-and-sell timing resulted in missing big chunks of the enduring bull market. The entry in 1954 came almost exactly a year late. Buying in October of the preceding year (the best seasonal time frame regardless of the presidential cycle) would have captured a big move up.

1962–1982. During this time of essentially sideways and lackluster market action, the presidential cycle almost worked like dancing. Presidential cycle buys came at or near market lows, and sells came at or near market tops. Very serious and unnerving declines were avoided entirely.

1986–1989. The table does not reflect the huge run-up and the October 1987 market crash. The timing to buy was superb, but one should have heeded screaming sell signals in the fall of 1987 in order to avoid giving back a huge profit. The net result for this period, a gain of 15 percent, doesn't begin to reflect the dramatic market action that actually occurred. Stocks continued advancing strongly during 1987, until August, even as they faced the competition of strongly rising interest rates, discussed in Chapter 23. Selling in May and going away, as discussed below, resulted in missing the last stages of the bull market but it also averted the crash that wiped out most of the profit—if you failed to get out some time before stocks went into free fall.

1989–1990. The exit occurred almost at the top, and the new buy, almost at the bottom! Thereafter during the 1990s, periods out of the market missed a lot of the bull-market action, as they did in the 1950s.

1998–2005. Back to dancing again, as during the period between 1962 and 1982. The two round trips from bottom to top captured the greater part of the available points without having to endure much of the bear market. Ideally, the sell in January 2001 would have been taken earlier in response to strong sell signals, but the timing still worked very well indeed.

The performance of the technology-heavy NASDAQ 100 Index from the 1992 presidential election missed some of the best of the bull market. The exit in January 2001 was very late—by about a year—but it still did the job of avoiding the worst of the bear market. The timing to buy in October 2002 almost caught the exact bottom, and it may turn out that the exit in January 2005 was a good one.

The four-year presidential cycle can vary, depending to some extent on the specific economic and political conditions of the times, such as wars and the level and direction of interest rates. Lows have occurred six months to a year early, particularly when the market is seriously washed out after a substantial decline. Conspicuous year-early buy points occurred in 1898, 1904, 1908, 1921, 1949, 1953, and there was a prominent six-months-early buy in May 1958 rather than October. Early highs occurred in 1987 and 2000. A late high occurred in 1998, when there was a sharp but temporary four-month decline during the greatest bull market of all time.

Although it is generally profitable to follow the presidential-cycle template on its own, you can improve the results by using other indicators to confirm the entries and exits. Stochastics on the monthly chart, and Ws and Ms on the monthly line chart are particularly valuable for use in conjunction with Presidential-cycle timing. There was, for example, no W buy signal on the monthly line chart during the entire bear market from 1929 to 1932.

Sell in May and Go Away

Independently of the presidential cycle, there is considerable validity to the saying originated long ago in England, *Sell in May and go away.* Seasonally, a higher risk of owning stocks, and a lower prospect of gains, has extended throughout the summer and well into October, particularly during the negative period within the Presidential cycle. Although there have often been good summer rallies, their occurrence has been statistically unreliable, especially given the statistical probability of a substantial decline in September and October. Some of the biggest declines into a significant low have occurred in October including 1929 and 1987. The prominent lows 1990, 1998 and 2002 all coincided with Presidential cycle buy points that were exceptionally successful.

The sell-in-May timetable calls for selling on May 1 and buying in the last week of October. Starting at the end of October 1950, an assumed $10,000 invested in the Dow Jones Industrial Average only during the six favorable winter and spring months would have grown to $567,600 by 2005. On the other hand, starting on the last day of April 1950, $10,000 invested only during the unfavorable six months would have grown to just $11,400 by the end of October 2004. "There are periods where you are not going to get all of the gains," according to Jeffrey Hirsch, editor of *Stock Trader's Almanac* "but you miss 90 percent of the losses."[1] According to his newsletter, using MACD as an entry and exit signal (much as recommended in Chapter 6, but using different indicators) multiplies by three times the profit from investing only during the favorable months.

The results for the sell-in-May cycle from 1897 to 1950 show an almost equal performance for the favorable and unfavorable periods. However, there were considerable gains during the favorable periods and much smaller gains, when there were gains, during the unfavorable ones. The comparison is skewed by the fact that most of the huge gains from the favorable six-month periods were given back during the two favorable periods within the bear market from 1929 to 1932. For the period between 1897 and 1928—that is, excluding the big bear market— an assumed $10,000 increased to $106,900 by investing only during the favorable winter and spring months, and $10,000 increased to just $23,000 by investing only during the other six unfavorable months.

As one would expect, the most favorable (or least unfavorable) years for owning stocks from May to October are those when the presidential cycle is also favorable, and the least favorable, those when the timing for the presidential cycle is adverse. When the presidential cycle is unfavorable, but depending on chart signals, it may be better to sell earlier in the year, as in 2005, particularly if you own stocks representative of the general market.

If you bought the Dow in accordance with the seasonal cycle at the end of October 1929 (and disregarding the adversity of the presidential cycle), you would have bought just a few days before the low for the crash, and would have made a very small profit by selling at the end of

[1] *Barron's*, April 25, 2005

April the next year, as the market was beginning to slide again. How-ever, buying at the end of October 1930 would have got you in at 191, and the seasonal cycle would have had you sell at 151 at the beginning of May. The resulting 21 percent loss would have been painful but not devastating. However, a purchase in October 1931 results in a 45 per-cent loss—the biggest loss for as long as records are available.

At least since 1984, and presumably earlier, there has been a reason for the lackluster performance of stocks during the summer months. Mutual fund cash inflows have consistently run at a lower level between May and October, with a reliable dead zone between the beginning of July and the end of September. *It takes money to make the pony go!*

Opinion and Contrary Opinion

When there is a general optimism about the market, even for mistaken reasons, the market will go up. As with other technical indicators, you don't have to know why people feel good about buying and holding their stocks. It is enough to know what they are doing. Similarly, the market will go down when there is general pessimism. Both optimistic inclinations and pessimistic sentiment tend to last for a long time—*until they reach an extremity.* Extremities occur when the majority have already placed their bets on a rising market or have thrown in the towel in disgust on a decline.

The current readings from several followers of market sentiment are printed each week in the "Market Laboratory, Economic Indicators" sec-tion of *Barron's.* There is only so much that an ordinary investor can be expected to do without turning the operation into drudgery, but it can be worth the time and patience to chart one of these sentiment indica-tors. The Investors Intelligence service is currently doing this job and free, updated charts are available at the web site http://www.market-harmonics.com/free-charts/sentiment/investors_intelligence.htm

Other valuable Investors Intelligence services are available only by subscription. The full service provides, for example, long-term charts lined up with price charts.

Broadly speaking, for Investors Intelligence a reading of bullish sentiment (percentage of bulls) in the range between 40 and 60 per-cent is constructive. (The source data derives from the recommenda-tions of market advisors who, in the aggregate, are totally wrong at major tops and bottoms!) A reading above 60 percent is excessive. A reading below 45 percent is quite negative. A reading below 40 percent is starting to be extreme, and a level at or below 30 percent is so excessive that you can be fairly confident that most of the heavy selling has been completed. As with most indicators, including price, the trend is as important as absolute levels of enthusiasm. Except at extremes, rising sentiment means that money is going into stocks, and vice versa when sentiment is declining.

At the October 2002 low in price for the major stock indexes, Investors Intelligence percentage of bulls fell to a very rare extremity of 32. At the low in April 2003 the percentage of bulls stood at 38, a much higher level, although the indexes almost reached all the way down to the October lows. This *positive divergence* in percentage of bulls at the second low strongly suggested that a trend reversal in price would likely follow as a result of this marked improvement in sentiment. In January 2000 the percentage of bulls reached a very bearish level of 62 that was almost exactly coincident with the top of the market. In January 2005 the percentage of bulls also reached a level of 62. In July the level was only 55 despite the fact that the price level of the indexes was about the same for the Dow and the S&P 500 as it had been in January, although the small capitalization indexes were significantly higher.

Mutual Funds as a Contrary Indicator

As discussed in Chapter 26, mutual funds almost make a religion out of rejecting any form of market timing as part of their investment strategy. As noted above, the stock market tends to go up during the months when mutual fund inflows are highest and it tends to go sideways or down during the months when inflows are lowest. Therefore, there is a high probability that mutual funds will both buy and sell at bad times during the year.

What mutual funds are doing compares with other measures of market sentiment when cash levels are at an extreme. As with other indicators, the direction is important until an extremity is reached. A steady inflow of cash for new investment is bullish and a steady outflow is bearish: the more cash on hand, the more they have firepower with which to buy stocks. Fortunately, it is possible to calibrate extremities. For a long time it was considered bullish when mutual fund cash balances rose above 10 percent of assets. In 1990 mutual fund cash balances reached almost 13 percent just as the major bull market was about to get under way.

It used to be considered bearish when mutual funds held less than 8 percent of their assets in cash, but recent market behavior has led to a lowering of the number required for a bearish interpretation because too much firepower had already been invested in stocks. There have been just three times in market history when mutual funds cash reached a low of 4 percent of assets: 1972, 2000, and mid-2005! After the low in cash in 1972 the Dow fell by 45 percent from its then-record high. After the low in cash in 2000, the Dow fell by 38 percent from its now-record high. As this edition was going to press, the Dow was considerably short of its 2000 high, although the small-capitalization issues had exceeded the highs made in 2000. The lower high in the Dow in conjunction with the equal low in mutual fund cash suggests the kind of negative divergence that you get when stochastics make a non-confirming lower high.

Source data for mutual fund cash balances is widely available on the Internet and is published in the first edition of the month in *Barron's*.

Sometimes a Bell Rings

Those who say so misleadingly that you can't time the market overlook the fact that sometimes a bell really does ring at or near a market high or low. Sometimes there is such a glaring expression of excessive pessimism that it signals the fact that everyone desperate to sell has already done so. A classic example of such pervasive pessimism was the famous *BusinessWeek* cover story on August 13, 1979, entitled, "The Death of Equities." The cover is a photo of a downed paper airplane fashioned from a stock certificate. The subcaption decries, "How inflation is destroying the stock market." The downed paper (stock certificate) airplane in the picture was actually surrounded by the crumpled remains of other "crashed" paper airplanes. An excerpt of the article reads

> Wall Street looks beyond stocks; moving into options, futures; buying into insurance. The masses long ago switched from stocks to investments having higher yields and more protection from inflation. Now the pension funds—the market's last

hope—have won permission to quit stocks and bonds for real estate, futures, gold, and even diamonds. The death of equities looks like an almost permanent condition—reversible some-day, but not soon.

On publication day, the Dow stood at 875. It was to go down to 729, or 17 percent lower, in April 1980, but that was the low before the big bull market started in 1982.

Perhaps similarly, there have been two notable covers potentially signaling the end of the decline in the U.S. Dollar. *The Economist's* cover on December 4, 2004, had a cartoon of a Chinese silkworm eating a bil-lion dollars, with the headline, "The Disappearing Dollar." The apparent low for the decline occurred three weeks later. Then the March 21, 2005, cover of *Newsweek* had the headline: "The Incredible Shrinking Dollar: What It Means for America's Future—and Yours." The next day after the magazine's publication the Federal Reserve raised interest rates for the seventh time, and the dollar was to surge upward beginning a major rally if not reversing its three-year downtrend.

Euphoria at Market Tops

Near major market tops there is almost always euphoria or, to use Fed-eral Reserve Chairman Alan Greenspan's expression, *irrational exu-berance*, and sometimes there is a glaring expression of the obvious that is so obviously wrong that it lights up the *Game over* sign.

The technology boom was largely fueled by concerns, and corre-sponding investment, ahead of the millennium changeover, known as *Y2K*. There were widespread fears that any number of disasters might occur because of the inability of computers to recognize the changeover at midnight on December 31. Concern about the possibility of disasters was a major component behind the frenzied activity in the preceding months and the shoveling of money into the financial system by the Federal Reserve.

Almost as if programmed in advance, the high for the Standard & Poor's (S&P) 500 Index occurred on the first trading day in January. For the Dow Jones Industrial Average, it came on January 14, and for the NASDAQ indexes, it was delayed until March.

The *New Era* Syndrome in 1999–2000

New era is the standard phrase, along with *new paradigm*, that has been used to describe a structural change in the financial environment that negates all previous history of markets and their propensity to revert to the mean. The timing may not be exact, but any widespread acceptance and proclamation of a new era sounds the warning loud and clear that there is no such thing. The old era will do just fine, and markets will fool people, as they always do, by reverting to the mean.

Sure enough, in October 1999, a reputable economist at a reputable bank was saying, "There is no question that we've entered a new era." In fairness, he added, "The question seems to be how long it will continue, and the jury is still out on that one."

Many, many people in the investment industry were not hedging their bets as this person did. Many, many so-called financial advisors were selling mutual funds like ice cream on the fourth of July, promising returns of 15, 20, and 30 percent or as a conservative minimum at least a return of 10 percent.

Along with the *Y2K* bell, the prize for contrary opinion at the top of the bull market of the 1990s goes to James Glassman and Kevin Hassett, both of the American Enterprise Institute. Mr. Glassman is also a columnist for the *Washington Post,* and Dr. Hassett's credentials include working as a senior economist at the Board of Governors of the Federal Reserve System and associate professor of economics and finance at the Graduate School of Business of Columbia University. He received a Ph.D. in economics from the University of Pennsylvania. By almost uncanny coincidence, it was in January 2000 that their book, *Dow 36,000!,* was published.

The Top in 1929

As the first edition of this book recorded, every really big and long-lasting boom breeds the myth that this time is different. President Calvin Coolidge delivered a classic new-era story in his last message to the new Congress on December 4, 1928: "No Congress of the United States ever assembled," he said, "on surveying the state of the Union, has met with a more pleasing prospect. . . . The great wealth created by our enterprise and industry, and saved by our economy, has had the widest distribution among our people, and has gone out in a steady stream to serve the charity and business of the world. . . . The country can regard the present with satisfaction, and anticipate the future with optimism. . . ." It took 10 months more to arrive at the stock market crash in October 1929, from which point the Great Depression may be said to have begun. With the economy enjoying an apparently never-ending prosperity, stock prices in 1929 were extremely high relative to all reasonable expectations for earnings and dividends. At last, in June 1929, an economic slowdown began. Production was outrunning consumption, so manufacturers began to rein in production. As production faded, profits not only failed to maintain their rate of increase but declined. Declining profits led to lower expectations from the stock market. So investors and speculators sold. Some sold to take profits, some to meet margin calls, and some to enter short sales. The declining stock market made people feel less comfortable with their finances, so they spent less. The so-called wealth effect went into reverse, so profits declined further and stock prices declined further too. The depression fed on itself in a downward spiral that was the opposite of the preceding boom.

The lesson of magazine cover stories, the publication of books with amazing titles, and excessive optimism or excessive pessimism is this: *If it's that obvious, it's obviously wrong!*

CHAPTER 14

What Works—A Review and Prospects for the Future

Where to Start Looking

There are, of course, two ways to find stocks to consider buying. You can start by looking at market action, or you can start with the story. You can get an idea from any number of sources—from newspapers to research reports to tips from friends. Yes, sometimes tips can at least be worth checking out! Occasionally—very occasionally—a great idea emerges from a cocktail party, although usually only after everyone else has heard it and acted on it. Therefore, the stock goes down, not up, as soon as you buy it. In any case, it helps to know whether the story makes sense. It can help enormously, for example, if the concept captures investors' imagination—the *sex-appeal factor*—as Apple did with the iPod. On the other hand, there's also the law of contrary opinion that results in some of the most successful investments occurring in the most unlikely and overlooked places, such as coal and waste disposal.

Regardless of how convincing the story is, unless technical market action checks out, wait until it develops. As you have already seen, there is no point in buying a share stuck in a trading range, and the risk is almost always unmanageable in one that is skyrocketing insanely. Buying stocks without any regard to the technicals is like buying cows in the moonlight. It can be done, often successfully, especially in a bull market. Nevertheless, you can miss seeing things that are important. It helps, therefore, to have a good story, but when it comes to the crunch, you are more likely to buy a stock successfully by relying only on favorable market action and strong technical indicators than you are by relying only on the story, however well researched.

Some Old Indicators Don't Do What They Used To

It is easy to turn into an indicator *junky* because there is so much available, but much of it is of doubtful usefulness. It used to be that the advance/decline for the New York Stock Exchange showed the underlying strength or weakness of the market. In recent years, however, this has been ineffective mainly because of the inclusion of many preferred shares and fixed-interest-rate surrogates. There is a similar problem with the ratio of new 52-week highs to new 52-week lows, which loses its effectiveness unless you scrutinize which stocks are actually making those new highs or lows. All you can say about the bare statistics is that a strong market should continue to show a broad list of quality common stocks making new 52-week highs. When the breadth and quality of new 52-week highs are faltering, you have to question the staying power of an advance. Similarly, when there are fewer new 52-week lows being made by quality stocks, and some quality stocks are starting to make new 52-week highs, there is a reasonable expectation that a decline may be close to running its course.

Technical Alerts That Work

To some extent, this is a recapitulation and review of material contained in previous chapters, and to some extent, it provides new insights.

1. Volume Surges

A surge in volume, whether daily or for the week, means that a stock has become the focus of new buying or selling pressure. When the surge occurs in conjunction with an upward move in price, there is a high probability that big money is anxious to press the market to buy stock. It can be just as significant when there is a sudden surge in selling pressure. A volume surge often occurs in the early stages of a major move. Volume surges also occur at the end of a major move as a result of a terminal buying frenzy or a panicky selling climax. It is usually obvious whether the surge is occurring at the potential start of a move or, after having made a big moves already, its potential end.

The most dramatic volume surges generally occur in conjunction with a selling climax, whether in the overall market or in an individual stock—see number 3 below. One selling climax, however, does not even begin to suggest the end of selling until other indicators turn positive, although there may be a substantial but temporary rally after the immediate selling pressure eases. Newspapers print a list of the most actively traded stocks. Sometimes this can be the tip-off to check out the technicals.

2. Volume Fades

Other than when occurring after an apparent selling climax, volume fades are nowhere near as significant as volume surges, but they are the logical counterpart. It is bullish when there is lower volume on any second prominent low where price holds above an earlier one. However, it is easy to misinterpret a short-lived increase in daily volume, when you think it ought to fade, on what is no more than a routine retracement in price.

It is bearish when volume fades on rising price, as occurs often when price approaches a near-term top. Then there applies the reverse principle of what happens at potential lows. New highs in price are suspect when they occur on conspicuously lower volume than at the previous high, even if price is higher.

It not always easy to read what volume is indicating, and much of the time it says nothing. This is why on-balance volume (OBV) is useful. It brings order where much of the time there is only clutter.

3. Selling Climaxes

Major lows in the market occur relatively seldom and sometimes several years apart. Nevertheless, it can be immensely profitable to identify them as they are developing. Stocks bought then offer the potential opportunity of really getting in on the ground floor.

A selling climax is a prime characteristic of a durable market bottom, and a selling climax, by definition, occurs on massive volume far in excess of what happens in the ordinary run of market days. (As a reminder, there has to be a buyer for every seller. Panicked and aggressive selling may be putting stocks into the hands of those who have the stamina, the money, and the longer-term perspective with which to take the other side of the trade.) To be significant, a selling climax should still occur when other conditions lead you to expect a major low. In addition, it almost always pays to see what happens at the next low—to see whether there is lower volume, with price holding above that apparently climactic low.

The weekly chart for the Standard & Poor's (S&P) 500 Index shows the volume bars below the price chart (Fig. 14-1). The market low in July 2002 occurred in conjunction with trading volume not seen before or since. The bar for the week closed well above the low, and sure enough, there was a rebound over the next four weeks. However, there was no reason at the time to believe that this selling climax was enough to end the bear market. One month or one bar, in isolation, generates no more than a single piece of evidence: The balance of evidence to justify a conclusion about timing the market, or an individual stock, requires much more.

The next spike in volume occurred during October 2002, in conjunction with a powerful weekly upside reversal, and the index went up for the next six weeks before cresting. This was a very encouraging but by no means conclusive sign that the bear market might now be at or near its end. This move down had seen both a new intraweek low and a new end-of-week closing low, confirming the principle of bear markets that they comprise, by definition, a pattern of lower lows and lower highs.

In any case, it is a fundamental principle of technical analysis that any first upturn or first signal is likely to be negated or at least challenged. Therefore, even this second selling climax on lower volume occurred with more pieces to fall into place to confirm the end of the bear market.

In the event, the following March the S&P 500 had to come back to test the low made in October, and this time the volume at that low was less than at either of the two preceding selling climaxes. Also, the price now held above the October low.

4. Stochastics at Major Market Turns

As illustrated by the monthly chart for the S&P 500, stochastics at a very low level on the monthly chart can provide the first technical indication that a major turn can happen, but generally there must also be supporting evidence from other indicators (Fig. 14-2). Even in the severe bear market starting in 2000, however, stochastics on the monthly chart

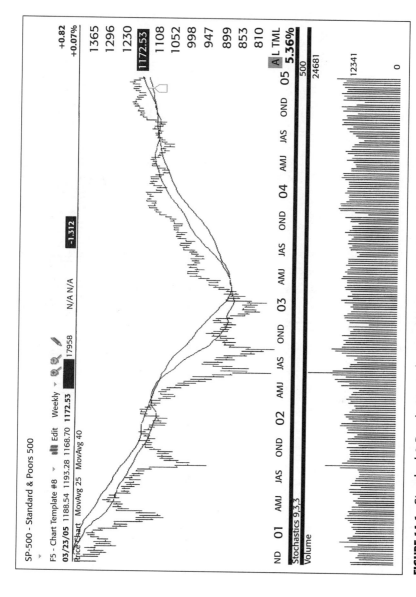

FIGURE 14-1 Standard & Poor's 500 Index Weekly Chart with 25- and 40-Week Moving Averages, and Volume Bars.

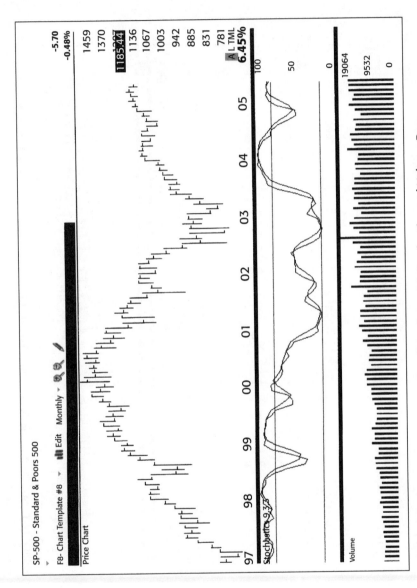

FIGURE 14-2 Standard & Poor's 500 Monthly Chart with Stochastics and Volume Bars.

for the S&P 500 failed to get below 20 (although they did, very much so, for the Nasdaq).

Stochastics developed a good W from a low level at the end of 2001, in conjunction with a year-end rally in 2001. However, many negating indicators remained in force, and the rally soon faded. Then a second double bottom and W came through in April 2003, and with other indicators confirming, the trend reversed, and the ensuing new bull market began.

Ominously, stochastics in early 2005 were bearish, as one might expect at this time in the presidential cycle. There was a considerably lower high than the one in February 1994, with stochastics now forming a big and very bearish M, even as price went a little higher.

5. Monthly Reversals, Double Monthly Reversals, and Lindahl Price Rules

Any monthly upside reversal in the direction of a strong and established trend generally provides an excellent signal to buy a stock, and vice versa when selling short in a bear market. A Lindahl price rule (rule 5) and a double reversal price rule (rule 8) are particularly powerful indicators of the potential for a stock to make a substantial move.

A single monthly reversal against the direction of the major trend may mean nothing when the overall chart is strong. A single rule 5 or rule 8 signal against the direction of an established trend may well mean that the stock is due for a rest. It may not be signaling that the stock is preparing to reverse direction unless there is an accumulation of other negating indicators and adverse market conditions.

In addition to showing how stochastics acted, the monthly chart for the S&P 500 shows completion of a powerful rule 5a Lindahl buy signal with a strong close at the end of April 2003. There was no earlier monthly buy signal. Any purchase of the general market through the S&P 500 Index, as a result of the selling climax alone the previous October, would have led to considerable backing and filling up to that point. A purchase of an index at the end of April, or of a representative basket of stocks, led to immediate gratification, and the market never looked back.

6. 52-Week Highs and Lows

One of the best technical alerts is the making of a new 52-week high for the first time. This means that on the day or week in question, the stock has reached a higher level than at any time during the preceding 52 weeks. It may or may not be an all-time high, depending on whether there had been a higher high longer ago than a year. A list of stocks making a new 52-week high appears each day in the *Wall Street Journal* and each week in *Barron's*. Also, any electronic chart service with a search option is certain to have this feature.

The mere fact that a stock makes a 52-week high may not mean that it will automatically continue to advance, let alone that it is timely to buy it at its current price. If the stock has moved too far too quickly, it may be temporarily overbought and it may therefore need to consolidate, or the upward move may fail altogether. When, however, a new 52-week high occurs in conjunction with a breakout from a long base, as discussed in Chapter 12, there is a high probability of the stock following through. There is also a reasonable probability of the stock continuing to go higher if it breaks above a previous high with a gap and a strong close or with an upside key reversal bar that closes at the top of the daily or weekly range.

Once an upward move gets under way, a stock will make a succession of new 52-week highs. The point of this indicator is that you have to put it in the context of the overall chart pattern. You don't arbitrarily chase a stock just because it makes a new high. Otherwise, you risk getting sucked in at the end of a surge rather than at the beginning of one. The same principle applies in reverse to 52-week lows.

7. Gaps

A stock that gaps shows that it has blown the gasket of normal day-to-day trading action. One gap in isolation within a consolidation may mean nothing, but there are two kinds of gaps that can be potentially exciting:

1. The stock is in an established bull market and has retraced significantly but without violating any of the definitions of a bull market. Stochastics readings reached a washed-out low level—generally at 20 or lower on the daily chart. The price gaps up from that low, leaving behind a bar representing the final throwing in of the towel by those unable to withstand the pressure of the retracement. Sometimes there may be several downward

probes on the daily chart with more than one upward gap. Then the significance of the gapping increases still further.

2. The stock has been in a trading range for some time and surges out of it to a new high, with a close at the top of the range. This may be a bandwagon to jump on! Hard as it may be to believe, the bigger the move out of the consolidation, the more likely the stock is to keep on going, particularly if it occurs on very high volume.

There is a rule of thumb that a good breakaway gap of either of these two flavors is likely to signal an upward continuation if it remains unfilled by a retracement for three market days or more. This shows that the breakaway is likely to stay broken away. Downside gaps work equally and opposite to upside gaps.

8. Islands

A gap up from a formation comprising one day or, ideally, several days of consolidation at the assumed bottom of a retracement is sufficiently significant to warrant special attention. The idea is that buyers and sellers have faced off and finished the business of wringing out weak holders and putting the stock into strong hands. Therefore, an island from which the price gaps up is particularly likely to signal an important low.

When a stock gaps down and leaves an island after a substantial blowoff upside run, it may mean that there is a high in place that will not be surpassed for some time, and the line of least resistance may now be downward. An island top often constitutes a prime signal to get out of a speculative stock that has had a parabolic advance.

9. 50 Percent Retracements

Look for retracements within an established trend to retrace 50 percent of the previous move from bottom to top in a bull market, and vice versa in a bear market. Many investors look at Fibonacci ratios[1] to guess how far a retracement might go. In round numbers, the percentages are 38, 50, and 62 percent. If a stock retraces more than 62 percent, it is likely to go the rest of the way back to where it started. If you know you want to own a stock (or to sell one short), you can sometimes trade into a 50 percent retracement without even waiting for a price

---

[1] The Fibonacci progression starts with 1 and adds the preceding number: 1, 2, 3, 5 etc.

rule to develop. Then you may enter at an excellent price with a very manageable stop.

10. Five Days Up or Down

A stock that goes up for five consecutive days, or more, is obviously being bought aggressively by people unwilling to wait for the price to subside after initial buying interest. The same applies in reverse, when there is persistent selling. Therefore, it is worth looking for an entry signal.

You should get on board a rapidly moving market as soon as possible, if you are ever going to. Otherwise, there may not be another timely signal, such as a reversal with the trend, for some time. By then, the price may have moved a long way. The remedy for peace of mind and responsible capital management is not to shun the stock but to buy only a small number of shares to start with, in case you have to carry them through a sharp setback.

Sometimes the price of a stock may go in the same direction for five consecutive days at the end of a major move. In this case, stochastics are almost certainly at an extremity. You can usually tell the difference quite readily between a possible starting five-day surge and a possible ending one.

11. Big Gainers on the Day

Stocks making big daily and weekly gains are always worth looking at, particularly when the gains occur on the first day out of a consolidation. Look for big daily and weekly gains to tie in with potential monthly reversals with the trend.

12. Look at Stock Group Subindexes

Stock group subindexes provide a shortcut to finding areas of the market where there are stocks with superior prospects for gains. They also show where there are stocks with little or no prospects of outperforming the market generally or which, on the contrary, may be candidates for short sales. There can be considerable variation in performance between individual companies within a group, but stocks within many groups move more or less together. For example, just a cursory look at a subindex for water utilities might direct you to stocks where you might otherwise not have thought to look, and it might suggest stocks far more promising than those in the auto industry.

Fundamental Factors to Look For

1. A Record of Success

There is a rough rule of thumb that the stock of a major corporation should have a record of success—rising profits and a record of an increasing share price over the long term. One is entitled to assume that it would not have established such a long-term record without having a sound, well-run business that has a solid franchise and is growing at least as fast as the economy as a whole. This rule may not be applicable to special situations where a new product is transforming a company's prospects or to some cyclic sectors. Nevertheless, the probabilities strongly favor the upward continuation over the long term of a stock that has gone up by at least four times over the previous 10 years. This rule of thumb will help you to differentiate between a great stock such as Johnson & Johnson and a dog such as General Motors, which has upward surges from time to time and then goes into its next successive round of decline.

2. Dividends

If a company pays a dividend, even just a minimally small one, it should show that it is generating real disposable income in excess of what is required to run the business and to replace its depreciating assets. Some businesses purport to be making money, but the reality may be that all or most of those reported earnings have to be ploughed back into research and development or marketing in order to keep the company in business for the long term. Many companies engaged in computer technology have to keep reinventing themselves entirely every year or two and are on a treadmill of constant renewal that might not continue in the years ahead.

There are, of course, some companies that do not pay dividends and which have performed wonderfully over the long term and, like Berkshire Hathaway, are likely to continue doing so. Failure to pay dividends may result, however, in retention of shareholders' just rewards in order to be squandered by megalomaniacal management. Many companies, such as BCE and Inco, have spent money foolishly that would have been better returned to shareholders as dividends instead of making disastrous acquisitions.

Payment of dividends is only a guide, and the lack of one does not by any means impose an embargo, except for those who must have dividends. A complete lack of a dividend or the foreseeable prospect of receiving one does not prevent a stock from going up by many times, as occurred for Microsoft and Berkshire Hathaway. It is worth repeating the axiom that it is better to buy a poor or an unknown, non-dividend-paying stock when the timing is right than it is to buy a great stock when the timing is wrong.

3. Dividend Increases

Following on from the last point, there is an aristocracy of companies within the S&P 500 Index that have raised their dividend payout year after year and some of them for 25 years or more.[2] When our technical indicators deliver buy signal, and as long as a bull market designation is in force, it will almost certainly be profitable to own shares in these companies. Note, however, that when there are sell signals, and especially when there is a general bear market, these stocks can go down along with the rest. After the top in 2000, many of these shares declined by 50 percent or more. Even in good times they may not be the fastest growing companies, but as a group, their reliability should continue. The dividend aristocrats include

Altria

Abbott Laboratories

ALLTEL Corporation

AmSouth Bancorp

Anheuser Busch

Archer Daniels Midland

Automatic Data Processing

Avery Denison

BancorpSouth

BB&T

Becton Dickinson

---

[2] Beware of the *dogs of the Dow strategy!* In the past, it has been profitable to own a basket of the 10 highest-yielding stocks in the Dow Jones Industrial Average. However, this strategy has not worked by a huge margin, it seldom meshes with market timing indicators, and it may not work in the future. There really are dogs that you don't want to own.

CenturyTel

Citigroup

Coca Cola

Comerica

ConAgra Foods

Consolidated Edison

CR Bard

Dover

Eli Lilly

Family Dollar Stores

First Tennessee National

FPL

Gallagher

Gannett

General Electric

Jefferson-Pilot

Johnson & Johnson

Johnson Controls

KeyCorp

Kimberley-Clark

Lowe's

Leggett & Platt

Marsh & McLennan

Masco

McDonald's

McGraw-Hill

Merck

National City

Nucor

Old National

PepsiCo

Pfizer

Pinnacle West

PPG Industries

Proctor & Gamble

Regions Financial

Rohm & Haas

RR Donnelley & Sons

Sara Lee

Sigma-Aldrich

SouthTrust

Stanley Works

Supervalu

Target

3M

US Bancorp

Universal

VF Corp

Walgreen

Wal-Mart

Washington Mutual

WW Grainger

Some Concepts for the Future

It is exceptionally difficult to forecast which areas might prove profitable long after this book is published. Nevertheless, certain areas may continue to prosper in the future as they have in the past. One concept that comes to mind, given the aging population, is everything to do with health care, medical appliances, pharmaceuticals, hospitals, and retirement homes. Of particular interest might be the low-cost makers of generic drugs.

As discussed elsewhere, one has to be hesitant about using the words *new era*, but it seems that the old era of cheap and plentiful energy may be ending, although even now the old era might have more life in it than many people suppose. Despite the apparent attractions of the energy industry, there are likely to be bigger fluctuations in supply and demand, and in price, than most forecasters were expecting in 2005. For example, the construction of natural gas pipelines from the arctic, the development of liquid natural gas facilities, and development of methane deposits could all contribute to a huge if temporary *surplus* of natural gas in the United States. The law of supply and demand works both on the supply side and on the demand side, with corresponding capital investment both overshooting and undershooting what is needed for a steady supply.

Modern technology and new discoveries could even now lead to a greater increase in production of oil and natural gas than is generally believed possible. There are still some major sedimentary basins, notably in India, Pakistan, and Bangladesh, as well as in central and South America where exploration has barely started. For example, in 1990 no one would have imagined that Vietnam might become, as it has, a net oil exporter. Nevertheless, it may be challenging for energy companies to replace reserves faster than they use them so as to be able to make money in real terms for shareholders. Attractive as petroleum companies may seem, oil service companies should do well under most foreseeable circumstances, including a moderate decline in the price of oil.

Coal should do well. It is available in almost unlimited abundance, and technology has made great strides in burning it without emitting anywhere near as much pollution as used to be the case. Also, the technology exists to make oil from coal, currently employed by South Africa's Sasol. It seems likely too that nuclear power will become widely accepted, as it has been for most of the electricity generated in France. Beneficiaries would be companies that build nuclear power plants and ones that supply uranium.

All aspects of waste management, water delivery, and environmental protection are likely to prosper. So are businesses engaged in all aspects of security, whether of people or computer applications. On the other hand, some businesses, such as financial institutions, transportation, and travel and leisure may be more vulnerable than has been supposed to lapses in security. They may also be more vulnerable than generally supposed if the American consumer demand slackens, as could occur in conjunction with baby boomers entering their retirement years.

Foreign Stocks

It is almost certain that there will be above-average growth and superior investment opportunities in some of the faster-growing emerging markets. India could well be the powerhouse of the future that does even better than China, where there are many and serious structural problems despite the rapid growth rate. Advantages include the English language, democracy (if imperfect), hard-working people, and the rule of law. Over the long term, the focus on high value-added information technology has to be a big plus over Chinese manufacturing. Other Asian countries, Mexico, Brazil, and the emerging economies of eastern Europe may all offer attractive investment opportunities. You can invest through the closed-end mutual funds listed each week in *Barron's* that are traded like any other stocks on the stock exchange. They are easy to buy and sell without paying inordinate entry and exit fees, and you can use stops. The risk in foreign stocks is that if the United States catches an economic cold, foreign economies succumb to double pneumonia. Foreign economies are dependent for their prosperity— even China—on the strength of the U.S. economy, with the result that foreign stocks could be more volatile in both directions.

CHAPTER 15

How to Manage Your Capital: Risk versus Reward

Many investment advisors and mutual fund sellers would have you put as much money into savings as they can squeeze out of you, particularly if they make more money from you by getting more money to work with. Yes, investment in stocks should form part of an overall financial plan—an essential part, obviously—but investing in stocks, or in anything, is not all that life is about. Therefore, you need to make a plan, and you need to review it periodically.

Depending on your circumstances, your plan may mean setting up a regular savings plan or setting aside capital all at once. Either way, it means setting up a budget as you would for any business venture. As with any business, you make capital investments, in this case by buying stocks or bonds. You also need to keep a reserve of working capital. You have to provide for unforeseen expenses or for significant new opportunities, ones unforeseeable when making your initial investments.

You expect profits, of course. However, you must also prepare to accept losses as well. As when setting up a clothing store or any other business, it is inevitable that some stock has to go on sale—and some at prices well below cost. The same thing happens in all business. No business is a one-way street to moneymaking. It is enough to make good profits overall.

Ideally, losers go out at prices near where you placed the initial stop loss (discussed in Chapter 18), but even with the best planning, the occasional bad loss occurs. It is important to internalize a state of mind that accepts the fact that some losses are a cost of doing any business of any kind, in the stock market as in any other aspect of life. In the overall scheme of things, this does not matter as long as there are major successes that more than offset the inevitable losses. Running profits and cutting losses should mean that some winners return huge profits, many times what you invest. You do not need many big winners to pay for the inevitable losers and to make big profits on balance.

Don't Invest All at Once

Never put a large amount of money into stocks all at once. There is hardly a more important rule than this. There is too high a risk of buying at a top, only to see the entire portfolio going down right after you buy. Statistically, the likelihood of buying at a long-term market top is small. Major tops do not happen often. Nevertheless, there is a great likelihood of buying at an intermediate top because things always look best at tops. It is no coincidence that mutual fund sales soared in 1999 and 2000, when enthusiasm and greed were peaking just as the bull market was about to reverse. If you placed a large amount of money in any representative basket of stocks or mutual funds, and especially ones selected from the then-popular technology area, you would probably have lost much of your capital over the next two years. From the top in January 2000 at 11,750, the Dow Jones Industrial Index fell to a low of 7,197, declining by 39 percent at the bottom in 2002. If you invested total capital of $100,000 in blue-chip, nontechnology stocks at the top, at the bottom you had lost $39,000—39 percent of your money over the two years. If you had put that $100,000 into a representative portfolio of Nasdaq 100 stocks, the result would have been truly disastrous. The decline from top to bottom was from 4,659 to just 795, declining by 83 percent. The record was actually even worse than that because several companies in the index went bankrupt and were replaced. Assuming a representative basket of Nasdaq 100 stocks, $100,000 invested at the top turned into just $17,000. There is no reasonable prospect of such a basket of stocks recovering to their former highs without having to wait for many years and possibly for a number of decades.

The point of going to such lengths about what happened in that bear market is to make it clear that it did happen, that it has happened in the past, and that it is certain to happen again sometime in the future.

The first edition of this book said, all too presciently, that it was an absolute certainty that in future there would be stock market declines similar to the one in 1987. Some would be more severe than the 1987 crash, and some would last much longer. Therefore, you would not even want to think of having all your investments going down the drain simultaneously from the top of the market.

Keep Capital in Reserve

There is a strategy for avoiding the disaster of investing all your money at or near the top of the market, and it is not simply to diversify into many different stocks and stock mutual funds. They are mostly variations on the same theme. The only meaningful way to handle the risks of the stock market is to invest only a part of your capital in stocks and to hold a significant cash reserve. Unless there is serious inflation, which is unlikely in the United States, there is almost no risk in holding cash or cash equivalents such as Treasury bills.

Buy bonds sparingly and only when they are going up (and interest rates are declining) or at least when they are relatively stable. Bonds are really worth owning only when they are in a bull market or when you need a regular income. You run the risk of tying up capital without having the flexibility of cash on hand with which to buy stocks. Buy bonds for retirement income when you are retired.

What Gerald Loeb Did

It is worth taking a leaf from the book of a great investor of the early twentieth century, Gerald Loeb. He never put at risk in stocks more than a portion of his capital, and he never bought on margin (using borrowed money). Despite his knowledge and closeness to market action, he thought there was too much risk of being wrong. He always kept substantial cash reserves, even during the roaring bull market of the 1920s. He aimed to find a small number of stocks with the potential to make very big gains. However attractive the prospects, he never invested more than a third of his money in any one stock. Then, if it went down instead of up, he had the cash and the flexibility with which to grasp new opportunities when they arose. Even more important, it was easy to take losses on the investments that failed to perform as expected. Losses never seriously dented his capital, but big gains often added to it enormously.

Loeb was delighted to put just 10 percent of his capital into one prime investment and see it double or triple in a year. In the unlikely event of losing all that 10 percent, his overall capital was essentially unimpaired. On the other hand, tripling 10 percent of his capital gave him an annual return of 20 percent overall for the year, assuming no return at all on the balance of his capital. In his book, *The Battle for Stock Market Survival,* Loeb was adamant that you must at all times maintain a cash balance so that you can grasp new opportunities when they arise. This is impossible if you are always fully invested in stocks and especially if much of your portfolio is underwater.

Loeb often invested on the basis of good information, and he generally put a huge amount of money into just a few stocks at any given time. In this respect, he was a precursor of Warren Buffett, intentionally not diversifying beyond what he could follow closely. He differed from Buffett, however, in that he was seldom a long-term investor.

You may never succeed in finding a single stock that triples in a year, and there is little point in looking for these stocks intentionally. The rule is that looking for long shots does not work over time. You have too high a percentage of losers, unless you are exceptionally lucky. Luck is different from probability theory. You cannot count on it with acceptable consistency as a useful component of the process of making investment decisions. Luck generally comes to people who are already doing the right things: chance follows design. Buy a stock with the potential to double within a few years, and you are likely to buy the occasional one that takes off like a rocket.

Don't Diversify Too Much!

There are some money managers looking after millions of dollars but who have fewer than 50 stocks, and some have as few as 20. There are about 30 major areas of the economy within which you might theoretically look to invest a widely diversified portfolio. Yet, at any given time, it is unlikely that more than a third of those sectors are really attractive, and it can be counterproductive to invest in a wide selection within that group. Even within an important sector such as banking, it would likely be sufficient for a large portfolio to include just two or three stocks such as Citigroup, KeyCorp, and perhaps one more.

In sum, it is simply not true that you need to diversify widely, and it is absolutely unnecessary to diversify through mutual funds into hundreds of different companies. Diversification can work against you just as much as it can work for you, by diluting your successes.

Routine Retracements and More Serious Ones

Chapter 18 discusses the stops that cut a loss when a stock stumbles as soon as you buy it. If the stock falls back by more than a routine retracement, you get out. This means defining what is or is not routine. Then you have to build into your capital management plan an allowance for the certainty that some stocks fail to perform as expected and have to be sold at a loss. Depending on the volatility of a stock, you have to allow for fluctuations against you of at least 10 percent of the price you pay but generally not more than 30 percent. A standard budget to allow for a retracement in a major stock should be about 15 percent.

If you invest $100,000 all at once, the chances are that you will be budgeting for stop losses that together put about $15,000 at risk. You have to assume the worst case: that every one of your selections is stopped out. If your total capital is $100,000, this is quite a serious loss. If you do not use a stop and have no mechanism for selling out of losing stocks, your loss theoretically could consume all your capital. On the other hand, if you start with total capital of $100,000 and initially invest only $30,000, perhaps $10,000 in each of three stocks, you are likely to incur a risk of losing $4,500 in the event that all three investments fail. This represents 15 percent of the $30,000 actually invested out of your $100,000 capital. A loss of this amount should not impair your ability to come back at the market with complete peace of mind.

Once the stocks you buy start going up, then you can venture a little more money into one or two more stocks. Ideally, you should be working with profits, incurring risks no greater than would put you back to the amount of money you started with. Once you get ahead substantially, you can tolerate greater fluctuations and truly live by the maxim of letting profits run.

Give Winners Room to Breathe

There has to be a trade-off between giving a stock room to breathe and living through a huge reversal. Any fluctuation back to an identifiable previous low, plus a small allowance for aberrations, may be normal backing and filling. All investments fluctuate and must be allowed to do so—but only within reason. Allowing stocks less room to fluctuate than 10 or 15 percent before you dump them is a strategy that incurs many unnecessary and debilitating losses. However, giving a stock too much room to fluctuate makes recovery difficult. Remember that it takes a 100 percent gain to recover from a 50 percent loss.

The mutual fund industry is correct insofar as it advises investors to accept the fact that stocks can go down as well as up, although they neglect to tell you anything about the difference between acceptable and unacceptable fluctuations. There is no getting around the challenge that any stock may set back quite a lot without violating a long-term upward trend. You have to accept that it is impossible to invest for gains of 100 percent or more in the long term without making allowances for as much as 30 percent setbacks on the way. Under normal circumstances in a bull market, few stocks in your portfolio should retrace simultaneously by so much. Nevertheless, this can and does happen sometimes. You must prepare for the real possibility of it happening by not going in too deep all at once.

Don't Average Down!

Logically, you might want to buy more of a good stock if it goes down, not throw in the towel. In the jargon of the industry, this is called *averaging down*. The mutual fund industry constantly recommends this approach to investing on the grounds that you cannot expect to time the market. Since—so they maintain—the long-term direction of stock is always upward, averaging down means that you make more money in the long run.

For all practical purposes, averaging down is a loser play. This logic is absolutely not recommended because of the risk of doubling a loss rather than doubling a profit.

Remember the futures trader's adage: *Never add to a losing position!* It seldom pays to depart from the principle of running profits and cutting losses. Buy more of a stock that is making money, not one that is losing.

When you buy a stock, ideally, it should go up right away. Realistically, this happens only about half the time. Sometimes you have to be patient. Capital management is also a function of patience. Even the strongest bull markets falter and sometimes fluctuate violently.

Think Positively in a Bull Market

Sometimes it is fairly clear that the stock market is going up and that you have a solidly based bull market. Then you can be a little more venturesome than at times when there is ambiguity. You might go to as much as 75 percent or so of your money in stocks. Nevertheless, you still need to maintain a cash reserve. You don't want to find yourself living through a normal setback only to find that you could not buy more stock even if you wanted to, but on the contrary, find yourself pressed by a margin call.

Margin is the money a broker will lend you to buy more stocks than you can pay for outright. You can normally borrow half the cost of stock you buy. If the stock goes down instead of up, the broker will call for more money if the loan exceeds 60 percent of the value of the stock. You can meet a margin call either by paying in more money or by selling stock. Selling stock may be an exercise in selling out at the worst possible time so that you lose money even though you are right on the stock.

When you identify a bull market and you see a stock going up, think positively. It is logical to ask the question: If I would like to own a stock, why don't I? If you see a great stock, it is not logical to wish that you owned it and not do something about it. The chances are that if the stock looks as if it is going up, then it will go higher still. Don't just lament the lost opportunity and do nothing about it. Buy just a little, however, unless there is a really strong signal and, in addition, overall market conditions are favorable. Ideally, you should look for a logical place, an entry signal, to buy after a retracement. However, if you have a $100,000 account, it is not too serious to find $5,000 to buy a strong stock right away, even without an entry signal. You just don't want to have several impulse buys on the go all at once that are not making money.

Think Defensively in a Bear Market

The other side of this coin is that you must be prepared to bite the bullet in a stock going against you. The absolute necessity of cutting losses, and of preserving capital, could not have been demonstrated more emphatically between 2000 and the end of 2002. During the bear market, many darlings of the preceding bull market came to serious grief, with several of the most prominent, such as Enron and MCI Worldcom, going to zero. Many shares in solid companies declined by 80 and 90 percent and were slow to recover after the general market stopped falling.

If you wish you didn't own a stock because it never stops going down, then sell it. As a rule, it practically never pays to hold a stock for recovery when the general trend for stocks is down. The probabilities are that a loss will become greater. The bigger the loss, the greater is the likelihood of it becoming bigger still. In the event of a rally, you may be tempted to hang on only to see the stock fall below the level where it first started troubling you. It is better to live by the saying: *First loss is best loss.* Like a toothache, a brief period of suffering soon ends once you get rid of the bad tooth. Then you can make new decisions objectively.

Remember the dynamics of a bear market. Once a bear market becomes entrenched, buyers hold off in anticipation of lower prices. More and more investors want to cash in their profits while they still have them, and they are relentless sellers. Those who bought stocks with borrowed money have to sell because their market value no longer supports the loans taken out to buy them. As prices sink lower, despair becomes the counterpart of the previous enthusiasm, and selling pressure swamps buying power.

The normality of bear markets is that they are a slow and grinding process. Inexorably declining stock prices lead to inexorably rising desperation. Mutual funds experience net outflows of money instead of net inflows. Therefore, mutual fund managers sell stock to meet redemptions, and their stock sales drive prices ever lower. A bear market creates a vicious circle. There have to be exceptionally good reasons to own any stock during a full-fledged bear market, and even then the winners are likely to be very sector-specific such as those related to housing or energy between 2000 and 2003.The upside of bear markets is that eventually they provide the opportunity to buy the best stocks at wonderful prices. Only those who have cash can profit from that opportunity. Plan to be one of them.

Separate Income from Capital

It used to be that there was income and there was capital. You could spend income, but it was a cardinal sin to spend capital. Spending capital was like eating your seed corn for the next crop. This approach is still valid.

Reality for pension funds, for most family trusts, and for many other investors is that people need income to live on. The capital and income returns from investment should therefore be separated. It is, of course, true that you can draw off money from either capital or income. However, the staff of life stands better when you live on income and leave capital to do its work. When the perspective is for retirement in years ahead, then the bias can be toward capital gains. When you need to increase income, then look for higher-yielding stocks that also have the potential for capital gain. When personal or general economic circumstances warrant, shift some money out of lower-yielding stocks and into bonds and higher-yielding stocks, preferably selling weaker stocks to do so rather than selling winners. You may not make superior capital gains in higher-yielding stocks and bonds, but the risk of losing either capital or income is generally lower. In any case, it happens surprisingly often that higher-yielding stocks also make superior capital gains, so you can sometimes have it both ways, often with lower risk. (In the years ahead, it will be interesting to compare the performance of Walgreen and SBC, discussed in chapter 12!)

If you plan to supplement income with realized capital gains, the result may be that you find yourself going through a time when there are no capital gains. Then you lose both ways, selling the capital that should be generating income. This is an exercise in killing the goose that lays the golden eggs.

Capital Management Summary

Here is a summary of the main points to remember when bringing decisions to buy or sell together with the amount of money available to do it. The list includes points already discussed, as well as some new ones that can be handled in point form.

1. It is too risky to put a large amount of capital all at once into stocks or into any other form of long-term investment. Start

small, and add to your winners while weeding out your losers. Put another way, fools and their money are soon parted.

It can be very difficult psychologically to sell out an individual stock, let alone a major portfolio of stocks (or bonds), when your investments are hopelessly underwater.

2. Keep a cash reserve. However favorable the market conditions and however well your stocks are acting, there will always be rainy days when you need cash for something else. Also, there will always be new and better opportunities for which you need money.

3. Do not buy too many different stocks. It is not necessary to diversify by owning, either directly or through a mutual fund, a large number of different stocks. Aimless diversification merely increases the likelihood of investing in fewer great stocks. This is the downfall of many mutual funds. Real diversification involves diversification between entirely different asset classes— between stocks and bonds or cash equivalents such as Treasury bills and the money market.

   Warren Buffett achieved success for Berkshire Hathaway by investing huge amounts of money in a relatively small handful of stocks. It can be enough, even for someone investing tens of millions of dollars, to own as few as a half dozen prime stocks as long as the market in them is reasonably liquid.

4. Run your profits and cut your losses! There is no way to put it better than to repeat this old chestnut.

5. Responsible capital management requires that you sell when the technical case for owning an individual stock, or for the market generally, is no longer favorable. It is infinitely easier to accept losses when they are small, when they represent a manageable proportion of your portfolio. Then you have the means to come back at the market again, with both cash and peace of mind. Remember how much money you can make when you are right!

6. Don't trust a mutual fund to preserve your valuable savings during a bear market. You cannot count on this to change. Ever. Here in his own words is what one fund managers was saying in

1999: "We are not market timers. . . . It's not our job to sell out during a bear market. We are always more or less fully invested all the time. . . ." Remember what they have in fact done in sector-specific funds they manage during bear markets in those sectors.

7. During a general bear market, put your money into cash equivalents such as Treasury bills until the storm blows over. The return always seems inadequate, but unless you are among the few prepared to sell stocks short, you are only looking for a parking place. The alternative, investing for the long term and staying in stocks during a bear market, is to go down with the ship.

8. International investment may constitute diversification, but you have to be aware of the additional risk that accompanies the prospect of additional reward. The world economy is increasingly interdependent. The United States has the world's strongest and most open economy and, for the most part, the best investment opportunities. After the decline in the U.S. dollar between 2000 and 2005, U.S. stocks are on sale for the rest of the world. They may take time to regain their popularity with overseas investors, but the U.S. dollar is sufficiently washed out that a further significant decline is improbable. In addition, with U.S. stocks, you can keep track of what your stocks are doing. While international diversification may appear attractive, there are more companies with a growth rate of 50 percent or higher in the United States than there are in all the rest of the world put together. Weaker economies can catch cold without infecting the United States. When the United States catches cold, other economies may get double pneumonia.

9. Don't be afraid to come back to the stock market after taking a bad loss or when all about you is doom and gloom.

10. Separate capital from income. Think in terms of spending income, if you want, or reinvesting it. Selling capital to live on or, worse, borrowing against your capital to live on may mean that you have neither capital nor income. Living off capital is like gambling with the rent money. You may be able to do it very successfully for a time. In bad times, however, the pressure to make money may guarantee that you lose it. The futures

trader has a valuable saying: *You can't trade scared money!* Trying to find surefire winners because you need to make money virtually guarantees that you will in fact buy losers, not winners.

Capital management is an essential component of the investment business. You must buy stocks when it is timely to do so, after working out how much you can sensibly afford to buy, given that the investment may not be successful. You must sell stocks when it is timely to do so, bearing in mind the duty to conserve capital for the long term. In sum, you must manage your capital responsibly, as if it were an independent business.

The next two chapters show how to set about buying a stock. You have to consider them in conjunction with Chapter 18, which deals with stops (or the stop loss) that protect you from ruinous losses. Chapter 18 also shows how to distinguish between setbacks that are acceptable and those that are not and how to use stops to protect your profits.

CHAPTER 16

Entry Checklist: Buy

Bringing the Signals Together

Most people find it difficult to pull the trigger to buy or sell: It is difficult to be completely objective, either hoping too much or fearing too much without good reason to act. Using a checklist imposes discipline and helps to avoid oversights. This is why airline pilots use them, even though they make thousands of flights over the years.

Often the greatest stocks to buy appear to involve a high risk because they have moved so far in a short time. Many people find it difficult to buy a stock that has gone up by 20 or 30 percent in a surge. Others cannot resist buying a stock that seems to be running away, although the prime entry point has long been left behind. Naturally, you do not want to buy a stock only to see it come all the way back again. Nevertheless, the one that shows that it can go higher is most likely to go higher still. The stocks that go on to double or triple or more should take care of the inevitable losses many, many times over. It is all too easy to buy a dog of a stock because you think there is a low risk. In fact, there may be a high risk and no corresponding upside potential to offset the risk.

No system is perfect. An entry checklist using the indicators described in this book provides the best available compromise between knowing that a stock can move and knowing that the reward-to-risk is favorable

ENTRY CHECKLIST: BUY

Stock	Price		Date
Confirming Indicators	Monthly	Weekly	Daily
1. W/Zigzag Line			
2. 25-Bar MA			
3. 40-Bar MA			
4. OBV 1			
5. OBV 10			
6. Fast MACD			
7. Slow MACD			
8. %K Turn			
9. %K Level (under 20)			
10. Price Rule			
11. Turn at MA/Trendline			
12. Key Reversal			
13. Double Reversal			
14. Chart Pattern			
15. Gap			
16. Island			
17. Market Conditions			
18. Value			
TOTAL			
Negating Indicators			
1. Adverse W/Zigzag Line			
2. Adv. 25 MA			
3. Adv. 40 MA			
4. OBV 1			
5. OBV 10			
6. Fast MACD			
7. Slow MACD			
8. %K Level (above 80)			
9. Resistance			
10. Channel Line			
11. Adv. T-Line Cross			
12. Value			
TOTAL			

relative to a reasonable stop loss. For easy use, photocopy the Entry Checklist to fill a full-size sheet.

Your entry checklist has three columns, one each for monthly, weekly, and daily indicators. The monthly list provides the essential information for the big picture whether you want to own the stock at all. The weekly checklist confirms the intermediate picture. Ideally, the monthly, weekly, and daily chart patterns should all confirm simultaneously whether the stock is a buy now, but the main thing is the monthly chart for the big picture and the daily chart for an actual entry signal. At different times, every variation in chart patterns can happen, so there is still an element of judgment required in many situations. Simultaneous new buy signals on the monthly or weekly list at the same time as a daily buy signal indicate that the probabilities are strongly favorable for the stock to start making money right away.

Place a checkmark beside an indicator when it confirms a buy, and leave a blank when it is negating it. Below the list of confirming indicators is a list of negating indicators to make sure that there is not a weight of evidence against the decision. You might think that it would be obvious not to buy a stock going down instead of one going up. Not so! A lot of people do it. Remember that someone has to take the other side of every trade. Otherwise, you cannot do business!

Normally, there should be about eight or more confirming indicators across the board. There should not be more than one or two negating indicators. There should be almost nothing ambiguous or contradictory about the best stocks to buy.

It is generally best to make out one or two checklists in addition to making out one for the specific stock that you are considering. Go through the entry checklist for at least one of the major stock market indexes, as well as for a sector index, if available. It may also be worth making out the entry checklist for more than one stock in a market group.

When one stock comes in with more positive indicators than another, go with that one. It seldom pays to depart from the rule that you should buy the strongest stock and sell the weakest. The strong stock may double from its current price level, even if it seems to have done a lot already, whereas the laggard goes up by only 50 percent. The psychology of expecting laggards to catch up is generally a loser play over the long term.

Confirming Indicators

1. **W formation/zigzag line.** There is no more powerful indicator of a bull market than an upward zigzag on the monthly line chart or a W to indicate the potential start of an upward zigzag. For all practical purposes, the probabilities seldom favor buying a stock unless there is an upward zigzag or a new W. A stock that has gone through a big correction within the major trend may actually have a negating zigzag on the daily chart. Severely oversold stochastics should offset this negativity.

2. **25-bar moving average.** The 25-month moving average should show an upward direction, and ideally, this average, as well as price, should be above the 40-month moving average. The 25-week and 25-day moving averages ideally should confirm when you buy a stock, but they may not necessarily do so when the stock is extremely oversold in the short term.

3. **40-bar moving average.** The 40-month moving average, for all practical purposes, always should be pointing up when you buy a stock. A wobbling 25-month moving average may show aberrations, but the primary indication of market direction by the 40-month moving average seldom fails unless the price has advanced a long way above it.

4. **OBV 1.** The direction of the simple unsmoothed line for on-balance volume (OBV) shows the immediate weight of buying or selling pressure in a stock. This line is particularly bullish when it defines its own upward zigzag pattern.

    There are two conditions in the action for OBV that you have to be careful with. When OBV 1 has moved a long way from its 10-bar moving average, it may indicate a buying climax rather than the kind of persistence that keeps a stock moving steadily higher. You also have to beware when price moves to a new high, but OBV makes a lower high.

5. **OBV 10.** The smoothed OBV line takes the wrinkles out of the ebb and flow of supply and demand. It shows persistence more reliably than does OBV 1. You want it to confirm direction.

    Although not required for the checklist, OBV generates a buy signal in its own right when it crosses over its 10-bar moving average. It is particularly significant when the crossover occurs after a period of rounding by the two OBV lines.

6. **Fast MACD.** Fast moving-average convergence/divergence (MACD) should be pointing upward for a confirming indicator when buying a stock. Sometimes this is a lagging indicator, and an upturn may occur after other indicators fall into place. Nevertheless, you generally can tell whether fast MACD is in the process of rounding upward and likely to run up.

   As with OBV, beware of buying a stock when MACD fails to make a higher high along with a higher high in price. It may be showing flagging momentum. The result may either be that the stock fails to follow through or that it is unable to move up significantly until MACD comes decisively back on side.

7. **Slow MACD.** Slow MACD should be pointing upward when buying.

   (Some of the biggest and best moves start from the time when fast MACD crosses the slow and they both begin a steady upward progress.)

8. **%K turn.** This indicator should be pointing up to confirm a buy. Unlike MACD, the fast stochastic %K is a fast-acting indicator.

   When a stock is under way, %K should show the likely direction of price, regardless of whether it is at a high or low level. Flagging action in %K may indicate that a stock is in need of a rest and may be vulnerable to a retracement. It does not by any means suggest an impending trend reversal, for which many indicators need to fall into place.

9. **%K level.** This indicator should be currently or have been recently below 20 to confirm a buy, thereby indicating the likelihood that a correction has been completed. When %K is at a level below 20 in a bull market, you may want to buy a stock before %K turns up. It may be enough that the stock has finished an intermediate correction or is imminently about to do so.

10. **Price rule signal.** You need to have a new price rule on the daily chart to pull the trigger to buy a stock. (Ideally, there should be a clear price rule signal in force on the monthly and the weekly charts when buying a stock. In practice, it is often enough to get a general impression that bars on the weekly and monthly

charts are favorable, with closes mostly in the upper end of their respective bars.)

11. **Turn at moving average/trendline.** There is a positive indicator when, after completing a retracement, the price stops and turns at a level at or near the 25 and 40 moving averages or at a clear trendline.

   There is high probability that the moving averages will contain the retracement. Therefore, a price rule signal at that level is much more likely to succeed than one occurring randomly. The 25 and 40 calibration may seem random. However, the probabilities tend to be more favorable on retracements to these levels for two reasons. First, they show that the stock is not exceptionally overextended and vulnerable to a retracement. Second, many traders watch the 25 and 40 moving averages, so their effectiveness in containing retracements tends to be self-reinforcing.

12. **Key reversal.** Count a favorable indicator for a key reversal. A key reversal with a strong close powerfully contributes to the probability of a stock continuing in the direction of the close. An upside key reversal provides the visible means of showing that weak holders have been flushed out at a bottom and that strong money has come in to buy.

   Key reversals on the monthly and weekly charts tend to show strong newfound power in a stock, especially when there have been one or more additional upside reversals recently. A key reversal occurring in conjunction with a buy signal on the daily chart increases the probability of a stock moving to a profit right away. A key reversal on the daily chart in a rapidly moving stock may provide a prime entry and do so in conjunction with a manageable stop placed below the low of the day.

13. **Double reversal.** Count a favorable indicator with this occurrence. A double reversal in the direction of an established trend and occurring within a few bars is as powerful as a key reversal, if not more so. The two reversals indicate cleansing of the market of weak holders and preparation for a strong upward move. A double reversal is much more powerful than a single one occurring at random.

14. **Chart pattern.** Count a favorable indicator when a stock is breaking out of a trading range or is completing a reverse head-and-shoulders pattern.

15. **Gaps.** Count a favorable indicator when there is an upward gap on the weekly or daily chart. Gaps on the weekly chart tend to have more significance than you might expect because of so many people who make their investment decisions over the weekend.

16. **Island.** Count a favorable indicator when the price has gapped down and then gapped up. Best of all is when there are several days of market consolidation underneath the market prior to a sharp upside resolution of the standoff between buyers and sellers. This can be one of the best indications to show that a retracement has ended.

    On the other hand, an island above the current price that results from downward gapping may show that the stock has exhausted its upside potential. Any consolidation below an island simply may be the harbinger of a further significant decline when new buyers find they are wrong.

17. **Market conditions.** It is essential to look at the bigger picture for the market generally, for interest rates, and for the group index for the stock that you are considering. When the stock market generally is going either sideways or down or is at a very high level, be careful. Depending on your interpretation of a necessarily subjective array of considerations, it means that you should buy lightly, not that you should pass when there is a strong signal to buy a specific stock.

    In a general bear market, be wary of buying any stock of any kind in any company. It is difficult to find the 10 percent of stocks that are going up in a general bear market. During the recent bear market, there were specific sectors that were extremely rewarding even as the overall market, and espcially technology stocks, were going down. The stocks that went up had very sepcific characteristics. They included the direct beneficiaries of the low interest rates with which the Federal Reserve sought to counter the recession and the implosion of the stock market, such as the housing and construction sector.

They also included oil stocks, which responded to rising oil prices, and gold stocks, which responded to the declining dollar versus the overseas currencies.

18. **Value.** The best stocks generally have an external reason to buy them—the sex appeal factor. You like the product. Or you think what they do seems to fit into the general pattern of society's needs or desires, such as for health care or hamburgers. If a business looks busy and prosperous, the chances are that it is well run, that it makes money, and that its stock will perform well. You don't have to be an accountant to sniff out a great business, particularly if the technical patterns on the charts look good.

Negating Indicators

1. **Adverse W/zigzag line.** It practically never pays to buy a stock unless there is an upward zigzag or a newly forming W on the monthly line chart. Lack of this confirming indicator amounts virtually to a total trade embargo. The weekly and daily charts may not have an upward zigzag pattern after a severe retracement. The main thing is to have a strong monthly chart pattern confirming a major uptrend.

2. **Adverse 25-bar moving-average direction.** A downward incline in the 25-bar moving average counts as a negating indicator. Many stocks take off before the 25-month moving average turns up, but the probabilities are not favorable for a sustained move, and the risk of a major retracement, if not outright failure, is high. As with an adverse W, lack of this confirming factor almost amounts to a trade embargo.

3. **Adverse 40-bar moving-average direction.** A downward incline in the 40-bar moving average counts as a negating indicator. Ideally, price should be above the 25- and 40-month moving averages for several months, say, five or more, unless there is a very pronounced rounding by both price and the moving average. An adverse close below rising 25- and 40-bar moving averages counts as a negating indicator.

4. **OBV 1.** When OBV 1 points down, count this indicator negative. The direction of the OBV 1 should be pointing upward or making

no more than a small downward incline in an overall bullish pattern. Also, a new high in price should be accompanied by a new high in OBV.

When OBV 1 is extremely overextended, this indicator may be showing signs of climactic buying rather than the kind of steady and persistent buying that confirms the strength of the stock.

5. **OBV 10.** Count this indicator negative when OBV 10 is pointing down. Ideally, OBV 1 should be above OBV 10. A single and short-lived adverse crossover of OBV 10 may mean little. When OBV 1 is persistently below OBV 10, the probabilities are that the stock is being sold and that a decline in price may go further than you expect.

6. **Fast MACD.** Count it a negating indicator when fast MACD is pointing down.

7. **Slow MACD.** Count it a negative indicator when slow MACD is pointing down.

8. **%K level.** Count it a negative indicator when fast stochastic %K is above 80 or higher. This condition often occurs when a stock is overbought and vulnerable to a retracement. It also occurs, however, in the fastest-moving markets and when a stock first breaks out of a consolidation. Therefore, a high %K level may be a sign of market strength. Thus you have to interpret this overbought level in the context of specific market action at the time.

9. **Resistance.** Resistance counts as a negative indicator when a stock is approaching a historic high where it previously turned down and began a major correction. It is easy to fear that the most recent high on the daily chart may signify a more durable top when no more than a temporary correction has occurred. Look for resistance on the monthly and weekly charts, for levels that have truly rebuffed attempts by the stock to go higher.

10. **Channel line.** Count this indicator negative when a stock is pressing against an upper channel line. Then there is a high probability of a retracement back to the upward trendline.

11. **Adverse trendline crossover.** Count this as a negative indicator when price is below a clearly identifiable upward trendline.

This means that the market has lost its immediate upward momentum. A strong stock should not require ever shallower trendlines.

12. **Value.** Count this indicator negative when there is no known fundamental value in a stock or there have been poor earnings results. Even the most ardent technician and antivaluation investor should have some general awareness of the difference between a Dow stock and a speculative new issue with no financial history. If the technical picture is good enough, the best thing may be just to buy a small number of shares rather than pass on buying the stock altogether.

Stops

See Chapter 18. Don't buy a stock without knowing where to place the stop! Remember that a 50 percent loss requires a double to get your money back. A loss of 20 percent requires only a 25 percent gain to get you back to where you started.

Case Study: How to Buy

The Entry Checklist for Whole Foods Market, Inc. (WFMI)

Even in the dark days of the bear market, after a year and a half of decline, you might have been looking for stocks to consider buying in October and November 2001, in anticipation of a worthwhile seasonal rally and possibly the end of the bear market. When considering those possibilities, you should have been looking for stocks already bucking the trend of the overall market and ideally ones that were still managing to maintain an established upward trend. The largest distributor of health foods in the United States, WFMI, fulfilled these criteria, in addition to being a remarkably robust company with a unique franchise.

The checklist for October 22, 2001, on page 201, shows how the indicators confirmed WFMI as a timely stock to buy.

Monthly Confirming Indicators

1. **W formation/zigzag line** (Fig. 17-1). Yes. The stock has been in a steady, if somewhat erratic, upward zigzag since making its low in March 1999. Curiously, this stock went through its own proprietary bear market in 1998–1999, when the stock halved as investors turned their attention toward the high-flying technology sector. After the low in March 1999, WFMI not only failed to

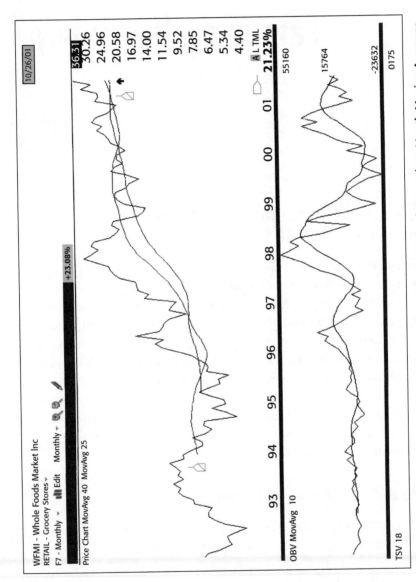

FIGURE 17-1 Whole Foods Market Monthly Line Chart with OBV and 25- and 40-Month Moving Averages.

follow the general market down but also succeeded in making a succession of higher lows, with the one in April 2001 holding perceptibly above the one in June 2000. Now the stock appears to be making a pronounced new upward zigzag on the monthly line chart, with a break to a new high above the one in 1998.

2. **25-month moving average.** Yes. Price is above this average and has been for six months, with a recent successful test and rebound.

3. **40-month moving average.** Yes. The direction of the 40-month moving average has confirmed a major bull market since 1995, and it did not even turn down at the low in 1999, although the stock traded briefly below it.

4. **OBV 1.** Yes. On-balance volume (OBV) fell rather hard when the price of the stock declined into its low in April, but since then, it has been developing a very satisfactory upward zigzag.

5. **OBV 10.** No, but OBV1 has just crossed to the upside, which is a positive sign.

6. **Fast MACD** (Fig. 17-2). Yes. On the monthly chart, fast moving-average convergence/divergence (MACD) turned up over a year ago and crossed above slow MACD a few months later. Note the recent correction and the new upturn above slow MACD, which forms its own small W.

7. **Slow MACD.** Yes. This configuration is superb, with fast MACD trending steadily above slow MACD. This pattern suggest that WFMI could be starting a significant move up, as occurred during the move that began in 1997, when the stock tripled in price.

8. **%K turn** (Fig. 17-3). Yes. %K got down to quite a low level at the last low, and it has risen steadily. The incline may be somewhat mature, but, as occurred in 1997, the strong move up may indicate that the stock itself is strong.

9. **%K level.** No. Count this indicator neutral. It does not give a positive reading after being oversold, below 20, but it has been low enough to suggest that an important low may have been put in place. It has just about reached an overbought reading at 80, but this should not be a deterrent to buying the stock.

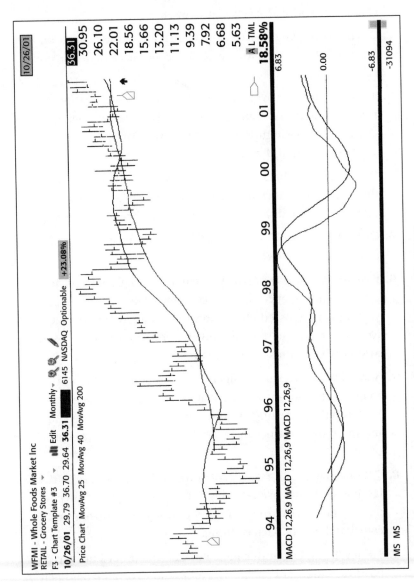

FIGURE 17-2 Whole Foods Market Monthly Bar Chart with MACD.

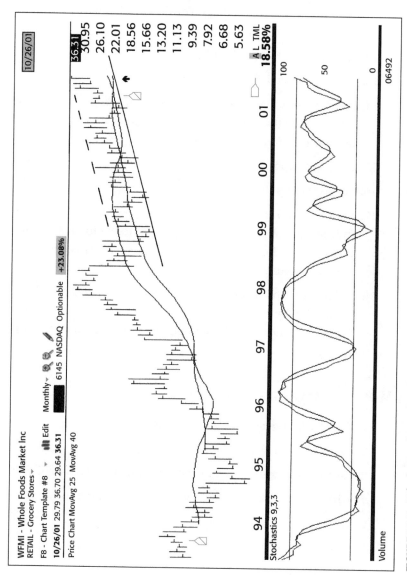

FIGURE 17-3 Whole Foods Market Bar Line Chart with Stochastics.

10. **Price rule.** Yes. Count a rule 2 price rule in effect from August and note the powerful new high/low upside reversal bar.

11. **Turn at moving average/trendline.** Yes. The price held at a fourth point of contact on a shallow trendline from the low in 1999, and at the low, it dipped only briefly below the upwardly inclining monthly moving averages.

12. **Key reversal.** Not applicable.

13. **Double reversal.** Not applicable.

14. **Chart pattern.** Yes. Count as positive. There is a powerful coiling action within the monthly chart that suggests that the stock can move strongly out of the three-year-long basing formation.

15. **Gap.** Not applicable.

16. **Island.** Not applicable.

17. **Market conditions.** Yes, but extremely doubtful. The major indexes (not shown) look as if they are trying to take a stand, but it is still a bear market. Count this indicator negative, subject to these reservations.

18. **Value.** Yes. Count this indicator positive. This company has a wonderful franchise and is not subject to serious competition. The stock is not cheap, but there might never be a better time to buy it.

Monthly Negating Indicators

1. **Adverse W/zigzag line.** Not applicable.

2. **Adverse 25-month moving-average direction.** Not applicable.

3. **Adverse 40-month moving-average direction.** Not applicable.

4. **OBV 1.** Not applicable, but not exactly confirming strongly.

5. **OBV 10.** Negative.

6. **Fast MACD.** Not applicable

7. **Slow MACD.** Not applicable.

8. **%K level.** Negative.

9. **Resistance.** None. WFMI is just now clearing resistance.

10. **Channel line.** Negative. The stock is right at the upper channel line opposite the trendline from the 1999 low. It looks as if it will push on through. We have to count this a negative and be prepared for the stock to have to do some work at this level before gaining upward momentum.

11. **Adverse trendline crossover.** Not applicable.

12. **Value.** Covered on the monthly confirming list.

The confirming indicators are so strong that there is little risk in overriding negative to neutral readings for %K and the channel line.

Weekly Confirming Indicators

1. **W formation/zigzag line** (Fig. 17-4). Yes. The stock looks great. You might be wary of the fact that it has come so far in a relatively short time during the year from its low at the $21 level to the current $34 level. Since the zigzag is so powerful, the pattern suggests that there should be a new upward surge beyond the recent high as great as the amplitude of the last retracement. This chart suggests a target toward the $40 level.

2. **25-week moving average.** Yes. The stock crossed over with a powerful surge, then settled back to be cradled by the moving averages, and then went on its way again.

3. **40-week moving average.** Yes. Confirms with the same positive indications as the 25-week moving average.

4. **OBV 1.** Yes. OBV confirms with a very steady and reliable upward zigzag.

5. **OBV 10.** Yes. Confirms with an OBV 1 crossover and a turn at OBV 10.

6. **Fast MACD** (Fig. 17-5). Yes. Confirming beautifully, although possibly a little overextended in the near term.

7. **Slow MACD.** Yes. Although it is a bit high, it is interesting to see that it never came close to the low reading in 1999, and it is possible that it could develop an upward swing comparable with that downward one.

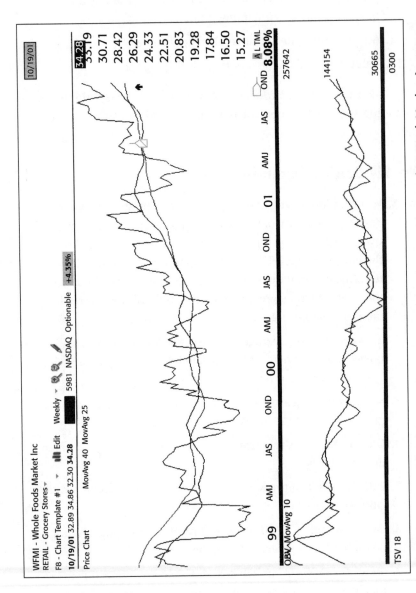

FIGURE 17-4 Whole Foods Market Weekly Line Chart with OBV and 25- and 40-Week Moving Averages.

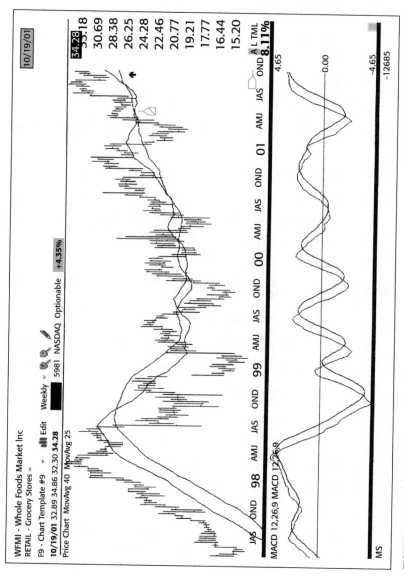

FIGURE 17-5 Whole Foods Market Weekly Bar Chart with MACD.

8. **%K turn** (Fig. 17-6). Yes. Count %K positive, with a good W pattern.

9. **%K level.** Yes. This looks just fine with the recent crossover and plenty of upside room before reaching 80.

10. **Price rule.** Yes. Count a rule 2 price rule two weeks ago that is still in force and a strong current bar.

11. **Turn at moving average/trendline.** Yes, a beautiful turn at the assumed new uptrend line.

12. **Key reversal.** Not applicable.

13. **Double reversal.** Not applicable.

14. **Chart pattern.** Yes. Count positive. The weekly chart is strong without being overextended.

15. **Gap.** Not applicable.

16. **Island.** Not applicable.

17. **Market conditions.** Yes. Covered on the monthly list.

18. **Value.** Yes. Covered on the monthly list.

Weekly Negating Indicators

1. **Adverse W/zigzag line.** Not applicable.

2. **Adverse 25-week moving-average direction.** Not applicable.

3. **Adverse 40-week moving average direction.** Not applicable.

4. **OBV 1.** Not applicable.

5. **OBV 10.** Not applicable.

6. **Fast MACD.** Not applicable.

7. **Slow MACD.** Not applicable.

8. **%K level.** Not applicable.

9. **Resistance.** None.

10. **Channel line.** Not applicable. The assumed upper channel line intersects with a price projection far above its current level.

11. **Adverse trendline crossover.** Not applicable.

12. **Value.** Not applicable.

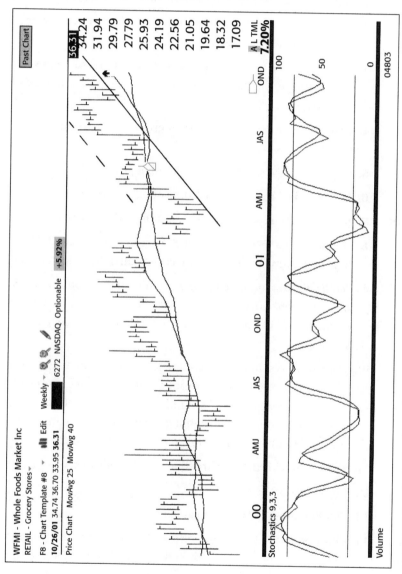

FIGURE 17-6 Whole Foods Market Weekly Bar Chart with Stochastics.

Daily Confirming Indicators

1. **W formation/zigzag line** (Fig. 17-7). Yes. It has been a bit erratic, but there's a new upturn, and the last retracement did no damage because it held at the level of the previous low.

2. **25-day moving average.** Yes. Just turning up now after price has consolidated above it.

3. **40-day moving average.** Yes. Confirms with the same positive indications as the 25-week moving average, if a bit behind in responding.

4. **OBV 1.** Yes. OBV confirms strongly now, having had a few bumpy weeks.

5. **OBV 10.** Yes. Confirms, although rather grudgingly.

6. **Fast MACD** (Fig. 17-8). Yes. Confirming beautifully.

7. **Slow MACD.** Yes. Confirming beautifully, with superb rounding.

8. **%K turn** (Fig. 17-9). Yes. Count %K positive, with a good W pattern after a very small downward correction quickly righted itself.

9. **%K level.** No. Count negative. As noted on the monthly checklist, an overbought stochastic reading is often a sign of strength, not of vulnerability, when other indicators confirm strongly.

10. **Price rule.** Yes, but not as completely clear as one might wish. There has been a succession of strong bars since the recent lows, including a powerful Lindahl buy signal with a strong upside key reversal when coming out of the low. Count a rule 5 price rule with a small key reversal on the entry day.

11. Turn at moving average/trendline. Not applicable.

12. Key reversal. Yes.

13. **Double reversal.** Not applicable.

14. **Chart pattern.** Yes. Count positive. The daily chart is making a small W with the second low significantly higher than the first one.

15. **Gap.** Not applicable.

16. **Island.** Not applicable.

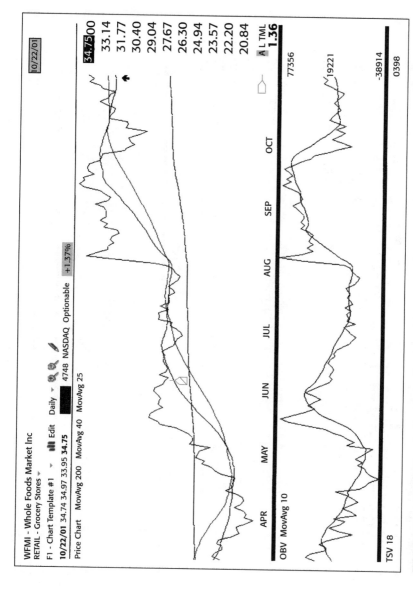

FIGURE 17-7 Whole Foods Market Daily Line Chart with OBV and 25-, 40- and 200-Day Moving Averages.

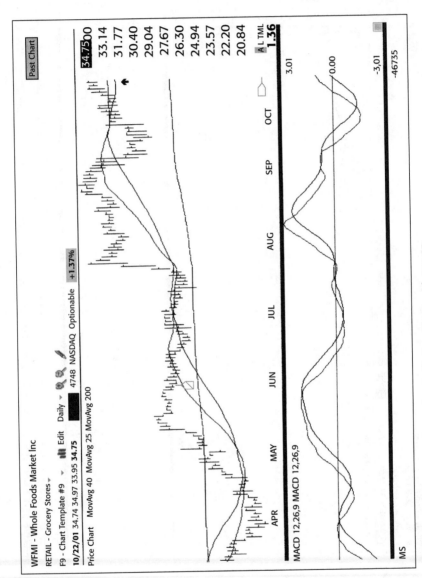

FIGURE 17-8 Whole Foods Market Daily Bar Chart with MACD.

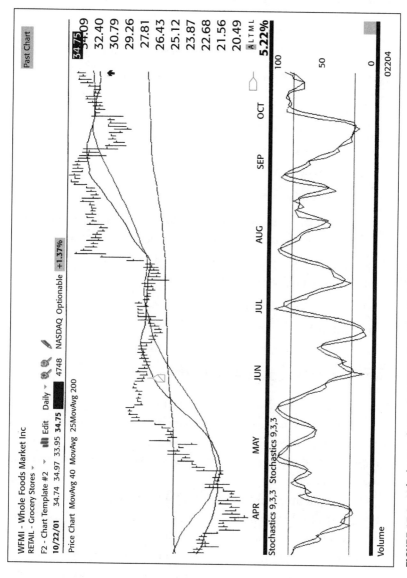

FIGURE 17-9 Whole Foods Market Daily Bar Chart with Stochastics.

17. **Market conditions.** Yes. Covered on the monthly list.

18. **Value.** Yes. Covered on the monthly list.

Daily Negating Indicators

1. **Adverse W/zigzag line.** Not applicable.

2. **Adverse 25 moving-average direction.** Not applicable.

3. **Adverse 40 moving-average direction.** Not applicable.

4. **OBV 1.** Not applicable.

5. **OBV 10.** Not applicable.

6. **Fast MACD.** Not applicable.

7. **Slow MACD.** Not applicable.

8. **%K level.** Not applicable.

9. **Resistance.** Yes. The price has to move conclusively out to a new all-time high, but there is no reason to expect that it will have more than temporary difficulty in doing so, if any.

10. **Channel line.** Not applicable.

11. **Adverse trendline crossover.** Not applicable.

12. **Value.** Not applicable.

The Stop (discussed in Chapter 18)

This is such a strong stock that it seems appropriate to give it room to move. The best available compromise for the stop looks to be at $29.75, below recent significant lows on the daily chart, below the $30 round number, and allowing about 13 percent of the value in the event that the stop is activated.

As it turned out, a purchase of WFMI in October 2001 would have put you into the stock at an extremely good price relative to what it was to do subsequently, even though you would have bought when it had already come a long way. You can see from the monthly chart carrying forward to 2005 that there was a steady move from our assumed entry price around $35 to a price just above $100 over the three and half years (Fig. 17-10). At that price, the stock was expensive, with a price-earnings

ENTRY CHECKLIST: BUY

Stock CCI	Price	Date	
Confirming Indicators	Monthly	Weekly	Daily
1. W/Zigzag Line	✔	✔	✔
2. 25-Bar MA	✔	✔	✔
3. 40-Bar MA	✔	✔	✔
4. OBV 1	✔	✔	✔
5. OBV 10		✔	✔
6. Fast MACD	✔	✔	✔
7. Slow MACD	✔	✔	✔
8. %K Turn	✔	✔	✔
9. %K Level (under 20)		✔	
10. Price Rule	✔	✔	✔
11. Turn at MA/Trendline	✔	✔	
12. Key Reversal			
13. Double Reversal			
14. Chart Pattern	✔	✔	✔
15. Gap			
16. Island			
17. Market Conditions	✔	✔	✔
18. Value	✔	✔	✔
TOTAL	12	14	12
Negating Indicators			
1. Adverse W/Zigzag Line			
2. Adv. 25 MA			
3. Adv. 40 MA			
4. OBV 1			
5. OBV 10	✔		
6. Fast MACD			
7. Slow MACD			
8. %K Level (above 80)	✔		✔
9. Resistance			✔
10. Channel Line	✔		
11. Adv. T-Line Cross			
12. Value			
TOTAL	3	0	2

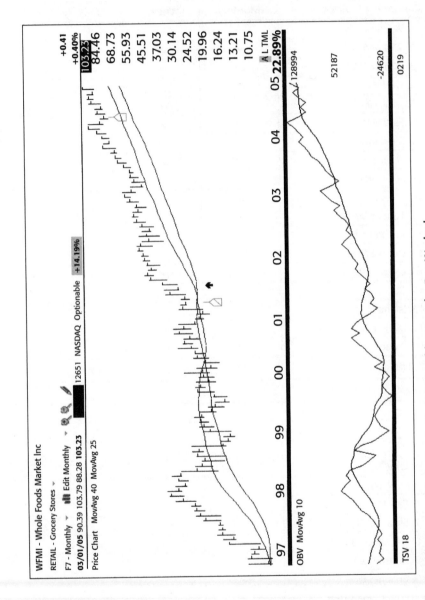

FIGURE 17-10 Whole Foods Market Monthly: How the Buy Worked.

ratio of 46, and it seemed overdue for a more significant consolidation. However, corporate performance kept on coming through, so in due course the stock could be expected to grow into its market price. This case study for WFMI shows that a stock in a long-term uptrend that is well bought offers a superb ratio of reward to risk: Risk 10 percent or so in the hope of doubling or even tripling your money eventually.

WFMI combines the characteristics that we look for both for buying into an established trend and for buying into a long-term breakout. The bear market never damaged the long-term uptrend, and the sideways action since the high in March 1998 established a base for projecting the substantial move that was to follow through.

Protect Capital with a Stop Loss

The Importance of Stops

This chapter discusses one of the most important challenges facing investors: *stops*, also known as the *stop loss*—starting with the *initial protective stop* (IPS) and then, as the price moves up, the *trailing protective stop* (TPS). Most people know that you can make disastrous mistakes in the stock market, and indeed, most people will have had bad experiences. Only chart-based technical analysis provides a reliable and methodical approach for avoiding ruinous losses and protecting profits.

The Psychology of Stops

The first lesson of stops is that if you don't know where to place the stop, discussed below, then perhaps you should not buy the stock at all. Or else you should buy only a small number of shares to start with so that you really can live with whatever happens, including carrying the shares down to zero. Capital conservation requires putting a handle on potential losses, if only for disaster insurance.

Many investors learned to their cost and dismay during the recent bear market that it can be a serious challenge to deal with a loss or a forgone profit that has gotten away on you. You often hear people say something like, "Oh well, I'm in it for the long term, so I might as well stay with it. I am sure it will turn out all right in the end. At least a company like that isn't going out of business." The trouble is that you *cannot* be so certain that it will turn out all right in the end.

Logically, for the fundamental analyst, a stock that you can buy cheaper is a better buy than when you bought it at a higher price. However, markets can remain irrational longer than you can remain solvent! The stock of a fine dividend-paying company can go down by 75 percent or more, as was demonstrated between 2000 and 2002. Even if you are right about the underlying value of a stock that is going down, that doesn't mean that it will stop going down, let alone that it will actually go up. Buying more shares if the price goes down rather than getting stopped out can be ruinous. It violates the successful investor's saying: *Run your profits and cut your losses!* A better strategy than buying more of stock that goes down is this: If you buy two stocks and one goes up and the other goes down, buy more of the one that goes up, not the one that you can buy cheaper. The first is what winners do. The second is a standard loser play.

Apart from the practical problem of risking a doubled loss when doubling up on a loser, there is another problem. Psychologically, it is much more difficult to take a big loss than it is to take a small one. Even under the best of circumstances, when you think that you have the best possible information, there will be times when you miss some vital piece of the jigsaw puzzle. Sometimes there may be nothing wrong with the stock that goes down. It is just that the stock has become too expensive for now, and the current price attracts more aggressive sellers and less aggressive buyers. As discussed elsewhere, sometimes you inadvertently find a stock such as Nortel that never stops going down, even before the full extent of corporate business problems becomes known. As a reminder, from a high of $89 in August 2000, Nortel ratcheted down to an eventual low of just 43 cents in October 2002.

First Loss, Least Loss

There's a saying about cutting losses that is worth remembering: *First loss, least loss!* You have to internalize the fact that it is far less difficult to get out of an investment in the early stages of a decline than it is later on, and if the stock is losing money, you had better take it when it's small and manageable. Once an unplaced stop point has been taken out or an exit signal has been missed, the psychology of getting out goes something like this: You expect a retracement to get out at a less bad price. But it doesn't come back, and the less the stock is worth, the more reluctant you are to cash it in. When at last there is a rally, it never goes far enough. All it does is to induce the false expectation that this time the market has really turned at last. Then the stock turns down again, and determination to stay with it takes on a new conviction. That, of course, is how a bear market works. Which bring us back to where we started: You cannot count on things working out in the end.

Many investors find it very difficult to be disciplined about selling a loser, but there is consolation: *Remember how much money you can make when you are right!*

The Initial Protective Stop (IPS)

The idea behind stops is that you enter an order with your broker to sell shares if the price falls below your predetermined tolerance level. For example, you buy shares at $10, hoping that they will go to $15 or $20 in due course. This might not happen for many unforeseeable reasons. Worse, the stock might go down to $5 or even to zero. To protect yourself from the risk of a devastating loss, you are prepared to accept one that is moderate. Therefore, you decide to tolerate a retracement to $8.75, budgeting for a loss of $1.25 per share if it doesn't go up. If the shares sell down to $9.25 or even to $8.76, you still want to own them. The moment a price of $8.75 is touched, the broker acts on an order to sell at the best possible price, which may be at your price of $8.75 or the best that is obtainable below that level.

Sometimes really bad news strikes between the close of one day and the opening of the market the next day. It could be something like the announcement of a reduction of the dividend or the loss of a major contract. In that case, the stock might open the next day at a price significantly below $8.75. It might even open at $7.75, a full dollar below your stop. Never mind! This price action has knocked the stuffing out of any technical justification for continuing to own the stock. Bad news practically never comes in isolation any more than does one cockroach. The shares may or may not go down farther but this doesn't mean that the reason you bought them—that they will increase in price—will happen any time soon.

In sum, stops get you out of a share before any decline from its current price becomes expensive.

In the recent bear market, many, many investors would have saved themselves from devastating losses had they used stops to protect their capital. It is simply not true, and never has been, that you can buy and hold any and all stocks for the long term without heeding their market action. (Remember what Benjamin Graham actually said, quoted in Chapter 1, and not what financial advisors say that he said about holding stocks for the long term!) It has happened often in the past that a stock has a wonderful story and has continued to pay a good dividend, yet it lost 75 percent of its value. Even if the business remains sound as ever, which may or may not be the case, but you find out only much later, business and financial conditions may be changing for the worse so that the market values all shares at a much lower price.

The Trailing Protective Stop (TPS)

Although not of the same order of necessity as an IPS, you also need stops to protect profits when a stock goes up. This is the *trailing protective stop* (TPS). Say that you buy that stock at $10 and it goes up to $20. Then you fear that it might make a round trip back to what you paid for it. You enter a TPS to protect some profit, leaving the stock room to move, and let the profit run so that it may double again. You might place the TPS just under $15. Then you protect a profit of almost $5 rather than give back all of the $10 profit or, worse, see a profit turn to a loss.

Where to Put the Stop

There is an irreconcilable conflict about stops that costs you money unnecessarily some of the time although, ultimately, protecting your capital all the time. Putting the IPS close guarantees a larger number of relatively small losses compared with allowing a stock more latitude to move against you. Putting stops more distant means that losses are fewer, but they will be bigger.

These four approaches to placing a stop make sense:

1. Allow a stock to retrace by just 10 percent or so and no more and no less, except for putting it below any obvious round number—thus at $9.95 rather than at a round $10. This approach imposes

a discipline that prevents bad losses, but it is arbitrary, sometimes allowing for too much and sometimes not enough.

2. Place a stop beyond the technical formation that activated the initial entry. Any retracement toward that level may be no more than a routine consolidation, even if the price goes back to test the low. If the price level below the entry formation is violated, it means that the stock has violated the near-term bull market requirement of maintaining a pattern of higher highs and higher lows.

   Say that you act on a signal to buy CR Bard (BCR) at $59.64 on December 8 as a result of a rule 2 reversal rule buy signal (Fig. 18-1). The low for the buy rule formation is at $58.18, the low of the previous day. It would be reasonable to put a very tight stop below that low, say, at $57.95. In the event, this works just fine because the stop was never threatened (although, obviously, at the time, you could not know that it would not be). This allows for a loss of just 3 percent in the event that the stop is activated.

3. Look for chart support, and place the stop beyond that level. The chart for BCR shows that the price gapped up on November 2, from the previous day's close at $56.70, leaving the entire earlier formation behind, and you can now see that it is staying left behind. The stock might still test back into that gap, but if it goes much beyond, then the entire breakout may not have been valid. Therefore, a stop at about $55.95 does the job. This allows a budget of approximately 6 percent from the entry for the loss in the event that the stop is activated, which is very reasonable.

   Use this approach for all support areas, particularly including trendlines, and move the stop up as the price goes up. For an initial entry on the basis of the daily chart, you could use a trendline on that daily chart. However, when looking to hold a stock for the long term when there is no particular reason to expect a trend reversal, using an uptrend line on the monthly chart generally does the best job of keeping you in and getting you out when things may be starting to go wrong.

4. Put a stop beyond the most recent monthly reversal, whether a closing price reversal or a high/low reversal, or the most recent prominent spike on the monthly chart (Fig. 18-2). This is the best available all-weather stop when taking a long-term view, and it works very effectively both as an IPS and as a TPS.

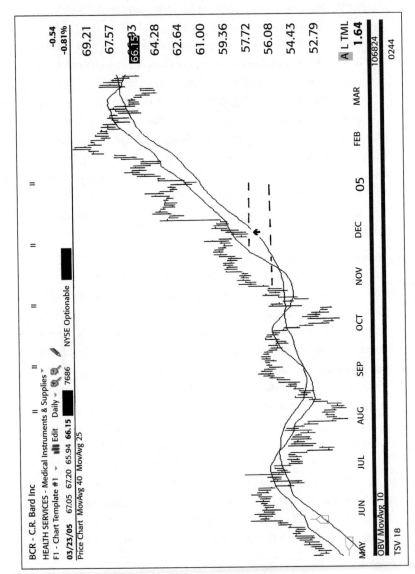

FIGURE 18-1 CR Bard Daily Bar Chart with Stop Levels.

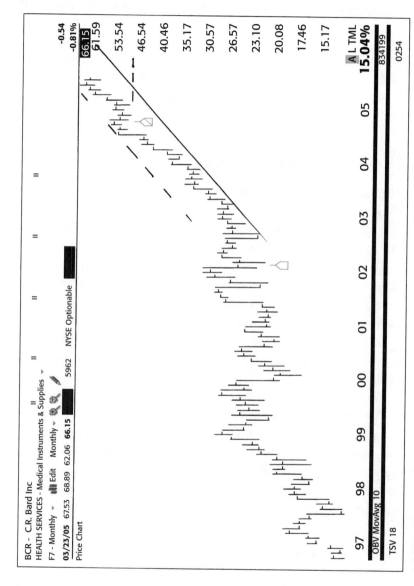

FIGURE 18-2 CR Bard Monthly Bar Chart with Trendline and Stop Level.

Assuming, as before, the purchase of BCR at $59.64 on December 8, you see that there has been a monthly low, tested twice at the $51 level. Assuming that you have a high level of confidence in the long-term prospects for this stock, you could place a stop at, say, $49. This allows for a loss of some 20 percent from your entry price, but it is very unlikely indeed to be activated unless something goes badly wrong. You can see that all the way up the stock has pulled away from those downward thrusts and has then kept on going up. The trend in force ought to remain in force!

Stops for a Runaway Market

The daily chart for Apple Computer (AAPL) shows how the stock kept going up in a series of steps, with each one well above the previous one (Fig. 18-3). Although the fluctuations amount to quite a lot of money and a significant percentage of the value of the stock at any time, there is no real substitute for giving the stock room to move. This is the kind of stock that doubles and doubles again and may even double a third time before running out of steam. Accordingly, you can protect most of your profits with a series of stops under each successive low after the stock has moved to the next higher level. The chart for AAPL demonstrates the principle that trying to count on capturing all of your profit at any time practically never works because you almost always sell prematurely, and miss out on the next leg up.

Trendlines do much the same job except that you can see how the steeper upward trendline between the identifiable lows in October and December was exceeded quite soon without meaning that the upward trend had stopped. If you had been stopped out, it might have proved difficult to get back in, although, obviously, with the wisdom of hindsight you would have been right to do so.

Be Prepared to Buy Back

Just because you owned a stock once doesn't mean to say that you can't own it again. In fact, if the grounds for owning the stock in the first place were good, there's a high probability that those reasons are still

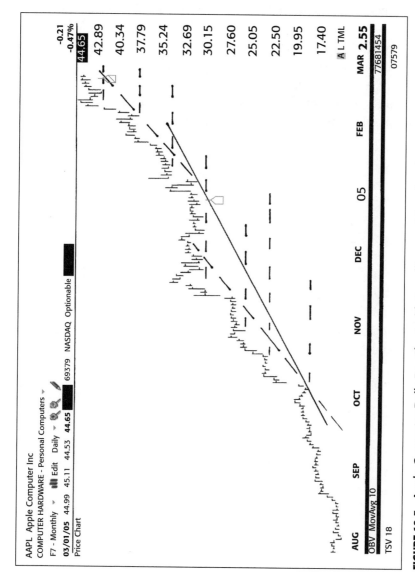

FIGURE 18-3 Apple Computer Daily Bar Chart with Trendlines and Stop Levels.

good. It is essential, therefore, never to regard any stock as a one-trade deal. If you sell a stock on a stop or for any other reason, then buy it back if it turns around and generates a new buy signal. Buying and selling stocks is always an imperfect art, and one of the most conspicuous imperfections is the inadvertent selling of a stock that you still want to own. Never mind! This is better than incurring the risk of staying wrongly in a stock that sets back substantially or, worse, goes down the tube altogether.

You may buy and sell a really good stock such as BCR several times over a number of years. If you have to buy back a stock for more than you sold it for, it probably means that it is going higher still.

CHAPTER 19

When to Sell

Reasons to Sell

Sometimes you have to sell. Sometimes you have to sell not just a single stock but every stock you own. The bear market in 2000–2002 demonstrated conclusively, as occurs with a regularity of about once every 30 years or about once every generation, that there can be general market declines of such severity that retention of stocks can be ruinous. Even in normal times there is one question you can ask yourself about a stock that may seem simple and even simplistic, but it comprises much wisdom. Ask yourself whether you would buy more of a stock that you own at its current price. If the answer is no, then you should at the very least undertake a review.

If in Doubt, Run Profits but Cut Losses

It is much easier to buy than it is to sell. You do not set sail or buy a stock without checking for fair weather. Selling requires interpretation of a wide range of unpredictable variables. What looks initially like a summer shower may be the start of a hurricane. A severe squall that looks like the start of a hurricane may be no more than an unpleasant but isolated interruption that soon passes.

When in doubt, it generally pays to stay in a stock in which you have a good profit, and it generally pays to sell one in which you have a loss.

This is the exact opposite of what comes easily to most people. When there is conflicting evidence, it generally pays to live by the principle of running profits and cutting losses. But this doesn't mean that you should give back all of a big profit by staying in a stock long after the technical indicators have turned negative.

There are four primary reasons to sell a stock.

1. You See Something Better to Do with the Money

There is always the risk of constantly seeing something better to do with the money. It is all too easy to turn into a trading junkie. When, however, you see a really good stock that is timely to buy, it makes a lot of sense to weed out one or more weak stocks and upgrade the quality of your portfolio. Many investors do the opposite, taking profits in order to buy stocks at an earlier stage of development. This is almost invariably a loser play. It seldom pays to sell a stock such as Whole Foods Market in order to buy one like General Motors (GM), however seductive GM might seem to look in terms of defensive value or a chart pattern in the early stages of developing strength.

There is, of course, a conflict that cannot by any means always be resolved successfully. There are certain to be periods of consolidation even in the finest stocks, but if you sell them hastily, it may be difficult to buy them back, particularly at a lower price than you sold them for. It is a characteristic of all investment that you tend to make money in surges, and if you are not positioned in a stock when it starts moving, it may be difficult both technically and psychologically to find a reentry point.

2. The Stock Runs Its Stop

The stop is either an initial protect stop (IPS) or a trailing protective stop (TPS). As discussed in Chapter 18, placing stops is a challenge but also a necessity: When you buy the stock, it is an absolute necessity.

Paradoxically, it is easier to move stops when a stock such as Whole Food Markets establishes a clear and strong uptrend and you are making a good profit. More difficult is the challenge of using stops when you get stuck in a stock that doesn't seem to want to get going. But this is exactly when you need to be the least tolerant. Many people find it psychologically difficult to stay in a stock making money and psychologically easier to be patient with a malingering stock on welfare—the exact opposite of what is required for maximum success in the long run.

You seldom go far wrong by setting either an IPS or a TPS at a level below the most recent reversal or identifiable spike on the monthly chart.

3. The Stock Breaks the Trendline on the Monthly Chart

A close at the end of the month below a long-term trendline on the monthly chart is for all practical purposes an iron-clad and mandatory sell signal. This simply doesn't happen to the best stocks to own. True, the broken trendline may signify no more than that the stock needs a short rest in order to let the fundamentals of its business catch up with its share price. However, as we have seen with many of the best blue chip stocks, as well as those of intermediate-sized companies such as St. Jude, once a stock starts going sideways, it can become a long-lasting habit, sometimes lasting for a decade.

The monthly and weekly charts for General Electric (GE) both show the same trendline *A-B*, which signaled a mandatory exit in November 2000 at approximately $50, after retracing from its all-time high at $60.50 (Figs, 19-1 and 19-2). It is essential to use a long-term chart because fluctuations on a daily chart covering just a year or two can give a very misleading view of the big picture.

4. Warning Signs and Sell Signals

Here are some of the things to look for when taking a more aggressive or vigilant approach than simply waiting for stops to be activated. When pulling the trigger to sell a stock, it is generally best to do so on activation of a daily price rule signal to sell. This probably shows that the price is indeed heading lower, at least in the near term.

1. **Adverse monthly reversals, double reversals, and Lindahl sell signals.** One adverse monthly reversal means nothing, two mean little, but a succession of them shows that waves of buying or selling pressure are running into the readiness of people to take the other side of the trade. Figure 19-1 shows a succession of monthly downside reversals in GE (both closing price reversals and high/low reversals), marked with arrows, as the price was approaching its high and when the decline was getting under way.

   If you failed to sell GE as a result of its breaking its long-term upward trendline in November 2000, you should unquestionably have heeded the downside key reversal bar completed in

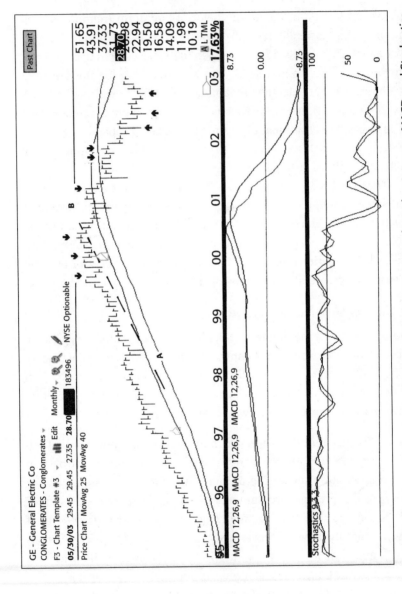

FIGURE 19-1 General Electric Weekly Chart with 25- and 40-Week Moving Averages, MACD, and Stochastics.

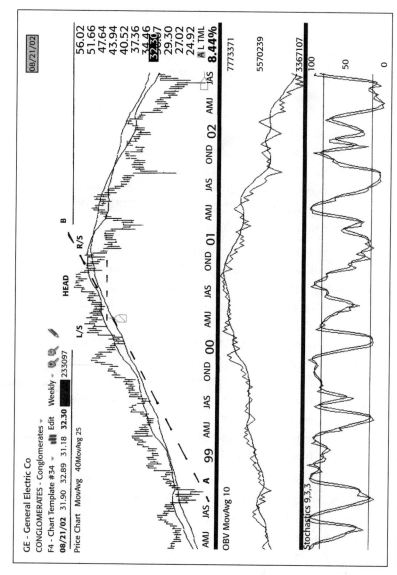

FIGURE 19-2 General Electric Monthly Chart with 25- and 40-Month Moving Averages, OBV, and Stochastics.

December, which also completed a Lindahl rule 5b sell signal. In the event, a sale at that price would have been at about $48, or only just below the level where the trendline could be declared broken.

In 2002, there began a series of upside monthly reversals that suggested that the decline might be close to running its course and that this was no longer a stock to sell short, even if buying it was almost certainly premature.

2. **OBV Failure.** A major warning signal sounds when on-balance volume (OBV) establishes a lower successive high even if the price has exceeded its last high. When OBV establishes an M, and especially when the next legs of a downward zigzag develop, it is almost always advisable to sell a stock right away.

OBV on the weekly chart for WMT shows a relentless decline even as price remained within its descending triangle in the middle panel of Fig. 19-3.

3. **Moving-average failure.** When considered in conjunction with other indicators, such as the breaking of an upward trendline and monthly sell signals, the rollover of the 25- and 40-week moving averages and price crossing underneath largely confirms the fact that it is time to sell.

The weekly charts for GE (Fig. 19-2) and Wal-Mart (Fig. 19-3) both illustrate this point. Once this pattern develops, it is likely to become entrenched. There is no reasonable prospect of an early worthwhile upward move, and the risk of a prolonged move down is substantial. Note, of course, that the 40-week moving average equates with the 200-day moving average that many people use to define a bull or a bear market.

4. **MACD failure.** When moving-average convergence/divergence (MACD) on the monthly chart starts topping out, there is a high probability that the stock price will begin to consolidate, if not necessarily change direction. Thus a weakening MACD serves initially as an alert, not an immediate call for action. The stronger a stock has been previously, the more it is entitled to a rest and, therefore, a weakening MACD. In this case, MACD may turn negative without forecasting a trend reversal. The good thing about a stock that has previously been persistently strong is that its

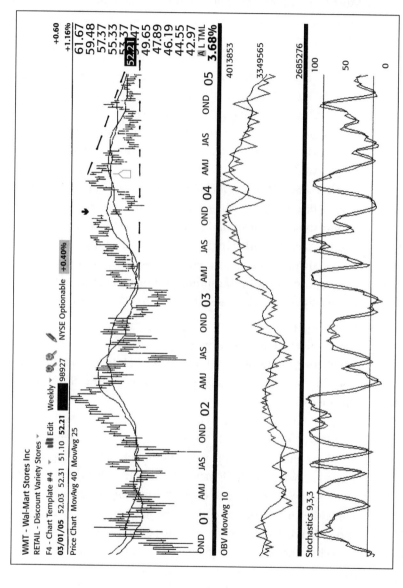

FIGURE 19-3 Wal-Mart Weekly Chart with 25- and 40-Week Moving Averages, OBV, and Stochastics.

fan club doesn't depart from the stock all at once, and there are plenty of newcomers ready to accept the transfer of stock from strong hands to weak. Consequently, there is plenty of time to act.

5. **Stochastics failure.** Stochastics are a much more sensitive indicator than MACD and are generally more useful at showing when a retracement in the major direction may be ending than at showing when a trend reversal may be imminent. Nevertheless, you can see in the bottom panel of Fig. 19-1 how stochastics established a triple top on the monthly chart for GE well before the price started breaking down. Stochastics then confirmed the early stages of the decline but became oversold and remained oversold long before there were any serious signs that the decline might ever finish.

On the weekly chart for GE (Fig. 19-2), you can see how high stochastics reached in the summer of 2001, when the stock was ending its savage bear market rally. The high stochastic reading and the fact that price had rallied to the declining 25- and 40-week moving averages showed that this was absolutely not time to get carried away by the enthusiasm that had brought the stock up so far from its recent low. It was a time to sell, not to buy.

6. **Adverse gaps.** As we saw in Chapter 11, gaps against you are bad news unless there is a fairly rapid recovery, and the level from which the gapping occurred is regained and stays regained. (Gapping can be positive when it goes your way and is the rationale for price rule 3.)

When there are several downward gaps, the assumption is that there are a lot of determined people more concerned with selling than whether they succeed in doing so at a good price. Gaps are particularly significant when they occur on the first day of the week or the first day of the month because those days coincide with market action following days when investors are more than usually diligent about reviewing what they own.

When there is a huge gap, you might feel like hanging on to see whether there is at least a partial recovery, or whether it might have happened as a selling climax. Don't do it! The probabilities favor biting the bullet and getting out right away. Even if the stock stops going down, which is not what market action suggests is likely to happen, the probabilities have turned against the steady upward move on which owning the stop was predicated when you bought it. Therefore, get out, let the dust settle, and then, if you really want to, come back to review the stock some time later—probably several months later.

As with all indicators, a succession of signals pointing in the same direction cumulatively reinforces the likelihood of price going in the direction indicated. Despite it being such a wonderful company that has done so well for investors over the long term, the weekly chart for Wal-Mart shows a number of downward gaps (marked with arrows in Fig. 19-3). In light of this evidence, the probabilities cannot be considered favorable, and it is almost certainly better to sell and see how market action develops.

7. **The head-and-shoulders top.** As discussed in Chapter 12, but worth repeating here, the head-and-shoulders top is one of the most reliable of all chart formations. It comes in all shapes and sizes on every chart. On the weekly or monthly chart, it often serves to warn of a substantial trend reversal, as illustrated by the weekly chart for GE (Fig. 19-2). If such a strong, bellwether stock shows that trouble may be brewing, you had better pay heed to any weaker stocks that you own. (On the other hand, of course, when a stock such as GE starts to show resilience after a long decline, it may mean that you can start looking forward to better days ahead.)

The idea behind a head-and-shoulders formation is that the stock surges strongly to a new high, making in the process the left shoulder. Then it settles back and surges again to a higher high, making the head, before settling back yet again. Next, it surges a third time to make the right shoulder. This time the stock fails to exceed the previous high before turning down again. Confirmation of a head-and-shoulders formation occurs when the stock breaks below the so-called neckline, shown on the chart for GE with the line of dashes. Once broken, a sharp decline often occurs, and any subsequent rally is unlikely to exceed the breakdown level by much, if at all, before the decline resumes. To signify a top with the greatest reliability, the pattern should take a significant time to form on the monthly chart, often a year or more. It should also be as symmetrical as possible, and ideally, the right shoulder should be equal to or lower than the left one.

8. **A descending triangle.** The descending triangle is a powerful indicator of a market preparing to break down, which, in addition to the downside gapping, is also illustrated here by the weekly chart for Wal-Mart (WMT). Support holds tenaciously for a time, but the rallies off that support become weaker and weaker until they stop altogether. Then the line of least resistance is a downward break and, often, the start of a substantial move down. The descending triangle is the equal and opposite of the ascending triangle discussed in Chapter 12. It is likely that market action within this descending triangle, as with a head-and-shoulders formation, will lead to a downside break at least equal to the height of the triangle at its base. The chart for Wal-Mart suggests that a downside break of $6 to the $46 level could occur some time before the price action finally reaches the apex of the triangle. A break of that amplitude is indicated by the amplitude from the low at the $52 level in September 2004 and the high at the $58 level in November 2004. Such a break could signal the start of a more serious decline even if the stock were to rally back to the breakdown level at $52.

Selling, even more than buying, is an art more than it is a science. It is guaranteed that there will be many frustrations when selling. You keep a stock only to see its price fall apart. You sell a stock only to see its price turn around and continue higher. As a rule, it is better to keep a great stock and give it room to move. On the other hand, it is best to act as soon as possible on strong signals to sell. Of course, these two guidelines often seem contradictory in practice. You cannot avoid this altogether. Nevertheless, these approaches to selling are likely in the long run to work a lot better than mindlessly holding stocks forever or else constantly getting in and out of the market.

Of course, a stock well bought is likely to cause less difficulty when deciding to sell. It is always easier to make good decisions when you are making money.

Don't forget that you may buy and sell a stock many times over the years. If you have done good homework and have a sense that you know about the company, then you should not be deterred from buying it back when the technicals say you should, even if you have to pay much more for it than you sold it for.

Selling Stocks Short

Sell First, Then Buy

You may not want to sell short, but you should know what selling short is all about. If there is one thing the recent bear market should have made abundantly clear, it is that stocks go down as well as up. Therefore, you don't want to own stocks that others see as such prime candidates to go down that they want to sell shares so as to buy them back later on at a lower price. In sum, you don't want to be their bag holder.

The standard investment approach is, of course, to buy a stock, expecting it to go up. However, there are times when an individual stock or the general market is going down, not up. Owning stocks then is an invitation to lose money. As discussed in Chapter 19, the obvious remedy for avoiding losses or the disappearance of profits is to sell. Logically, it makes equal sense—no more and no less—to make money when the market goes down as when it goes up.

After identifying a stock that is going down or is likely to go down, it is both logical and possible to sell a stock you don't own and then buy it back at a profit when the price is lower. This is what selling short is. Few people sell short mainly because so few people know how to do it. Unquestionably, this is an operation for more adventurous and more aggressive investors, and it certainly requires a high degree of vigilance in case your short sale starts going violently against you. However, learning how to sell short successfully is by no means as difficult as you might believe.

No doubt you will have noticed that losses seem to come fast and profits from stocks you own tend to come more slowly if they come at all. There is a reason for this. It takes new money coming into the market to make a stock go up. All it takes for a stock to go down is for the inflow of new money to fade. As a result, a stock often goes down between two and three times as fast as it goes up.

Short-Sellers Perform a Service

Many people think selling short is unethical. Not so. Selling short is something many businesses do, in effect, as a matter of course. A business often delivers goods or services, such as an airline ticket or a tailor-made suit, after the customer has placed the order and paid for it. A short sale in the stock market does essentially the same thing. Nor is the effect of short selling entirely negative for those who own a stock. Although it is likely that well-reasoned short selling will cause a stock to go down, if that short selling is misguided, then the stock may have to be bought back in a rising market. One of the reasons why a selling climax works to establish a durable low is that it will certainly have sucked in new short-sellers, driven by their emotions rather than by reason, establishing new short positions at the bottom.

One reason why an apparently irrational stock keeps blowing off into the stratosphere may be that aggressive short-sellers thought that the stock was absurdly priced and should go down—except that it didn't. Therefore, they have to buy back under pressure when the stock keeps on going up. This explains why you have to sell a high-flyer only when the back of an irrationally skyrocketing stock has been well and truly broken. It also explains why it generally pays to stay in a stock that is doing well until the technicals tell you to sell. Even a stock that you own that appears to be very overvalued may have more upside potential than you would ever have thought possible. Besides, there may be corporate developments that you don't know about yet that will actually justify what currently seems to be an absurd price.

As for the morality of selling short, short-sellers perform a useful service by providing the liquidity that makes it possible to do business on the stock exchange with a reasonable spread between the buying price and the selling price. Many market-makers and specialists have the job of making it possible for people to buy and sell readily, and they can almost as readily have a net short position in a stock as a net long position.

Risk and Reward

There is a common belief that selling short is very dangerous or, in any case, that it is not worth the risk. If you sell a stock short, the most you can make is the total amount you sold it for. Since a stock sold short can go up by several times instead of going down, the potential for loss is unlimited. It is natural, therefore, to think that the odds are heavily stacked in favor of buying and heavily stacked against selling short. This is true as far as it goes, but it is an extreme oversimplification. The risk depends on market conditions and how you set about selling short.

Consider the difference it makes whether you buy or sell short a stock that goes down. Say that you bought Nortel at $80 in 2000. You rode the stock down to $40. Finally, you threw in the towel and suffered a loss of $40 per share. You lost 50 percent of your investment. It has gone down the drain forever. However, if you sold the stock short instead of buying it, then you had a profit of $40 per share, not a loss. To make the same money by buying the stock at $80, it had to go up to $120.

Occasionally, you can sell a stock short and see it decline by much more than 50 percent. It can happen, and it did happen to many stocks in the recent bear market that went to zero. But even the most wretched dogs generally make a bottom eventually. Nortel made its high in July 2000 at $89, and in September 2002, its low was just 47 cents. From there it rallied to a short-lived high of $7.96, where it was 17 times its price at the low but still only 9 percent of the price where it stood at its high!

In a normal bear market, about 90 percent of all stocks go down. This compares with the 70 percent of all stocks that are normally rising at any given time in a strong bull market. Nevertheless, there may still be some stocks that buck the trend. Therefore, you have to do good homework to find which stocks to sell short. In the 2000–2002 bear market, there were beneficiaries of the force-fed low interest rates, such as housing, and proprietary bull markets began in certain commodity-related sectors such as petroleum. Those stocks you did not want to sell short!

Stocks Not to Sell Short

Many people think that selling short means selling stocks that are absurdly high on the assumption that they are worth only a fraction of their current price. A stock captures the public imagination and seems to go to the moon for no good reason. You find a company with a million dollars a year in sales and a market capitalization of a billion dollars. The stock has assets behind it of 50 cents, but it sells for $50. How can it not be a short sale? Sure as you try to sell that stock short, the chances are that it will go on to $75 or $150. There is no price so high that a stock cannot go higher still, most especially when a lot of people sell it short. Then buying back by those who sold it short drives the price higher still. Here are three categories of stock to avoid selling short:

1. **High-flyers.** Don't break this rule: *Don't even think of selling a high-flyer short until it has had its back well and truly broken.* It should have broken upward trendlines, and it should be trading below declining moving averages. Moving-average convergence/divergence (MACD) should confirm a declining market and certainly not a rising one. The $50 stock that has gone up on helium and hype may be a short at $30 or at $15 when it has been truly busted and is heading back to earth—and possibly to zero.

2. **Stocks you may not be able to buy back.** Don't sell short the shares of a small company where the market for the shares is thin. You know that there will always be plenty of activity in a billion-dollar stock in the Dow Jones Industrial Average or, in fact, in most indexes. Thus you can readily put on the short sale, and you can just as easily get out of the position. Don't even think of selling short a penny mine or a startup technology stock having a market value of less, say, than $50 million or so. The reason you need liquidity is that you have to be able to get back out of a short sale. The shares of a small company can be subjected to what is called a *short squeeze* if a lot of people all want to cover their short positions at the same time. Then the buying frenzy feeds on itself without there having to be any justification for the actual price of the stock.

3. **Possible takeover targets.** A company may appear to be in poor financial condition in a sector that is doing poorly. Yet it may be asset-rich or have some special reason to be attractive to a buyer in the same industry or to outsiders wanting to shake up the management and sell

underutilized assets. Such a company may be a target for a takeover at a price significantly higher than the current market. You have to weigh the risk and avoid potential targets for merger or acquisition. The announcement of a takeover can raise the price sharply overnight.

Short Sale Candidates

Corrections in a bear market may be extremely severe. Therefore, you have to reverse your thinking compared with buying in a bull market. Sell short on rallies when, for example, daily stochastics are at a high level and not already in the basement and when price has rallied back to a downward trendline or the declining moving averages. You can sell on a breakdown, but the risk of doing so and of having to withstand a rally against you increases exponentially when you sell into a short-term bottom rather than at the crest of a rally. With this reservation, opportunities for short sales fall into four categories:

1. **A general bear market.** Sell short a stock that is in a clear bear market and when, in addition, stocks generally are in a bear market. When both these conditions are met, there is relatively little risk in selling short. The biggest challenge, however, is not to succumb to believing that there is a general bear market when there is no more than a correction in a continuing bull market.

2. **A stock-specific or sector bear market.** Sell a stock short that is carving out its own proprietary bear market or a stock in a sector that is in a bear market even as stocks generally are rising or going sideways. Normally, there are conspicuous business problems behind stocks carving out their own proprietary bear markets. Ideally, the company represented by the stock should be losing money, and there should be little prospect of that changing soon. Ideally, too, the company should be in an industry plagued with chronic overcapacity and low profit margins, and the entire subindex for the group should be in an entrenched bear market. Most gold stocks met these conditions from 1996 to 2000.

3. **An emerging bear market.** Sell a stock short as it is *completing* a long, drawn-out distributional top.

    At major tops there is often a distributional phase that is the counterpart of the long-term base-building or the reverse head-and-shoulders from which come many of the most substantial bull markets. There are various topping patterns, but the best of all is generally the head-and-shoulders pattern. For some reason it tends to work even better than any random double, triple, or even quadruple top. Sometimes you see rounding, like an upside-down saucer, that is the counterpart of the rounding bottom when a stock is starting to turn up and gather speed as it takes flight.

4. **Sell short to spread or hedge.** There are two main reasons for considering the short sale of one stock while owning another one, putting on what the professionals call a *spread:*

   a. **Sell short a weak stock while simultaneously owning a strong stock.** You might, for example, consider buying Southwest Airlines while selling short Northwest. Or you might own Toyota and simultaneously hold Ford short. This approach seldom has much to recommend it unless the case for both the long and the short can be justified, solidly, on their own merits. It may simply offer two opportunities to lose money.

   b. **Sell short another stock as a deliberate strategy for protecting profits in a stock you own.** Then you may be able to delay payment of the capital gains taxes that would result from selling a stock that has made a lot of money. When a stock has gone up by several times and there is a sell signal but you expect only temporary weakness, you may want to make an offsetting short sale of a closely related stock so as to lock in the profit. If both stocks go down by roughly the same amount, you may be able to bank a profit on the short that is roughly equal to what you lost on the stock that you still own.

   This approach is sometimes used in order to avoid paying capital gains taxes on a stock that has made a lot of money and which you may want to continue to own for the long term. As a general rule, however, it generally pays better in the long run and is psychologically more liberating to clear the decks by banking a profit and to accept the fact that you have to pay some taxes. Otherwise, you may find yourself married to an investment in a market sector where the sun is no longer shining. The main thing when banking a profit is to make sure that you also take losses to offset the gains. If you have to pay taxes, so be it. It shows that you have done well.

The Short Interest Ratio

When everyone wants to sell short, in all likelihood the market will be at or near an important bottom, and a short-sale candidate may be more likely to go up than down. When any investment concept becomes too popular, firepower may run out at any time, causing a sharp reversal. Logically, most short selling should happen at secondary market tops, not at bottoms, but investors driven by their emotions tend to do the opposite. When it comes to selling short, logic generally rules the professional market-makers and more astute investors. Emotions rule an uninformed public at bottoms as at major market tops.

Some technicians use the short interest numbers as a contrary indicator with which to measure investment sentiment. Although not a timing indicator as such, it often works in the big picture. The list of short interest in stocks, published monthly in *Barron's,* represents a useful but by no means infallible guide to the advisability of selling short any individual stock.

This list shows net changes since the previous report, as well as the ratio of the number of stocks shorted compared with the average daily volume for the stock. Thus, if there is a short interest of 200,000 shares and average daily volume is 100,000 shares, the ratio is 2. The most desirable stocks to sell short generally have a short interest of between two and four days' average daily volume. When the ratio is too low, it means that few people want to sell the stock short, and it is probably unwise to do what few other people want to do. When the short interest ratio is too high, it may mean that selling that particular stock short may be excessively popular. There may therefore be a short squeeze: Any rally may start a scramble in the stock that leads to a big upward surge in price that goes far beyond your comfort level.

Short Sale Procedures

There are some minor procedural differences between selling a stock that you own and selling a stock short. Ordinarily, when you own a stock and want to sell it, you just do it. When you sell a stock short, you have to tell the broker that you are selling short. Since you have no stock to give to the buyer, the broker has to borrow stock to deliver to the buyer for you. Most likely the stock comes from the margin account of another client. It may come from stock owned by the firm, or it may even be borrowed from another firm. The important thing is that, except by special agreement, you cannot keep the buyer waiting for delivery.

Occasionally, the person from whom you borrowed the stock may want it back. Your broker may then be unable to borrow stock elsewhere to cover your short sale. This situation generally occurs only in a thinly traded stock. However, it can happen that aggressive buyers wanting to push the price higher refuse to lend stock to be sold against them. When there is an extreme imbalance of demand over supply, holders of short positions unable to borrow stock may be forced to buy in the stock in which they are short. One way or another, they must either borrow the stock or pay it back. Regardless of how much the short-seller has to pay, in a short squeeze there may be no choice but to pay up to buy the stock back, however much it costs to do so. For all practical purposes, a short squeeze never occurs in a stock that a prudent investor would ever normally want to sell short. But you have to know what a short squeeze is.

After selling a stock short, you are responsible for making good the value of all dividends and any other benefits of ownership issued to stockholders by the company. If the stock pays only a small dividend or none, this obligation counts for little. If the stock pays a large dividend, the obligation may be heavy. It is generally better to avoid selling short stocks that pay a good dividend unless you have a strong reason to believe that the dividend will be cut or omitted. Dividends tend to hold up the price of a stock.

There is a technical requirement for execution of a short sale on the exchange. Regulations require that a short sale occur only by an uptick. It is allowed only after someone is prepared to pay more than the price of the last trade in the stock. It can happen occasionally in a rapidly falling market that you cannot execute a short sale. Every trade is at the same price or lower, so your order is never filled. If you do get a fill, it may be only at a price far lower than you expect, especially when the market is falling apart all around you. To avoid getting an appalling fill, give the broker a limit below which you do not want to sell.

There is no time limit for covering a short sale (by buying back the stock). You can stay short for as long as you like unless the person from whom you borrowed the stock wants it back, and the broker cannot find a replacement borrowing. Occasionally, you may want to hold a short position for years. If the company issuing the stock you sold short goes bankrupt, you never have to cover the short position.

Short Sale Margins

Margins work differently when selling short than when buying on margin. When buying a stock on margin, the broker requires the account to have cash equal to half what you pay for the stock. The other half is advanced as a debit balance on which you pay interest. Even if the stock goes up by several times, you still owe the same amount of money to the broker. When a stock bought on margin goes up enough, you can, of course, use the excess to buy more stock.

When you sell short $10,000 worth of stock, you must put up cash of $5,000, or 50 percent. When you sell, $10,000 in proceeds from the sale is deposited in your account, so you have on hand $15,000 in cash. Instead of owing 50 cents for each dollar of stock that you buy on margin, you own $1.50 in cash for each dollar of stock that you are short. Some brokers will pay interest on all that $15,000. It is hard to find one that will, but it is worth working on when interest rates are high. Normally, brokers keep the interest earned on that credit balance in exchange for the favor of finding the stock for you to borrow. This is why some brokers execute short sales without charging any commissions at all.

As when buying a stock, you have to budget for a short sale not to work. The broker allows a rise in price against you until your margin falls from 50 percent down to 40 percent. This is roughly equivalent to a 10 percent rise in price against you. It means that you lose $1,000 of the $5,000 that you started with. You will not have a margin call if you have other money or stocks in the account. In that case, you have to do your own homework to monitor your short sale.

If, as intended, the stock you sell short goes down by 50 percent, it takes only $5,000 to buy back what you sold for $10,000. To be fully margined at 150 percent, the broker now requires only $7,500 in the account, representing $5,000 for the market value of the stock and $2,500 of your margin money. You can stay in your short position and draw off your entire profit of $5,000 as well as the $2,500 representing half the $5,000 that you put up as margin in the first place.

Calculate the Stop Loss

Instead of a sell stop below the market, as when you buy a stock, when selling short, you place a buy stop above the market. Depending on the chart pattern for the stock, you might place a stop 10 percent above your selling price.

Before selling a stock short, work out where the stop has to be, as you would before buying. Then consider how much of a loss you can withstand, both financially and psychologically, in the event of the stop being activated.

You have to work out your own tolerance for losses using the total value of your portfolio as the starting point. Say that you have a portfolio worth $100,000. A short sale of $10,000 worth of stock represents a 10 percent commitment of your total funds to the market, as it would when buying an equivalent amount of stock. If the stop dictates getting out when the stock goes up by 20 percent, you lose $2,000, or 2 percent of the total value of your portfolio. This should be acceptable for most people.

As when you own a stock, you must give a short sale room to move. In addition, you must allow for contingencies. Every venture into the stock market, whether you buy or sell, involves the risk of a market accident. When you own a stock, there can be an announcement of some devastating piece of corporate news that sends the stock plummeting. When you are short a stock, there can be an announcement about the launch of some wonderful new product or a bid for the stock from another company. Most surprise announcements have an impact on the stock price that falls within about a 30 percent range up or down for the stock. You should, therefore, budget to absorb a sudden 30 percent loss on a single short sale that backfires.

Start Short Sales Slowly

When starting to sell short, sell only half of what you think you can handle. Remember that the great market operator of the 1920s Gerald Loeb seldom put at risk more than one-third of his total capital at any one time or more than 10 percent in a single stock. This is a reasonable maximum exposure for most accounts selling any stock short. Some people plunge into selling short, learning the hard way. Even if you are successful, at some point the probabilities are likely to turn against you if you overtrade or take a bigger position than you can afford should things go wrong.

As well as learning the mechanics of how to do it, almost everyone needs to get the psychological hang of short selling. As with all investments, it is worth remembering how much money you can make when you are right. There is no point in risking a squeeze that endangers the overall value of your investments.

It pays to set about short sales with the mind-set that the general direction of stocks over the long term is up, not down. If you buy a stock at a bad price, things may turn out all right just by holding on until it comes back. You cannot make this assumption about a short sale. A short sale that runs your stop could, instead, be a stock to buy. You may have sold toward the end of a move down, and the next significant move could be higher, possibly very much higher.

It is essential to look at the big picture for the overall market. Selling any stock short in a general bull market is an invitation to lose money unless the case for doing so is overwhelming. In a bull market it is generally much better to stay with the major uptrend, looking for stocks that are timely to buy rather than seeking out short sales.

On balance, professional traders who sell short tend to be better versed in market timing than the majority of investors. They tend also to be better traders, whether buying or selling, because they use the techniques of market timing. They understand the meaning of the truism that the stock market fluctuates and does so within the confines of an uptrend or a downtrend within the channels established by bear markets as well as bull markets.

Even in a clearly established bear market, it seldom pays to be greedy when selling short. Powerful bear market rallies can come out of nowhere even in stocks having the weakest chart patterns and the most hopeless fundamentals. The rallies may be completely illogical, but that's almost the point. At least in the short term, if it's obvious, it's obviously wrong—because too many other people have the same idea and have already done all the selling they are going to.

CHAPTER 21

Entry Checklist: Sell Short

Differences Compared with Buying

The checklist for selling stocks short is almost identical to the one for buying stocks except that the overbought and oversold indicators are reversed.

Short sales having the highest probability of success occur normally in an established bear market. Ideally, there should be a downward zigzag that has established a minimum of a triple top or a double M. Larger M's developed over a longer time are more significant than smaller ones.

It is not mandatory to have the 25- and 40-month moving averages already pointing downward, with price trading below them, but these confirmations reinforce the likelihood of success and lessen the risk of failure.

If a downtrend in the monthly moving averages is not yet established, there should be strong evidence of an extended distributional top forming. On-balance volume (OBV) and moving-average convergence/divergence (MACD) should show clear evidence of the potential for a decline in price. One of the best indications of an impending top is a long, drawn-out head-and-shoulders formation. It can be lethal to own a stock that completes a big head-and-shoulders top. The other side of the coin is a corresponding prospect of a big gain from a short sale. This pattern can be a very rewarding place to start looking for potential short sales.

As when buying, there is always a trade-off between entering a short sale early or late. Enter early, and you have a manageable stop. Enter later, and the evidence of a breakdown is much stronger. However, the distance from a reasonable stop requires a bigger budget in case the short sale aborts. When a decline is under way, it is generally better to sell into rallies than into breakdowns unless the breakdown is decisive and the decline is at an early stage of development.

As when buying, it is not necessary for every indicator to confirm, although the more indicators that confirm, the better is the probability of success—but only up to a point. If you wait until every possible indicator confirms, there is a high probability of an imminent retracement, if not necessarily a trend reversal. You can have too much of a good thing.

Confirming Indicators

1. **M formation/zigzag line.** There is no more powerful an indicator of a bear market than a downward zigzag on the monthly line chart, preferably with markedly lower highs and lower lows. You can identify an emerging bear market when there is an M on the monthly line chart. The bigger it is and the longer it takes to form, the more likely it is to signify an important top. An M occurring in conjunction with a head-and-shoulders formation is particularly powerful.

2. **25-bar moving average.** The 25-month moving average should show a downward direction, and ideally, it should be below the 40-month moving average.

3. **40-bar moving average.** The 40-month moving average takes longer to turn down than the 25-month moving average. Tops often form too fast for confirmation by the 40-month moving average. However, a declining 40-month moving average shows a solidly entrenched bear market.

4. **OBV 1.** The direction of the simple unsmoothed line for on-balance volume (OBV) shows the immediate weight of buying or selling pressure in a stock. This line is particularly encouraging for downward continuation in the price of a stock when it comprises its own downward zigzag pattern.

There are two conditions in the action for OBV that you have to be careful with. When OBV 1 has moved a long way from OBV 10, it may indicate a selling climax rather than the kind of persistence that keeps a stock moving steadily lower. You also have to beware when price moves to a new low but OBV makes a higher low.

Although not included on the checklist, this indicator delivers a sell signal in its own right when it crosses below its 10-bar moving average. It is most significant when the crossover occurs after a period of rounding by the two OBV lines.

5. **OBV 10.** The smoothed OBV line takes the wrinkles out of the ebb and flow of supply and demand. It shows persistence more reliably than does OBV 1. You want it to confirm direction.

6. **Fast MACD.** Fast moving-average convergence/divergence (MACD) should be pointing down. This is often a lagging indicator when buying, but it seldom pays to go against its direction when selling. The best short sales have MACD solidly zigzagging down.

7. **Slow MACD.** This indicator should be pointing down. Some of the biggest and best declines start when fast MACD crosses below the slow MACD, and they both begin to move hard down.

8. **%K turn.** The %K fast stochastic should point down to confirm, regardless of whether it is at a high or a low level.

9. **%K level.** This indicator confirms when %K is above 80 in a clearly defined bear market. Stochastics are the single most important technical study to enable a sale at the crest of a rally and for avoiding a sale at the bottom of a valley. In a confirmed bear market, and despite the fact that it still is a confirmed bear market, there are almost always substantial retracements that run out of steam eventually. Think of the exercise of selling into the crest of a bear market rally as being similar to getting on a surf board at the crest of a wave just as it is set to take you surging forward.

10. **Price rule signal.** You need a new price rule on the daily chart to pull the trigger to sell. Ideally, there should be a clear price rule signal on the monthly and the weekly charts in force when selling a stock short. In practice, it is often enough to get a general

impression that bars on the weekly and monthly charts are bearish, with closes mostly in the lower end of their respective bars.

11. **Turn at moving average.** Count this indicator positive when the price stops and turns at a level at or near the 25- and 40-month moving averages after completing a retracement. Then there is a very high probability that the moving averages will contain the retracement, and there is a much higher probability of success than when a price rule occurs randomly.

    The 25 and 40 calibration may seem arbitrary. Nevertheless, the probabilities tend to be more favorable on retracements to these levels for two reasons. First, they show that the stock is not exceptionally overextended and vulnerable to a retracement. On the contrary, it has returned to an equilibrium level within the major trend. Second, many traders watch the 25 and 40 moving averages so that their effectiveness in containing retracements tends to be self-reinforcing. And as we saw before, the 40-week moving average equates to the much-heeded 200-day moving average.

12. **Key reversal.** A key reversal with a strong close increases the probability of a stock continuing in the direction of the close. A downside key reversal provides the visible means of showing that buyers have failed to turn the market up. Also, timid shorts have probably been flushed out of the market.

    Downside key reversals on the monthly and weekly charts tend to show a weak stock, especially when there have been one or more additional downside reversals recently.

    A key reversal occurring in conjunction with a sell signal on the daily chart generally provides a much-enhanced probability of a stock moving sharply lower right away.

13. **Double reversal.** A double reversal in the direction of an established trend is as powerful as a key reversal, if not more so. They both indicate cleansing of the market of weak holders and preparation for a strong continuation of the move.

14. **Chart pattern.** Count a favorable indicator when the overall chart pattern is clearly bearish. For example, count a favorable chart pattern when a stock is breaking out of a trading range or is completing a head-and-shoulders pattern.

15. **Gaps.** Count a favorable indicator when there are downward gaps on the weekly or daily charts. Gaps on the weekly chart tend to have more significance than you might expect because so many people make investment decisions over the weekend.

16. **Islands.** Count a favorable indicator when the price has gapped up and then gapped down. Best of all is when there are several days of market consolidation above the market prior to a sharp downside resolution of the standoff between buyers and sellers. This can be one of the most favorable formations for selling at the end of a retracement in a bear market.

    On the other hand, an island below the current price that results from downward-upward gapping may show that the stock has exhausted its downside potential.

17. **Market conditions.** It is essential to look at the bigger picture for the market generally, for interest rates, and for the group index for the stock that you are considering. When the stock market in general is either going sideways or is at a very low level, be careful. A *low level* is defined by distance from the moving averages and by oversold stochastics, particularly on the monthly and weekly charts. This means that you should sell lightly, not that you should pass when there is a strong signal. In a general bull market, be wary of selling any stock short.

18. **Value.** The best stocks to sell short generally have an external reason to sell them. It should be obvious that the company is badly run, is not making money, and has little prospect of doing so. Ideally, the stock should represent a company in an industry that has substantial overcapacity. On the other hand, beware of selling a stock so beaten down that it could be a takeover target.

Negating Indicators

1. **Adverse M/zigzag line.** It practically never pays even to think about selling short a stock without a clearly defined downward zigzag on the monthly chart, or at least the beginning of one. Lack of this confirming indicator virtually amounts to a total embargo. However, a very overbought condition in a bear market

can establish an adverse zigzag on the weekly chart or even more frequently on the daily chart.

The weekly and daily charts may not have a downward zigzag pattern after a severe retracement but the downward incline on the monthly chart should still be in place

2. **Adverse 40 moving-average direction.** An upward incline in the counts as a negating indicator. Many stocks sell off before the 40-month moving average turns down, so this indicator may take some time to come on side.

3. **Adverse 25-moving-average direction.** An upward incline counts as a negating indicator.

4. **OBV 1.** When OBV 1 points up, count this indicator negative.

5. **OBV 10.** Count this indicator negative when pointing up.

6. **Fast MACD.** Count this a negating indicator when it is pointing up.

7. **Slow MACD.** Count this a negative indicator when it is pointing up.

8. **%K level.** Count this a negative indicator when the fast stochastic %K is at 20 or lower. This condition often occurs when a stock is oversold and vulnerable to a retracement. It also occurs, however, in the fastest-moving markets and when a stock first breaks out of a consolidation. Therefore, a low %K level may be a sign of a stock capable of collapsing. Therefore, you have to interpret %K in the context of specific market action at the time.

9. **Support.** Support counts as a negative indicator when a stock is approaching a historic low where it has previously turned up.

10. **Channel line.** Count this a negative indicator when a stock is pressing against a lower channel line. Then there is a high probability of retracement back to the downward trendline.

11. **Adverse trendline crossover.** Count this a negative indicator when price is above a clearly identifiable downward trendline. This means that the stock has lost its immediate downward momentum. A strongly downtrending stock should not require ever shallower trendlines.

ENTRY CHECKLIST: SELL SHORT

Stock	Price		Date
Confirming Indicators	Monthly	Weekly	Daily
1. M/Zigzag Line			
2. 25-Bar MA			
3. 40-Bar MA			
4. OBV 1			
5. OBV 10			
6. Fast MACD			
7. Slow MACD			
8. %K Turn			
9. %K Level (above 80)			
10. Price Rule			
11. Turn at MA/Trendline			
12. Key Reversal			
13. Double Reversal			
14. Chart Pattern			
15. Gap			
16. Island			
17. Market Conditions			
18. Value			
TOTAL			
Negating Indicators			
1. Adverse M/Zigzag Line			
2. Adv. 25 MA			
3. Adv. 40 MA			
4. OBV 1			
5. OBV 10			
6. Fast MACD			
7. Slow MACD			
8. %K Level (under 20)			
9. Support			
10. Channel Line			
11. Adv. T-Line Cross			
12. Value			
TOTAL			

12. **Value.** Count this a negative indicator if the stock represents a company that is asset-rich and merely going through a bad patch that may only be temporary.

Stops

Don't sell a stock short without knowing where to place the stop. You must also, of course, enter the order with the broker. You cannot live without disaster insurance!

CHAPTER 22

Case Study: Sell Short

General Motors in Decline

You would be hard pressed to find a major corporation with better technicals, at the right time, for selling the shares short than General Motors (GM) in June 2004. From time to time, various brokers' research departments have favored the reputed value of the underlying business and especially the value of the financing arm, General Motors Acceptance Corporation (GMAC), the company that provides the credit for people to buy the vehicles that GM makes. Regardless of any apparent merits of the balance sheet or of improved quality of the product, there are many conspicuous challenges. First, there is immense worldwide overcapacity in the industry—possible to the extent of 30 percent or so, even in good times—and capacity never seems to stop growing, most recently in China. Second, foreign auto makers operating in the United States have relatively newly hired workers that come only with their much-delayed heavy costs for pensions and higher-cost health care in their retirement years. Third, better-built cars last longer, so the replacement market tends to keep lengthening. All these factors suggest that GM faces serious challenges even in good times. In bad times, the company may have difficulty making enough money to meet underfunded health liabilities, never mind for renewing their investment in the business and paying dividends.

We look now at the case for selling GM short, on June 28, 2004, at $46.51 as marked on the checklist on page 261.

Monthly Confirming Indicators

1. **M formation/zigzag line.** Yes. The monthly price line for GM shows big sweeping upswings and downswings since the high in April 2000, with a number of intermediate blips on the way (Fig. 22-1). The feeble attempted rally and new downturn in the monthly line chart put a confirming M in place.

2. **25-month moving average.** Yes. This average has been pointing hard down from the end of 2000.

3. **40-month moving average.** Yes. This average has also been pointing hard down since early 2002, turning decisively down a full year later than the 25-month moving average.

4. **OBV 1.** Yes. After an extremely strong upward surge as the price rose to the recently completed peak, the first on-balance volume line (OBV 1) shows that heavy cumulative selling has brought this indicator down hard.

5. **OBV 10.** Yes. OBV 1 is again under OBV 10 and likely to continue staying there.

6. **Fast MACD.** No. Fast moving-average convergence/divergence (MACD) is still going up, and on its own, this indicator suggests that there could well be an upward extension in price, although the strongly negative divergence of price and other indicators suggest that fast MACD is more likely to come on side by rolling over soon (Fig. 22-2).

7. **Slow MACD.** No. Even slower to turn than fast MACD, this indicator shows no sign whatever of ending its upward momentum.

8. **%K turn.** Yes. This indicator is screaming that there is no near-term upside momentum left in the stock (Fig. 22-3).

9. **%K level.** Yes. %K has been above 80, where it made a double top, although with the second one higher. Now it has fallen below 80 after summarily turning back under %D.

10. **Price rule.** Yes, but not conclusively. It's a bit of a stretch to count a single monthly downside reversal at the top as a valid signal, but we go with it, given the agreement of so many other indicators.

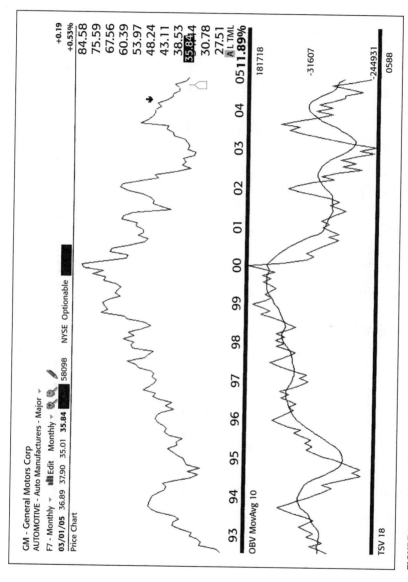

FIGURE 22-1 General Motors Monthly Line Chart with OBV.

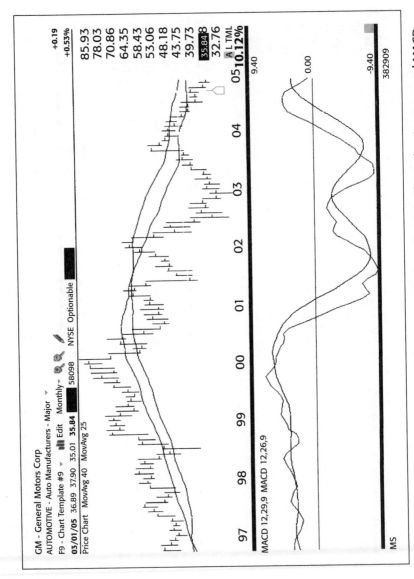

FIGURE 22-2 General Motors Monthly Bar Chart with 25- and 40-Month Moving Averages and MACD.

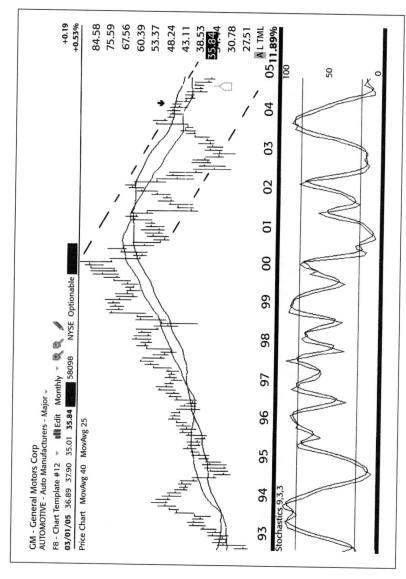

FIGURE 22-3 General Motors Monthly Bar Chart with Stochastics.

11. **Turn at moving average/trendline.** Yes. This situation is enough to make one quite enthusiastic about a short sale around here. Price has rallied almost exactly to the assumed downward trendline from the highs in 2000 and early 2002. You can be certain that every market-maker in GM on the floor of the New York Stock Exchange knows where that trendline is, along with every other trader and investor with any awareness of technical trading. This conjunction of price and the downward trendline is likely to induce enough selling to make the validity of this trendline self-fulfilling.

Similarly, the conjunction of price and the declining 25- and 40-month moving averages also confirms a high-probability, low-risk attempt at a new short sale.

12. **Key reversal.** Not applicable.

13. **Double reversal.** Not applicable.

14. **Chart pattern.** Yes. There is an overall downward zigzag but nothing special to note.

15. **Gap.** Not applicable.

16. **Island.** Not applicable.

17. **Market conditions.** No. Indexes such as the Standard & Poor's (S&P) 500 have rallied very strongly from the lows in 2002 and 2003 and may be considered somewhat vulnerable. But it is essentially a bull market.

18. **Value.** Yes. As noted earlier, the fundamentals for GM appear to be overwhelmingly negative.

Monthly Negating Indicators

1. **Adverse M/zigzag line.** Not applicable.

2. **Adverse 25-month moving-average direction.** Not applicable.

3. **Adverse 40-month moving-average direction.** Not applicable.

4. **OBV 1.** Not applicable.

5. **OBV 10.** Not applicable.

6. **Fast MACD.** Yes. This indicator is against the trade.

7. **Slow MACD.** Yes. This indicator is against the trade.

8. **%K level.** Not applicable.

9. **Support.** Not applicable.

10. **Channel line.** Not applicable.

11. **Adverse trendline crossover.** Not applicable.

12. **Value. Not applicable.** Covered on the monthly list.

The case for selling GM on the basis of the monthly chart looks good. There is an overwhelming preponderance of confirming indicators and almost a complete absence of negating indicators—only MACD is unfavorable.

Weekly Confirming Indicators

1. **M formation/zigzag line.** Yes. A new M (Fig. 22-4).

2. **25-week moving average.** Yes. This average has just rolled over and is pointing down (Fig. 22-5).

3. **40-week moving average.** No. Not the direction, but price has just crossed under it.

4. **OBV 1.** Yes. This is just turning down after a strong rally (see Fig. 22-4).

5. **OBV 10.** Yes. OBV 10 has never wavered in its downward direction for the past six months. The upside crossover by OBV raises the question of whether there is a temporarily over-bought situation prior to a new downturn—the more likely—or whether it is an early warning of the stock's attempt to stabilize.

6. **Fast MACD.** Yes. Fast MACD on the weekly chart has now been hard down for several weeks and alleviates much of the concern one might have about the fact that it is not confirming a short sale on the monthly chart.

7. **Slow MACD.** Yes. This indicator is flat with a slight upward bias, but the fact that it is decisively below the zero baseline suggests that there is no reason to expect renewed strength in the stock.

8. **%K turn.** Yes. The new downturn at the same level as the last one confirms it (Fig. 22-6).

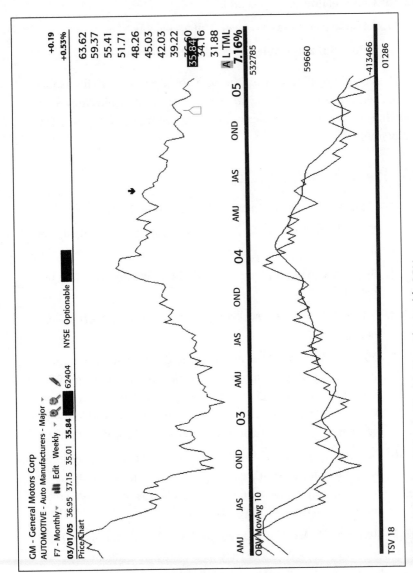

FIGURE 22-4 General Motors Weekly Line Chart with OBV.

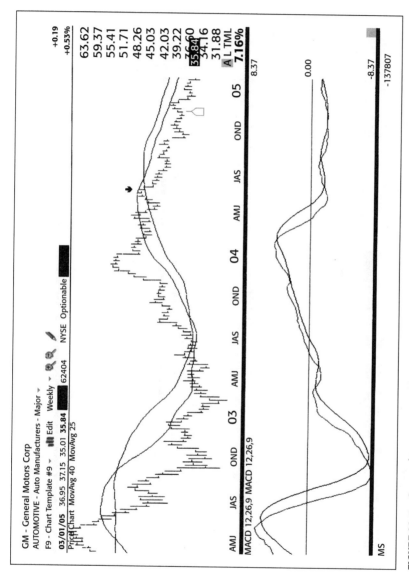

FIGURE 22-5 General Motors Weekly Bar Chart with 25- and 40-Week Moving Averages and MACD.

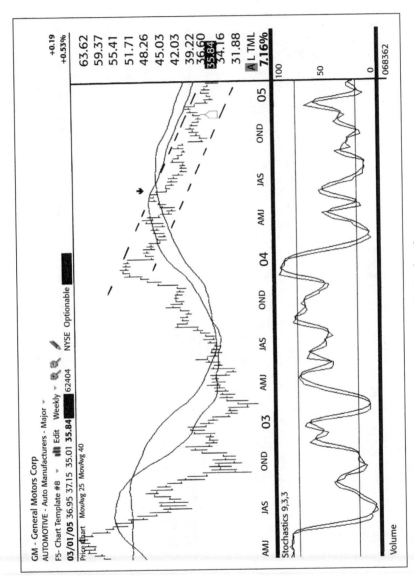

FIGURE 22-6 General Motors Weekly Bar Chart with Stochastics.

9. **%K level.** Yes, with reservations. At the end of 2003, %K was extremely overbought. Then it reached deeply oversold, and now it is in neutral territory but quite satisfactory for a sale in a confirmed bear market.

10. **Price rule.** Yes. There is a good solid rule 1 sell signal preceded by a rule 2b reversal sell signal.

11. **Turn at moving average/trendline.** Yes. This is a superb confirmation of the newly assumed downtrend line on the weekly chart and also at the now-turning 25-week moving average.

12. **Key reversal.** Yes, completed on June 20.

13. **Double reversal.** No.

14. **Chart pattern.** The overall chart pattern is superb.

15. **Gap.** Not applicable.

16. **Island.** Not applicable.

17. **Market conditions.** No. Covered on the monthly list.

18. **Value.** Yes. Covered on the monthly list.

Weekly Negating Indicators

1. **Adverse M/zigzag line.** Not applicable.

2. **Adverse 25-week moving-average direction.** Not applicable.

3. **Adverse 40-week moving-average direction.** Yes. Count negative.

4. **OBV 1.** Not applicable

5. **OBV 10.** Not applicable.

6. **Fast MACD.** Not applicable.

7. **Slow MACD.** Not applicable.

8. **%K level.** Not applicable.

9. **Support.** Not applicable.

10. **Channel line.** Not applicable.

11. **Adverse trendline crossover.** Not applicable.

12. **Value.** Not applicable. Covered on the monthly list.

Daily Confirming Indicators

1. **M formation/zigzag line.** Yes. There is a perfect new M with a break below the recent middle (Fig. 22-7).

2. **25-day moving average.** No. This average is still pointing strongly upward. The question is whether this situation expresses an overbought condition or whether the upward thrust is likely to fail (Fig. 22-8).

3. **40-day moving average.** Yes. This moving average has been acting as something of a median line, and it looks as if price should now go at least as far below it as it has just been above it. Note that price may be just about to cross below the slow-moving 200-day moving average.

4. **OBV 1.** Yes.

5. **OBV 10.** Yes, with a new downside crossover.

6. **Fast MACD.** Yes, with a new downturn (see Fig. 22-8).

7. **Slow MACD.** No. But with fast MACD turning down at a moderately high level, slow MACD will probably top out here.

8. **%K turn.** Yes. The succession of four highs in momentum and the pronounced downward zigzag now forming are strongly bearish (Fig. 22-9).

9. **%K level.** Yes. %K has been high enough for long enough to suggest that the price on the daily chart is likely to decline.

10. **Price rule.** There is a great rule 2 price rule with a reversal the preceding day and now a powerful downside break on extremely heavy volume.

11. **Turn at moving average/trendline.** Yes. We assume a new downturn and a third point of contact at the new donwtrend line.

12. **Key reversal.** Not applicable.

13. **Double reversal.** Not applicable.

14. **Chart pattern.** The overall chart pattern is fine.

15. **Gap.** There has been a gap down versus the close two days before.

16. **Island.** Not applicable.

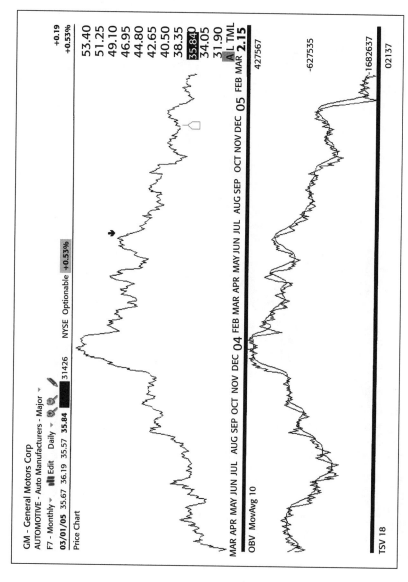

FIGURE 22-7 General Motors Daily Line Chart with OBV.

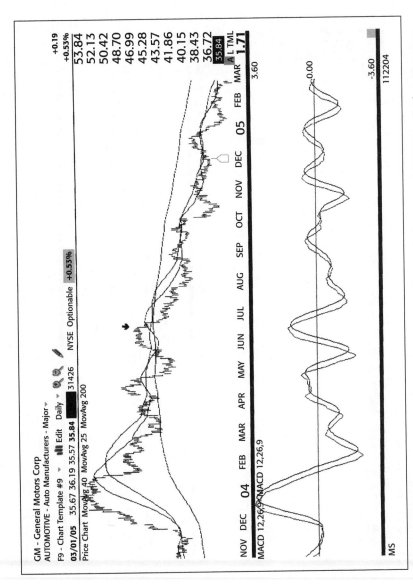

FIGURE 22-8 General Motors Daily Bar Chart with MACD, and 25-, 40- and 200-Day Moving Averages.

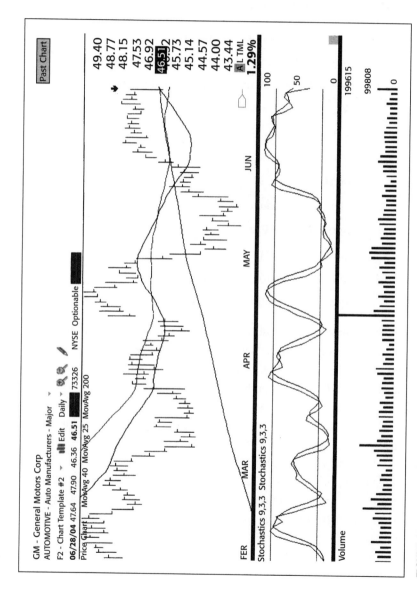

FIGURE 22-9 General Motors Daily Bar Chart with Stochastics, Volume Bars, and 25-, 40- and 200-Day Moving Averages.

17. **Market conditions.** No. Covered on the monthly list.

18. **Value.** Yes. Covered on the monthly list.

Daily Negating Indicators

1. **Adverse M/zigzag line.** Not applicable.

2. **Adverse 25-day moving-average direction.** Not applicable.

3. **Adverse 40-day moving-average direction.** Yes.

4. **OBV 1.** Not applicable.

5. **OBV 10.** Not applicable.

6. **Fast MACD.** Not applicable.

7. **Slow MACD.** Yes.

8. **%K level.** Not applicable.

9. **Support.** Not applicable.

10. **Channel line.** Not applicable.

11. **Adverse trendline crossover.** Not applicable.

12. **Value.** Not applicable. Covered on the monthly list.

The overall case for selling GM short is conclusive—around the $47 level at the end of June 2004. Subsequently, there were numerous new entry signals, and only a very nervous or impatient investor would have twitched during the relentless decline. However, on May 4, 2005 GM was to gap by $5 in response to a bid for some of the stock. This market action called for immediate covering of the short sale on the close for that day, at $32.80, which was near the high.

At $32.80, a short sale at $46.50 would represent a gain of $13.70 per share on margin of $23.25 per share, or 58 percent on the initially required 50-percent margin. This result was achievable between the end of June 2004 and the beginning of May 2005, a period of about nine months.

This short sale of GM could be regarded as quite a conservative trade. Arguably, this trade was both safer and more reliable than the purchase of its counterpart, the great General Electric (GE). As an alternative to selling GM short, you could have bought GE at $32.50 at the

ENTRY CHECKLIST: SELL SHORT

Stock	Price		Date
Confirming Indicators	**Monthly**	**Weekly**	**Daily**
1. M/Zigzag Line	✔	✔	✔
2. 25-Bar MA	✔	✔	
3. 40-Bar MA	✔		✔
4. OBV 1	✔	✔	✔
5. OBV 10	✔	✔	✔
6. Fast MACD		✔	✔
7. Slow MACD		✔	
8. %K Turn	✔	✔	✔
9. %K Level (above 80)	✔	✔	✔
10. Price Rule	✔	✔	✔
11. Turn at MA/Trendline	✔	✔	✔
12. Key Reversal		✔	
13. Double Reversal			
14. Chart Pattern	✔	✔	✔
15. Gap			
16. Island			
17. Market Conditions			
18. Value	✔	✔	✔
TOTAL	**11**	**13**	**11**
Negating Indicators			
1. Adverse M/Zigzag Line			
2. Adv. 25 MA			
3. Adv. 40 MA			✔
4. OBV 1			
5. OBV 10			
6. Fast MACD	✔		
7. Slow MACD	✔		✔
8. %K Level (under 20)			
9. Support			✔
10. Channel Line			
11. Adv. T-Line Cross			
12. Value			
TOTAL	**2**	**0**	**3**

end of June 2004. On May 4, 2005, the stock was at $36.20, for a gain of $3.70, or 11 percent. This gain in GE is barely enough to cover trading slippage and less than you might budget for a stop loss.

Stops

A stop on a closing basis could be placed above the recent highs in GM—the formation that justified the short sale—and just the other side of the new downward trendline—say, at $51—to budget about $4 per share, or about 10 percent, in the event of the stop being activated.

CHAPTER 23

Interest Rates, Inflation, and Stocks

Where Interest Rates Come From

There are always minor variations in the business cycle and the fortunes of the stock market, and sometimes major variations, but the same patterns generally recur. In general terms, these are the factors determining interest rates:

1. The *interest rate* is the price lenders charge borrowers for loans. Demand for loans comes from consumers financing the purchase of things such as cars and houses or from businesses financing accounts receivable or buying capital equipment. Interest rates rise when demand for money increases beyond the readily available supply. When demand for loans eases during an economic slowdown or a recession, the price goes down, as represented by lower interest rates—and higher bond prices (the price of bonds moves in the opposite direction to interest rates).

2. Short-term interest rates are controlled by the U.S. Federal Reserve (Fed). Lowering short-term rates increases the supply of money. However, long-term rates are set by supply and demand in the marketplace.

   Too much money supplied by the Fed—at any price—is perceived as inflationary. This ocurs when the federal government prints money to pay its bills instead of raising money by taxes or by borrowing. Therefore, cheaper short-term rates and more plentiful money actually can raise long-term rates: The bond vigilantes sell rather than hold bonds, and instead, they may buy hard assets such as gold or foreign assets. On the other hand, rising short-term interest rates are perceived as countering inflation so that bond yields may remain steady or even decline, as was happening during the first half of 2005. It is normally a sign of an impending recession when short-term interest rates exceed long-term rates—the so-called inverted yield curve.

3. Buyers of bonds hope to receive a rate of return that is higher than the rate at which the value of their capital is depreciating in real terms, although they don't always succeed in getting it. Therefore, a high and accelerating rate of inflation leads directly to higher interest rates and lower bond prices, and vice versa when inflation is decelerating.

   1981 marked the end of a 20-year *secular* age of inflation and declining bond prices. In all likelihood, similarly rampant inflation will not recur in the foreseeable future. Most likely, long-term interest rates will fluctuate between, say, 3 and 6 percent, but it is unlikely that they will exceed 10 percent, let alone the 14 percent reached in 1981. In the past, there have been periods lasting many decades when long-term interest rates fluctuated marginally on either side of 4 percent.

Interest Rates and the Stock Market

This is how interest rates and the stock market generally interact:

1. There is constant friction between interest rates and stock prices. When interest rates are high, competition from bonds for investors' money tends to keep a lid on stock prices, which may go sideways or down. When interest rates are very high, as occurred during the 1970s, dividend yields tend to be very high and stock prices depressed, regardless of growth in profits and dividends. On the other hand, stocks can compete successfully with moderately high and rising interest rates when demand for money is an expression of profitable business conditions.

2. The most profitable time to buy stocks is at the bottom of a bear market, as discussed in Chapter 13. Then stock prices are, of

course, low, and interest rates are low—bond prices having risen during the bear market in stocks.

It is, however, difficult to buy stocks at or near the bottom, for two reasons, one psychological and one practical. Things always look and *feel* worst at the bottom of a bear market, and pessimism is rampant. The practical problem is that investors are right to be pessimistic until there are technical signals to suggest, if not necessarily to confirm, that the tide of the bear market has gone out far enough. Fortunately, bottoms at the end of a bear market usually take time to develop, as demonstrated in earlier chapters. The far greater risk for investors not using market-timing techniques is to be much too early in assuming a potential low at the end of a bear market. Stocks can go very much lower than most people expect, and they may start looking cheap long before reaching their eventual low. However, stocks generally will turn up before there is evidence in the real economy of any pickup in demand, which is another reason why you have to rely on technical indicators.

3. The next best and, arguably, even better environment for the stock market is to have stable to slightly rising interest rates. This occurs in the early stages of an economic expansion and in the early and middle stages of a bull market. This environment can continue for a long time—from many months to several years, which is why there is no need to plunge into stocks before technical indictors suggest quite strongly that a new bull market may be under way. Investors expect profits and dividends to increase moderately for a long time without significant inflationary pressures.

4. In the final stages of a bull market, stocks may be soaring even as interest rates are rising sharply—and bond prices are falling. This period is accompanied by complacency, and there is no fear. It is psychologically easy to buy stocks, and selling is difficult.

5. In due course the economic expansion and the bull market in stocks become too much of a good thing. Interest rates start going up, with bonds competing progressively more for investment with stocks, and the bull market tops out. Sometimes the stock market, or an individual stock, can fall sharply after a speculative blow-off, but more usually the topping process is drawn out over a longer period, which may last for a year or more.

6. Once the stock market tops out and starts going down, and the economy starts contracting—not necessarily at the same time or in that order—interest rates start falling, and bonds start going up.

7. Finally, the business contraction starts easing, and consumers and businesses start using money that can now be borrowed for low enough cost to make the expenditure attractive, whether for consumption, such as the purchase of cars or houses, or for capital investment. Business owners and those in the know stop selling shares, and they start buying a few shares, if only tentatively at first, when they see the order book showing signs of improvement or more goods moving out of the factory. As a result of these perceptions and corresponding buying in the stock market, share prices generally start rising as much as 6 months before a change in sentiment starts to become evident to economists.

How Stocks and Bonds Interact

The monthly chart for U.S. Treasury bonds since 1980 shows an erratic long-term uptrend (Fig. 23-1). To put the chart in perspective, you need to remember that there was double-digit inflation for several years during the 1970s, which pushed bond yields to 14 percent at their high in 1981. Over the next 22 years, bonds advanced by three times from their ultra-depressed level in 1981. However, the apparently huge gain of tripled bond prices during that period was reduced in real or inflation-adjusted terms to just 50 percent because inflation almost exactly halved the value of money, as measured by the CPI.

From 1981 to 2003, both bonds and stocks were working erratically higher together in a secular bull market, reversing the unfavorable conditions induced by high levels of inflation during the previous 20 years. Within this secular bull market there were periods when interest rates rose, but stocks seldom set back substantially, except, notably, in October 1987. Mostly, stocks merely went sideways until the pressure of higher interest rates eased, and then they continued going higher. There were extended periods when both stocks and bonds went up together, when it was said that stocks had the "wind behind them." In more normal times, stocks and bonds tend to go in *opposite* directions in response to recessionary and expansionary forces in the economy and the intervention of the Fed.

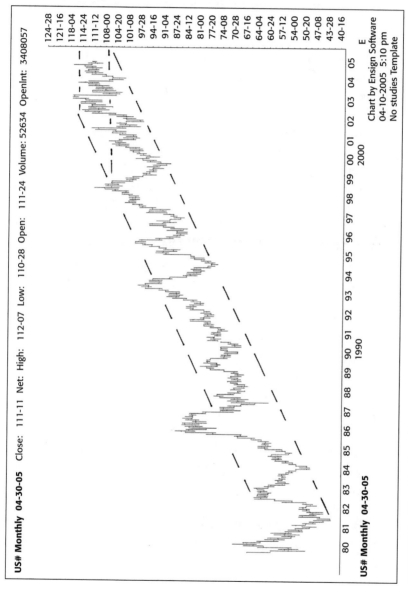

FIGURE 23-1 Monthly Chart for U.S. Treasury Bonds from 1980.

267

The split monthly chart shown on top in Figure 23-2 is the ACM Government Bond Fund, a surrogate for long-term interest rates, with the Standard & Poor's (S&P) 500 Index below. This chart shows how the respective appeal of stocks and bonds tends to alternate in normal market conditions. You can readily see four successive phases in the course of interest rates. The first, in 1994–1995, saw rising interest rates as the Fed sought to dampen the ardor of the economy. Investors foresaw the end of rising interest rates before it happened, and the S&P 500 started going up before the final downward spike in bonds. When bonds started going up, with interest rates declining accordingly, the wind was in the sails of the bull market for stocks until the short-lived setback in 1998.

After that, interest rates started rising again, but it was ever on the upward trend for stocks until it all became, at last, too much of a good thing. The stock market choked on its excesses, as bonds started competing for investors' money. Once the stock market turned down in January 2000 and recession began to squeeze the economy, investors in the bond market were delighted at the prospect of lesser inflationary pressures and, in any case, were seeking an alternative place to invest other than stocks.

The extension of the bull market in bonds was stimulated beyond the experience of many decades by the Fed lowering short-term interest rates to the multiyear low of 1 percent. This had the impact of buoying the housing and construction sectors that are particularly sensitive to interest rates, as well as providing the fuel for an immense boom in commodity prices, including oil.

In due course, the bear market in stocks ended, possibly brought to a premature end before the excesses of the preceding boom had really been purged. In any event, it was not long before the decline in interest rates and the bull market in bonds began to fade in parallel with the strong upturn in the stock market.

The weekly chart for bonds shows their bull market in more detail (Fig. 23-3). The low occurred in the third week of January 2000, whereas the top in the Dow Jones Industrial Average had occurred the week before. Stocks and bonds were to continue fluctuating erratically in opposite directions for the next three years. From top to bottom, the Dow fell by 39 percent, and coincidentally, bonds advanced by 39 percent from bottom to top. A hypothetical $1,000 retained in the Dow

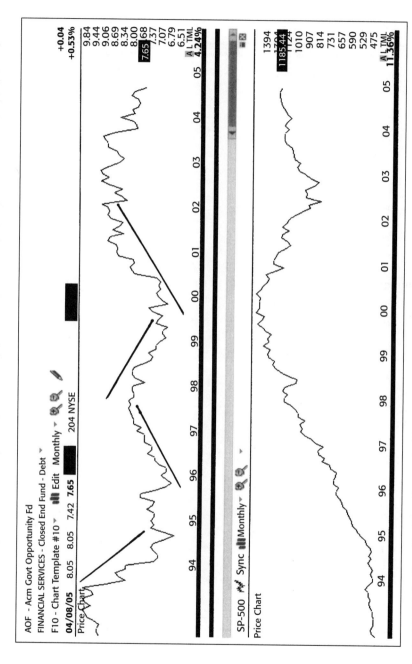

FIGURE 23-2 Monthly Chart for ACM Government Fund and the S&P 500 Index.

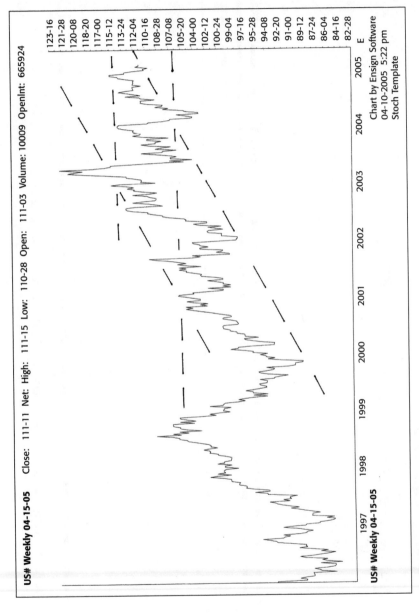

FIGURE 23-3 Weekly Chart for U.S. Treasury Bonds.

went down to $610 at the low. If sold out at the top and put into bonds, that $1,000 was worth $1,390 when bonds peaked in June 2003. Obviously, you would have had to be nimble to capture a good part of the difference from this switch. However, the need for agility does not detract from the proposition that there really are times to sell stocks and to buy bonds with the proceeds. You had more than three months to get out of bonds and back into stocks after the Dow had made its final low. From their high, bonds then burst their own proprietary bubble with a tumble of 17 percent in just 2 months.

Inflation and Stock Prices

Logically, inflation should be a fairly universal phenomenon. If the supply of money doubles, the price of bacon and beans also should double, along with wages and everything else, including the price of stocks. By extension, both capital values and dividends, in the aggregate, also should double—no more and no less—except insofar as they are influenced by productivity or other special factors. Therefore, the test of stocks' overall performance relative to inflation is one of capital values, without reinvestment of dividends, relative to the value of money. (The investment industry is accustomed to measuring the long-term performance of stocks on the fallacious assumption of reinvesting dividends, as if you had to keep feeding eggs back to the golden goose in which you invest. This is clearly both misleading and self-serving.)

Table 23-1 shows what happened in real terms if you invested in the Dow Jones Industrial Average at the 1929 high. In 1949, you had lost well over half your money in real terms, and despite the strong bull market of the 1950s, you still only got your money back in real terms by 1959, only to lose half of it again over the next 20 years. The only period that showed real gains was between 1989 and 1999, and those gains were substantial, if not altogether lasting, over the next six years. The case for passive investing needs these reality checks:

1. The table confirms academic studies that found that stock prices, in the aggregate, keep up with inflation and sometimes exceed inflation significantly, but the lags can be very long indeed.[1]

[1]James R. Lothian, *Equity Returns and Inflation: The Puzzlingly Long Lags.* New York: Fordham University Graduate School of Business Administration, 2001.

TABLE 23-1 The Dow Jones Industrials, the Consumer Price Index (CPI), 1967 = 100, and the Inflation-Adjusted Dow, 1929 = 100

Date	Index	CPI	Base 100
1929	386	51.3	100
1939	150	41.6	48
1949	199	71.4	37
1959	672	87.3	102
1969	776	109.8	94
1979	852	217.7	52
1989	2,709	365.2	99
1999	11,225	488.0	306
2005 (Feb.)	10,503	555.0	252

2. The lags are not as surprising as you might think. During times of high inflation, the dividend yield on stocks has to compete with high yields on bonds stocks. Therefore, the market value of stocks actually may decline, as occurred very substantially at various times between 1960 and 1981. Importantly, however, dividends do a much less erratic job of keeping up with inflation.

3. You had better try to avoid investing at the top of a bull market. If you invested in 1927 in the Dow at 193 or two years before and at half the eventual high for that bull market, you would have made twice as much money at every stage along the way, but never any more than twice. The returns depended on your entry level.

4. A portfolio replicating the Dow Jones Industrial Average is not a particularly good investment vehicle for protecting the real value of capital over the very long term. Most of the time you can expect little better in real terms than retaining the purchasing power of your money. There may be surges, as during the 1990s, but there also may be periods when the portfolio goes under water in real terms and stays there for a long time. Therefore, you need to look for ways to do better than following blindly a buy-and-hold investment strategy.

5. Even if the Dow Jones Industrials do no better than hold their own in real terms, they beat bonds hands down over the long term. The capital value of a bond, assuming the same approximate market price in 2005 compared with 1929, was reduced to the corresponding base 9 (or just 9 cents on the dollar) compared with the Dow's $2.52 versus the original dollar.

6. Stocks could give back all the apparent real (inflation-adjusted) gains between 1989 and 1999 and revert to the long-term mean of just keeping up with inflation. This could occur either by way of inflation or by way of declining stock prices or a combination of these forces.

Measuring Inflation

In fact, using the consumer price index (CPI) as a benchmark for the value of money in real terms is far less satisfactory than Table 23-1 might suggest. It doesn't adequately reflect what people actually buy in order to live, or the rising standard of living. It is artificially lowered by productivity improvements in manufacturing, as is readily evident from the way the real cost of computers has always declined precipitously. Wages of nonmechanized jobs such as waiting on tables and providing legal services, as well as the cost of housing, represent much better measures of the underlying value of money over the long term.

Investors cannot be complacent about inflation by any measure. If you get an after-tax return of 3 percent and inflation is 3 percent, the purchasing power of both the capital and the income is declining by 3 percent in real terms. Even with a relatively low inflation rate of 3 percent annually, the value of money declines by 50 percent every 24 years. Therefore, money managers for the likes of family trusts and pension funds face a challenge in order to maintain the real value of their bond portfolio: Investing in bonds for the long term really requires that you set up a sinking fund that puts as much income back into the capital account as the current rate of inflation. It has happened often that there was not enough interest paid to cover that real depreciation, never mind paying out any income. Looking at it the other way around, from the perspective of a borrower, as most home buyers know, you have often been able to buy assets that increase in value faster than the interest that you have to pay. There is a structural difference between earlier times and the present that may keep inflation above long-term historically average levels. In earlier times, there was almost no long-term inflation. Periods of declining prices followed periods of rising prices, and overall, the purchasing power of money remained more or less constant. These days the Fed massages the economy and the level of employment as its first priority, and the long-term purchasing power of the currency takes a back seat. The reduction of short-term interest rates to 1 percent was a deliberate exercise in preventing the deflationary forces that might have caused a more severe recession but that would have helped to preserve the value of money.

Recent Bubbles and the Prospect of More

As the first edition of this book warned, there is now general agreement that the bull market in stocks during the 1990s, and especially the bull market in technology stocks, was a classic bubble and that it was fueled by excessively plentiful money from the Fed.

It came, painfully, to its predicted end. In the past, burst bubbles led to an equal and opposite debt liquidation and deflation—a process that lasted for several years and was very painful. Obvious examples include the Great Depression that followed the stock market peak in 1929 and the implosion of the Japanese economy in 1989, which, arguably, may still not have finished running its course in 2005.

Since the stock market crash in 1987, the Fed has loosened credit dramatically in response to a succession of crises in financial markets. After this meltdown in stocks, there was the savings and loan crisis in 1989–1990. Then there was the European exchange-rate mechanism (ERM) in 1992. Next, in 1994, there was the implosion of the Mexican economy. The Asian financial crisis in 1997–1998 seemed to have the potential to capsize the world economy, as did the crisis at Long Term Capital Management, which had leveraged exposure to an amazing multiple of its equity. After the bursting of the stock market bubble in 2000, the Fed's response was to lower interest rates to just 1 percent— their lowest level in half a century.

What happened between 1987 and 2005 is well known, and many observers are almost certain to be right about the dangers of further emerging bubbles, including a continuation of the rebound in the stock market, the real estate bubble, and the expansion of the hedge funds industry, as well as the explosion of arcane strategies in the multi-trillion-dollar financial derivatives markets—the area of speculation that brought down the Long Term Capital Management hedge fund.

The Risks of Easy Money

There are certain economic principles to be learned from the long-term history of financial markets that suggest that the risks in financial markets may be underappreciated. These principles are as follows:

1. As Nobel Laureate Milton Friedman has observed, writing as the period of very high inflation and high interest rates in the 1970s was winding down: "Inflation is primarily a *monetary phenomenon,* produced by a more rapid increase in the quantity of money than in output. . . . A[n] instructive analogy is between inflation and alcoholism. When the alcoholic starts drinking, the good effects come first; the bad effects come only the next morning when he wakes up with a hangover—and often cannot resist easing the hangover by taking *the hair of the dog that bit him.*"[2]

2. The asset bubbles since 1987 took the place of consumer price inflation of the preceding decades and, as such, was perceived by Fed Chairman Alan Greenspan to be of little relevance given the apparent improvements in productivity in the economy. The Japanese experience suggests that there is a high risk of a general implosion of asset values in due course, as well as a serious recession or, worse, a new depression.

3. Using expanded credit to deal with a financial crisis or the deflation of a bubble merely leads to the inflation of further bubbles. The bailout of an individual company, the stock market, or the government of a bankrupt third world country seldom leads to well-founded prosperity and stability. On the contrary, the attempt to create stability is often a complete waste of money that creates far more serious problems than would have occurred by allowing the crisis to blow itself out.

[2]Milton and Rose Friedman, *Free to Choose.* New York: Avon Books, 1981, pp. 252, 255.

4. Credit used to salvage insolvent institutions or bubble-bursting phenomena hinders the adjustments necessary for a well-managed and financially sound future. It is argued, for example, that the bailout of Chrysler in the 1980s contributed to the difficulties now faced by Ford and General Motors. In part, the bailout may be said to have been an exercise in subsidizing the competition with money that Ford and GM had paid in taxes.

5. Booms can continue only as long as credit continues to expand.

6. It takes an increasing volume of credit to achieve the same economic growth.

7. Artificially low interest rates cannot last because the corresponding excess of money is inflationary. That excess has to find a home. It may go into consumption of consumer goods, whether made domestically or imported. It may go into the stock market or the commodity market. It may go into housing or other tangible assets such as gold. It may go into capital investment that would be uneconomic if this investment had to earn its real cost of capital (as occurred with Internet investment). And it may go into outright speculation.

8. Ever-expanding credit encourages ever-greater risk-taking, which increases the chances of the next crisis.

What Could Go Wrong

It is always possible that U.S. and international financial markets and the overall economy can continue on a path of apparent prosperity for some considerable time. It is also possible that the huge imbalances in financial markets will come into better balance by a process of muddling through, as occurred between 1987 and 2005. However, there are dangers lurking of which investors should be aware. There having been a succession of crises, one or more additional ones are to be expected, possibly of enough severity to lead to a more serious economic implosion and a corresponding bear market in stocks. Dangers include

1. *Bursting the housing bubble.* On the positive side, there is a fairly credible case for saying that the risks are overrated. Housing in

the United States is not priced hugely above replacement cost, as it is in England. New construction has not been exceeding family formations by a wide margin, and the apparent excess almost certainly arises from the fact that some new housing merely replaces housing that has been demolished. Also, some of the apparent increase in housing values has occurred as a result of renovation and upgrading of neighborhoods.

On the other hand, the housing bubble has been an important source of money for robust retail sales as a result of home refinancing based on price appreciation and low interest rates. Over 40 percent of new private-sector employment is related to housing. Forty-two percent of first-time homebuyers have been able to buy with zero down payment. In 2005, 28 percent of the mortgage market was subprime, compared with just 5 percent in 2000. The housing boom has been fueled by prices rising 6.7 percentage points faster than income. A perpetual extrapolation of this gap is mathematically impossible. The corollary is the risk of massive defaults on mortgages and credit cards and, by extension, of mortgage lenders and the entire banking industry. In 2005, the chart for the federally sponsored mortgage lender Fannie Mae was beginning to suggest that investors were starting to be very concerned about these risks. Housing-related employment, home-buying capacity, and the financial health of mortgage lenders are all interconnected, and none can be healthy without the continuing health of all of them. The strength of the entire economy became dependent on the health of the housing industry. However, the affordability of housing for an endless lineup of new buyers requires, axiomatically, a balance between house prices and incomes, as well as stable interest rates. The entire housing sector is very vulnerable to rising interest rates. There is also a parallel risk in an overheated commercial real estate market, which is also vulnerable to a setback that could have a knock-on effect on financial institutions and the economy generally.

2. *A major hedge fund accident.* The number of hedge funds has been growing rapidly, doubling between 2000 and 2005. An estimated 9,000 in the United States and internationally control

untold trillions of dollars of investors' assets. The ripple effects of a hedge fund collapse could have a devastating impact on the global financial system.

3. *An oil accident.* It has been estimated that an oil price of $60 per barrel includes a risk premium of about $15, but that might be nowhere near enough in the event of a major political or terrorist upheaval that disrupts supply, as at the time of the Arab oil embargo in 1973.

4. *An accident in the financial derivatives market.* The demise of Barings Bank was confined to a loss of about $1 billion, but that disaster could be dwarfed if derivative markets started to unravel: One party's liability is another party's asset, so any widespread collapse in asset values could have an effect like a house of cards falling down.

5. *Baby boomers rein in.* Baby boomers were born between 1945 and 1965. The idea that demographic forces have an impact on economic activity and also the stock market has been around for a long time and can be observed for successive 20-year periods throughout the twentieth century, starting with a bulge in fertility between 1905 and 1925. Then followed a 20-year contraction in fertility.

The population bulge in the post–World War II baby-boom age group had an impacted on birthing and baby care, then the school system and higher education, and then the job market. There was a surge in automobile sales in 1962 when the first baby boomers reached the driving age of 16, and sales kept soaring over the next eight years. The record year for home building was 1972, at an annualized rate of 2.6 million units, occurring at almost exactly the time when the leading edge of this cohort reached the age of household formation. From 1981 onward they were able to buy investments, if largely with borrowed money. With the front end of this baby-boom generation reaching retirement age in 2006, this cohort may be looking for the security of income that comes from bonds and secure high-dividend-paying stocks. Superfluous consumption may start to wind down. An aversion to risk-taking may develop with respect to all aspects of life, including ownership of more speculative stocks, where the prospect of a higher yield is more distant. In sum, the front end of the baby boomers' arrival at retirement age could lead to a general reversal of excessive consumption, excessive indebtedness, and insufficient saving. A decline in the yield on stocks and bonds could lead to wholesale selling of stocks to make up for a shortfall in income. Hence a long-drawn-out bear market in stocks is possible, along with an economic slowdown and low and perhaps declining interest rates, as a result of renewed demand for bonds.

Stephen Roach of Morgan Stanley is one of a number of respected market commentators concerned with the possibility of deflation in the United States. He has written:

> But how relevant is the Japanese experience to the challenges now facing the United States and China? While asset bubbles in both the United States and Japan suggest that the two economies have many risks in common, there are some key differences that need to be stressed as well. In particular, Japan's excesses were concentrated in the corporate sector—financial and nonfinancial businesses alike. America's excesses, on the other hand, are concentrated in the consumer sector. For example, during its pre-bubble run-up, Japanese capital spending peaked out at 20 percent of GDP in 1990—well in excess of the 12.5 percent capital spending peak hit in the United States in 2000. Moreover, Japan's corporate debt kept surging in the early years of its post-bubble shakeout, peaking at 197 percent of GDP in 1996; by contrast, the U.S. nonfinancial business debt ratio hit a high at 67 percent in 2000. At the same time, the consumption share of U.S. GDP has averaged about 70 percent since early 2002—well above the 67 percent norm of 1975 to 2000. By contrast, in Japan, the pre-bubble consumption share of its GDP peaked at just 56 percent in 1983—actually slightly below the 57 percent average share recorded over the preceding 25 years. . . .
>
> On balance, the saving-short, asset-dependent American consumer has made a much more aggressive consumption bet than has been the case in either the United Kingdom or Australia.

As a result, there is good reason to believe that the U.S. economy would be much more vulnerable to a bursting of its residential property bubble than might be implied by experiences elsewhere in the Anglo-Saxon world. The United States relies on its property bubble far more than the United Kingdom or Australia to square the circle of excess consumption and weak internal income generation. This relative desperation of the asset-dependent American consumer should caution us from drawing comfort from the seemingly gentle aftershocks of other post-bubble workouts.[3]

Mr. Roach is wary of projecting how the many and serious imbalances in the United States and throughout the world might come back into better balance. However, elsewhere he has stated forthrightly that "the global financial system is digging its own grave." It might be even more apposite to say that it is the Fed under Chairman Alan Greenspan that is the gravedigger. He has deployed credit to such an extent that the intended cure, by way of easy money, is likely to lead to a more serious contraction, and a corresponding bear market in stocks, than is generally thought possible: The law of unintended consequences has not been repealed. It may not happen, but the risks are real, and investors must be as prepared to protect themselves, as they should have been in 1999 and 2000, in the event that market action suggests that the bear market may resume. The price of financial security, as for freedom generally, is eternal vigilance.

[3]Stephen Roach, *Economic Forum*. New York: Morgan Stanley, July 25, 2005.

CHAPTER 24

What Does Value Really Mean?

The Historical Perspective

A lot of stock analysts working with financial statements and other fundamental information labor mightily to come up with forecasts for stock prices, but the inescapable fact remains that the connection between value and price is nebulous. It exists at the exact moment when a buyer and a seller make a deal. Perceptions may change the instant the deal is consummated. The buyer determines value on the basis of both current price and future prospects of reward or enjoyment, but once committed, price may change even if the perception of value, at least initially, does not.

Intrinsic Value, Discounted Value, and Market Value

So-called intrinsic value may be what you could get if you could sell underlying assets, but this doesn't mean that shares have to sell at or above their intrinsic value. It has often happened, even in recent years, that shares sell for less than their prorated share of cash in the bank, with all the other assets thrown in for free. However, if the company is losing money or you can't get at that intrinsic value, go back to where you were before: Value is the price at which willing buyers and willing sellers are prepared to do business.

The counterpart of intrinsic value is so-called discounted value. The idea is that you can project what a company is expected to earn in the future and then give it a cash value by discounting against a certain rate of interest. With so many variables, this is a contentious exercise. The one criterion for discounted value that stands the test of time is that it is reasonable if a stock sells with a price-earnings ratio equal to its expected growth rate. If a company earns $1 per share and earnings are expected to grow at 15 percent annually, a reasonable price therefore is $15.

During the great bull market of the 1990s, the criteria for valuing stocks were said to have changed, and value could now be seen in stocks selling for a hundred dollars that had perhaps a dollar or two in tangible assets, no sales, no earnings let alone dividends, and a business plan thrown together in an afternoon on a kitchen table. Value was based on assumptions of prospective growth that would have stretched credulity in the world of Hans Christian Andersen's fairy tale *The Emperor's New Clothes*. The case for buying and owning such stocks was based, in the final analysis, on greater fool theory: *Buy a stock that is going up because it is going up, and that is reason enough.* The overlooked second part of greater fool theory states that you have to sell to a fool greater than yourself, when you can, if you can.

After the end of the bull market of the 1990s, there was still a widespread view of value that departed from long-term historical criteria. Used as a benchmark by the Federal Reserve, the so-called Fed model rested on the proposition that earnings yield, as measured by the Standard & Poor (S&P) 500 index should equal the yield on the 10-year Treasury bond. Thus, at a yield on the bond of 4.5 percent the S&P 500 could have a price/earnings ratio of 22. This approach ignores corporate exposure to other liabilities and suggests that the corporate cost of capital should be the same as the risk-free rate. Given the propensity of both interest rates and, even more so, of profits to fluctuate wildly, valuation models based on these criteria are not only nonsensical but dangerous. A notable danger derives from the proposition that the over- or undervaluation of an individual stock may be considered relative to such a market model. This exercise ignores the fact that there may be good reasons why an individual stock may trade at its own ratio of price to earnings, and one that is quite different from the overall market. Whatever you think of their respective investment merits at any given price, it is fatuous to try to evaluate either Google or General

Motors on the basis of earnings relative to the yield on the 10-year Treasury note. In fairness to the Fed, their model simply represents what they observed had been happening in recent years, and not necessarily what ought to happen.

Historical Valuations for the Dow Industrials

Table 24-1 shows important milestones in market value during the twentieth century to March 2005. The table shows the dividend yield, the ratio of price to the book value of stocks in the index, and the level of the Dow Jones Industrial Average. The table also shows the inexorable stretching of valuations during the 1990s. It may be reasonable to assume that the concept of book values has changed as bricks and mortar count for less and information technology is worth more, but probably not to the extent that price/book value has changed

TABLE 24-1 The Dow Jones Industrial Average: Milestones in Market Value

Date	Dividend Yield	Price/Book	Dow Industrials
1929	3.1	2.2	380
1932	9.0	0.35	41
1942	7.8	0.8	95
1949	7.2	1.0	168
1972	2.3	2.2	1,020
1974	4.6	1.2	607
1982	5.8	1.2	770
1987	2.2	2.8	2,735
1993	2.3	3.1	3,754
1997	1.6	6.4	8,222
1999	1.3	6.8	11,497
2002	2.5	3.1	7,528
2005 (Feb.)	2.3	3.7	10,774

The numbers for 1932, 1942, 1982, and 1993 came when earnings were at their most depressed for the business cycle. The numbers for 2005 almost certainly express something close to peak earnings for the business cycle, as they did in 1999. You expect a substantial expansion of profits when the economy comes out of a recession, but most of that expansion happens relatively early in the cycle.

The best of all value during the century was available in 1932, in terms of both dividends and price-to-book ratio. You might have thought that there would be a total absence of dividends at the bottom of the slump, but this was not the case. Dividend yields were high in recognition of severe dividend cuts already made and the expectation that they would continue to be cut or eliminated. You needed to have faith that the world was not coming to an end in order to buy such good value. It was a function of immense pessimism that few people were prepared to take that risk, even for three times the yield obtainable from bonds.

Investment Trusts in the 1920s

The experience of the 1990s replicated what had occurred during the 1920s. The persistence of that bull market seemed to make traditional tenets inapplicable, as they also seemed to be in the 1990s. In the nineteenth century, a traditional tenet of trust management was to buy stocks in a depression and to sell them in a boom. Selling, however, is inordinately difficult when the boom lasts a long time, and the challenge lies in telling how long a bull market, or a bear market, will last. Selling during a boom may mean selling after a stock doubles once but before it doubles again one or more times. The twentieth century has shown how far stock market booms can go, as well as how low bear markets can go. The lesson of the 1920s, and the early 1970s and the 1990s is that eventually and invariably booms end.

Describing the approach taken by investment trusts during the 1920s, the equivalent of mutual funds of the 1990s, Graham and Dodd wrote in their book, *Security Analysis:*

> If a public utility stock was selling at 35 times its maximum recorded earnings, which was the pre-boom standard, the conclusion to be drawn was not that the stock was too high but that the standard of value had been raised. Instead of judging the

market price by established standards of value, the new era based its standards of value on the market price. Hence all upper limits disappeared, not only upon the price at which a stock could sell, but even upon the price at which it would deserve to sell.

What passed for wisdom in the 1920s also became generally accepted wisdom during the 1990s. The investment industry said that it followed Graham and Dodd's valuation criteria for buying and holding stocks for the long term However, people got away with saying that because few people had actually read Graham and Dodd, and because they were caught up in the emotional and sometimes dishonest hyperventilation of an irrationally exuberant market.

Valuations in the 1970s and Early 1980s

By contrast with the overvaluation of the 1920s, the early 1970s, and the late 1990s, there have been times of very low valuation, most notably in the early 1940s and the late 1970s and early 1980s. Polaroid, for example, rose from a low of $22 in 1965 to a high of $145 in 1973. The bear market then took the stock down to $17.50 at its low the next year. Polaroid was not an isolated example of market devastation. It was a representative one. The seemingly most solid and secure growth stocks of the early 1970s fell the most because they were the most overvalued. For technicians, at their highs they were also the most overextended on the charts. Almost none of the so-called *nifty fifty*, the one-decision stocks of that time, fell by less than 50 percent. From the 1972 market top to the 1974 low, declines of 75 percent or more were standard, as they were between 2000 and 2002.

In 1975, Hilton Hotels sold down to $10, where it had a dividend yield of 10 percent and a book value of $24. In the same year, Tiffany was selling for $7.50, although its headquarters building in Manhattan was itself worth more than the company's $17 million market capitalization. In 1978, Avon paid $40 per share to take over the company. In January 1980, Gulf & Western was at $16.25, after earning $4.13 the previous year, which gave the stock a price-earnings ratio of 3.93. From 1970 to 1980, earnings had been increasing at an annual rate of 9.5 percent and from 1975 to 1980 at a rate of 11.5 percent. Tangible book value was

$16.34. In 1979, the dividend was raised to 75 cents, making it the four-teenth consecutive year of dividend increases.

In March 1980, the Dow Jones Industrial Average was at 785. Its price-earnings ratio was 6.9, it had a dividend yield of 6.4 percent, and it sold at approximately 1.5 times book value. For a while the Dow Industrials responded to perceptions of value, rising to a high just over 1,000 in January 1981. From there, it was hard down again into the August 1982 low of 770, a decline of 23 percent off the top.

Low valuations from the mid-1970s to the early 1980s have to be put in the context of what happened earlier. The bear market that began in 1973, when combined with rising inflation and rising interest rates (and a corresponding collapse in bond prices), drove investors away from stocks. Having been burned so badly, it appeared too risky to go near the stock market. However, it was in this environment that Warren Buffett found the values that propelled the then-fledgling Berkshire Hathaway on its early flight path.

The Japanese Experience

At the extremity of overvaluation, it is hard to beat the initial public offer-ing (IPO) in Tokyo in February 1987 for Nippon Telegraph and Telephone. The stock was offered at the equivalent of $7,770 per share. Despite an expected drop in corporate earnings in 1987, the stock rose in a few weeks to the equivalent of $17,582, where it traded at 234 times questionable earnings. The London *Financial Times* quoted Peter Trasker of Kleinwort Benson International in Tokyo as saying: "We're talking about a social phenomenon. Everyone is buying because everyone is buying."

In due course, the Nikkei Average of Japanese stocks went on from the 30,000 level in 1987 to 39,000 in 1989. Then it began a protracted decline to 7,650 in April 2003. It was by no means clear even then that overall stock values in Japan had become cheap, although some stocks clearly had. It was hard to say that Japan's stock market was cheap when its entire banking industry was essentially bankrupt, largely as a result of the fallen stock market. This is how a downward spiral, a vicious circle, can feed on itself and can become the equal and oppo-site of an expansionary and virtuous one. By 2005 the Nikkei had grudg-ingly worked back toward 12,000 and was now, at last, looking very promising.

The Japanese experience suggests that the technology sector, as represented by the Nasdaq indexes, will also take a very long time to clamber back to their all-time highs.

The Value of Real Estate

The Japanese experience also illustrates the risk in thinking of real estate as the ultimate store of value, although it certainly has been in the very long term. As with anything else, you have to buy well, and returns are not guaranteed. Japan experienced a phenomenal real estate mania in conjunction with its stock market mania. At one point the value of real estate in Tokyo was estimated to be greater than that of all of California. This imbalance was corrected between 1990 and 1998 when the market value of much previously high-priced real estate declined by 90 percent, and many properties could not be sold at any price. Japanese banks were reported to be relieved if they could recover 20 percent of the value of a real estate loan.

Valuations: 1990 to 2005

During the 15 years to 2005, perceptions of value went from reasonable to a massive speculative overvaluation at the top of the bull market and then back to lesser unreasonableness at the low in 2002. Over the next three years, stock prices rose from a level that could not be regarded as cheap, even at the bottom, to a level in 2005 that appeared to discount an optimistic view of the future.

There was an extremity of high pricing in U.S. stocks in the 1990s, similar to what had happened in Japan. Internet stocks were capitalized in the billions, even when they had minuscule sales and, in many cases, no profits. Yahoo! was selling at 100 times revenues and 500 times profits. At least this company was the market leader, with a real business plan, in one of the fastest-growing industries of all time. If profits had stopped growing for some reason, however, you would have had to live to be 500 years old for the stock to earn what you paid for it. Yahoo! rose eventually to an ultimate high of $125 in January 2001. That it was an inherently sound business was not enough to prevent the stock from falling back to the bargain-basement $4 level in 2001 when the market sobered up.

As in the 1920s, book values seemed to have lost all meaning in the 1990s, with the Dow trading more than six times the reported book values on the balance sheet. Somehow Disney managed to show negative book value, which did not, of course, mean that the company was bankrupt. The balance sheet reflected markdowns of goodwill for tax purposes. By now, Hilton Hotels was yielding less than 1 percent, compared with 10 percent in 1980, and there were still analysts recommending it as a buy for a further 50 percent gain within a year.

In 1998, Coca-Cola stock sold for 50 times earnings when its reported earnings growth rate was around 18 percent. However, the company's reported growth rate considerably overstated what was really happening. After allowing for creative accounting of a kind not that different from what landed the executives of some failed companies in jail, the real long-term growth rate appeared to be less than 10 percent. The stock even sold at a multiple of more than five times sales, although unit sales growth was only 8 percent. Such a high multiple is generally attributable only to the stock of a dynamically growing company in some area of proprietary innovation.

The eventual height of unreality for Coca-Cola arrived when its stock topped out just short of $90. A better sense of reality and the ensuing bear market brought the stock back to a low of $37 in March 2003, from which level there was no strong rebound. At that level, one could now see, at least on a comparative basis, some semblance of value in a stock yielding 2.7 percent and having a record of increasing those dividends by 9 percent annually over the preceding five years.

Nortel Fools the Value Analysts

If Yahoo! was an exemplar for operating success, although still for absurd valuation, Nortel was an exemplar for disaster. From a low in 1989 of $1.78, the shares were to rise to an eventual high of $89 in 2000. As the shares approached their peak, the investing public was swallowing without question what the company said when it announced that sales in certain divisions could increase at a rate of 100 percent annually for the foreseeable future. In 1999–2000 it was indeed true that what were said to be sales had increased at that rate for the past year or so and looked to be increasing exponentially. The shares came to be valued at more than a hundred times reported earnings, and the company's market value rose to a level that represented one-third the value of all stocks listed on the Toronto Stock Exchange.

It eluded stock analysts that a significant part of Nortel's so-called sales were really an exercise in pushing product with no money changing hands. The new buzzword was *vendor financing*. When Nortel's customers finished burning through the cash raised to finance their stock promotion, there was nothing but debts and a pile of unsalable Nortel product. During the height of the apparent boom in sales, Nortel had a negative cash flow, only a small cushion of money in the bank relative to its level of business, and debts were mounting. The cost of making the product sold by way of vendor financing still had to be paid for, but there was no money coming in from those sales. More astute management could easily have raised billions to carry the company over by selling new equity when the opportunity was there to do so. But management didn't do that. After the market crested, and even the illusory vendor-financed sales imploded, the opportunity had passed. Nortel was forced to shrink and to shed good parts of its business that were essential for its ongoing renewal. Accordingly, the shares slumped, reaching at one point a low of just 45 cents.

By contrast, Amazon.com, the online bookseller, capitalized on an apparently absurd stock price to raise the billions of dollars to finance the cash-burn required to stay the course of huge losses until the company was able, eventually, to turn a profit.

Valuation Criteria and Normality

Despite the difficulty in establishing benchmarks for value, there are some rules of thumb that have stood the test of time. In the very long term, markets tend to fluctuate a very long way either side of these historic means, but here are some historic criteria:

1. Government bonds should yield 3 percent plus the rate of inflation.

2. When inflation is high and rising, bonds yield more. Rates also tend to be high after a period of inflation, when investors still fear its return. Rates tend to be lower after a period of stable prices or outright deflation, when investors do not fear inflation.

3. When prices are stable, no-growth stocks and commercial real estate should yield 25 percent more than long-term government bonds. Over the very long term this premium has been found necessary in order to provide an appropriate margin of safety. There were few really solid and stable no-growth stocks in the 1980s and 1990s, although some utilities, like The Southern Company, came close. Looking ahead, it may be that a former growth stock such as Merck may come to fit this designation. There have been long periods in the past when many companies simply marked time without profit growth. A yield higher than that from government bonds has been considered necessary in order to offset the perceived higher risk.

4. When prices are stable, a growth stock is assumed to represent fair value if its price-earnings ratio is equal to its expected rate of growth. If a stock earns $1 per share and growth is expected at 15 percent annually, by this measure a stock price of $15 represents fair value. It sells at 15 times earnings, or with a price-earnings ratio of 15. This multiple can grow as a good track record lengthens, but it cannot grow to infinity.

   The problem with a high multiple is what happens if growth falters. A share price based on a high expected growth rate is vulnerable. If a company with its stock selling at a price-earnings ratio of 40 or 50 starts losing money, the impact on the price can be devastating. As noted above, the recent bear market showed how even the stock of a prestigious company such as Coca-Cola can decline substantially when great expectations are confounded.

   In mid-2005 General Electric (GE), an unquestionably fine company, a market bellwether and component of the Dow Jones Industrial Average, was priced at about $34. At that price GE had a dividend yield of 2.6 percent and a price-earnings ratio of 20. However, its annual growth rate in earnings over the previous 5 years had been a mere 6 percent, as had its annual growth rate in dividends. If the company maintained a 6 percent rate of growth in dividends, it would take 12 years for the dividend to double. Even after allowing for a quality premium, GE provided a textbook example of a stock that could be said to be extremely expensive according to historic valuation criteria. Technical action appeared to be confirming this assessment.

5. During the twentieth century, the *normal* long-term average dividend payout for stocks in the Dow Jones Industrial Average was 50 percent, and its *normal* average price level was 23.7 times dividends, representing a dividend yield of 4.2 percent. In mid-1980, the Dow was trading at 18.5 times dividends. In 1999, it was trading around 77 times dividends, rising eventually to a high of 80 times at the crest of the bull market in January 2000. At the bear market low, the Dow had settled back to 43 times dividends, partly as a reflection of the Fed lowering short-term interest rates to just 1 percent. At that low, however, there was no provision in market pricing for the possibility or, indeed, the eventual inevitability of interests rising.

By March 2005 dividends had increased substantially from the time of the bear market low. With a dividend payout of approximately 40 percent of earnings, the Dow at 10,774 had a dividend yield of 2.27 percent and was therefore trading at 44 times dividends. Even after allowing for the fact that there had been considerable growth in earnings, this multiple was still at a level almost twice its normalized long-term average during the twentieth century. Normalizing the long-term relationship between dividends would have put the Dow Jones Industrial Average at the 5,800 level.

6. The yield on stocks has varied between about three times the yield on bonds, at the market low in 1932 and about one-quarter of the yield on bonds in 1999. In between these extremities there have been frequent and huge fluctuations.

As discussed in Chapter 23, when interest rates go up or down (with bond prices going in the opposite direction), there is, accordingly, more or less competition for investors' money. Thus, the criteria for most fundamental analysts' valuation models shift like goalposts moving all over the playing field. As has been famously observed, normality is for stock prices to fluctuate, and those fluctuations have little bearing on the new-found concept of valuation models.

Value Fails, Except Near the Mean

If fundamental analysis that is based on long-standing historical experience gets you out of a bull market far too early, it can be suicidal in a bear market. It leads you to believe that your seemingly great stocks should ride out the decline. This just does not happen in practice. Except for special situations, your chances of picking stocks that buck the downtrend are much lower when the majority of stocks are going down.

Benjamin Graham's own experience, as told in his memoirs,[1] is sobering. He recalls having a discussion with the great investor Bernard Baruch in 1929. They agreed how extraordinary it was that stocks at the time delivered a yield of only about 2 percent when a return of 8 percent was available in the money market. They both said that they expected that these returns would change places in due course. This happened over the next few years.

Baruch sold out of all his stocks in good time in 1929. Graham did not. He went on believing in fundamental investing and stuck with it throughout the bear market that began in 1929.

Graham admits in his memoirs that he should have taken his clients' money and his own out of the market and kept it out, but he did not. Emphasis on value meant that losses on his portfolio were limited to 70 percent, compared with the 89 percent decline in the Dow. During the decline, he continued to make quarterly disbursements of 1.5 percent of the value of the investments. As a result, by the end of 1932, only 22 percent remained of what he was managing in 1929. His loss in 1930 was 50.5 percent, in 1931 a further 16 percent, and in 1932 only 3 percent. During the following years, Graham recovered all his losses by sticking with his value approach to investing. He made the approach work for him again when the market was going up again.

In the final analysis, all that Graham and Dodd really proved was that fundamental analysis works spectacularly in a rising market and particularly when you start from a very low level.

Good News for the Long Run

On the Internet there is an academic study, *The Good News and the Bad News about Long-Run Stock Returns*, by Donald Robertson of the Faculty of Economics and Politics at Cambridge University and by Stephen Wright of the Department of Economics at Birkbeck College of the University of London. Setting aside the complex algebra, they

[1]Benjamin Graham, *The Memoirs of the Dean of Wall Street*, edited and with an introduction by Seymour Chatman, New York: McGraw-Hill, 1996

conclude that stocks go up over the very long term, going back 200 years. Most significant is their conclusion that there is a relationship between dividends and book value such that there is a tendency for them to revert to the mean. Therefore, the probabilities in favor of making money improve the longer your time perspective, even if you buy at the top of a market cycle.

Reversion to the Mean

History shows that the relationship between prices and valuation multiples always reverts to the mean eventually, however long it takes to happen. This is how it happens:

1. When stocks are very expensive in terms of the historic multiple of profits and dividends, and price-to-book value, there may be enough growth to bring those multiples more into line with historical normality so that the apparently high price level is justified in due course. Alternatively, stocks may decline so as to bring down historically high multiples.

2. When prices are low and stocks are cheap in terms of historic multiples, prices may rise as a result of increasing stock prices. Alternatively, profits, dividends and price-to-book value ratios may decline so as to fall in line with historic multiples.

Despite the draw of stock prices toward the mean of historical valuations, stock prices seldom stabilize close to the mean. There are huge swings from an extremity of high multiples to an extremity of low multiples. Therefore, you need to have some general awareness of underlying values for individual stocks that you are considering and the soundness of a company's operations. Many respected observers of the long-term history of stocks have noted that the recession and the bear market following the boom of the 1990s failed to correct the excesses of irrational exuberance of that expansion. Therefore, a new and possibly more severe bear market in stocks could get under way. That is not a forecast but merely an observation that since it has happened in the past, it could happen again: preservation of capital requires paying vigilant heed to market-timing indicators.

Lessons from the Long-Term History of Stocks

The Upward Trend Is Very Erratic

The trend in stock prices has always been upward, but sometimes with very long periods of going sideways, and there have been huge swings within those trading ranges. According to the Foundation for the Study of Cycles, stocks in general (but we don't know which ones) advanced by about 10 times from 1800 to 1900. During the nineteenth century there was almost no inflation so those gains were real.

During the twentieth century the challenge of owning shares represented by the major stock indexes was seriously compounded by inflation, and there were long periods when stocks lost money in real terms even when the market was going sideways or higher. The major stock indexes fail to reflect the divergence between new-economy companies and mature or obsolescent companies some of which drop from the indexes only when their best days are long past. Benjamin Graham, Warren Buffet and many others have proved that you can beat the indexes, as well as beating inflation, by a wide margin over the long term if you find shares in great companies, and stick with them as long as it is right to do so. The NASDAQ 100 stock index, comprising mostly technology stocks, advanced by almost 20 times during the 1990s. This performance eclipsed the major indexes until it fell back to the 2002 low. Then it was just four times its level in 1990, compared with a gain of three times for the Dow Jones Industrial Index.

Long-Term Problems with the Dow

The Dow Jones Industrial Average, at the time comprising 12 stocks, was at 41 at the low in 1903. By January 2000, it was at 11,750 for a nominal increase of more than 286 times. With stocks constantly coming and going from the Dow, all you can really say, though, is that stocks generally went up as the economy grew. You cannot say that any mindless buy-and-hold strategy applied to individual stocks held for eternity is effective. Capitalism has rightly been described as creative destruction, and entire industries, as well as individual companies, come and go.

There is no easy way to reconcile distortions caused by the departure of stocks from the Dow and the arrival of new ones. Of the original 12 stocks in the Dow in 1900, only General Electric remained in the index throughout the twentieth century. Compared with the constantly revised Dow, a portfolio invested in the Dow stocks of 1900 and never changed could show a much worse performance than the apparent result suggested by this index. You have to make a negative adjustment for bankruptcies and companies that fell into oblivion. You have to make a positive adjustment for reinvestment of the proceeds from Dow stocks taken over and bought out for cash.

The 25 years from 1972 to 1997 provide an example of the challenge of evaluating the performance of any stock index over the long term. Of the so-called nifty-fifty stocks of 1972, nine disappeared by 1997, or 18 percent of them. These included MGIC, acquired by Baldwin United, which went bankrupt, and Burroughs and Emery, which both fell into oblivion. A truly long-term investor has to include these stocks in the record as if they were still held, even if they became worthless. A buy-and-hold strategy applied only to the Dow as it once was would have you still owning many lackluster stocks and heavily weighted in steels and textiles, as well as some stocks worth no more than their value as collectible certificates. All Dow stocks should have been sold at one time or another. As we have shown, even General Electric doesn't only go up, and there was no reasonable way of knowing in advance that this single stock would come back after every bear market when so many apparently great stocks did not. A 1-in-12 probability of finding and holding for a century that one great stock is not good odds. In sum, there are good reasons to override a perpetual buy-and-hold strategy that relies on finding needles in haystacks.

Logically, you could sell stocks when they are dropped from the Dow and buy the new additions when they arrive. Owning the adjusted Dow has some merit for the very long term, and this strategy would produce better results than many money managers achieve. It would be an approach sharing a conceptual relationship with the objective of this book—to buy stocks on strength and to sell them on weakness. The problem is that the call for action occurs so long after weakness in a departing stock has become apparent. There is the same problem with the strength in a new arrival, which, like the newly arrived Microsoft, may have its best days behind it when it arrives in the Dow. In some cases Dow stocks have been dropped only long after the price has gone down the drain, as appears to be happening with General Motors.

In sum, if you simply buy the Dow, there is no provision in this approach for buying stocks performing better and shunning those performing worse or for avoiding major bear markets. All you can really say is that buying Dow stocks equally has the feeble merit of avoiding what many money managers do: sell winners seemingly overpriced and then buy losers.

The Big Market Swings

As illustrated by the chart for the Dow Jones Industrial Average from 1897 to 1934 (Fig. 25-1) and the chart for the Dow from 1916 to 2005 (Fig. 25-2), the stock market generally has gone up about two-thirds of the time and down or sideways about one-third of the time.

Between 1897 and 1925 the Dow fluctuated in a broad range between about 40 and 100, with a short-lived surge to 110 in 1916, and another to 114 in 1920. Even the top in 1920, however, was to be followed by a bear market that took the Dow back to a level just above 60, with a fairly normal bear market decline of 45 percent. Sideways action within this broad trading range was to last for 28 years before the big bull market surge was to get going between 1925 and 1929. In those four years the Dow more than tripled from the breakout level at 120 to an eventual, short-lived high at 386.

The extended sideways action between 1897 and 1925 might be regarded as inconsequential for the twenty-first century except for the fact it was merely the first of three long periods of backing and filling ahead of a substantial move to a new all-time high. Three occurrences don't

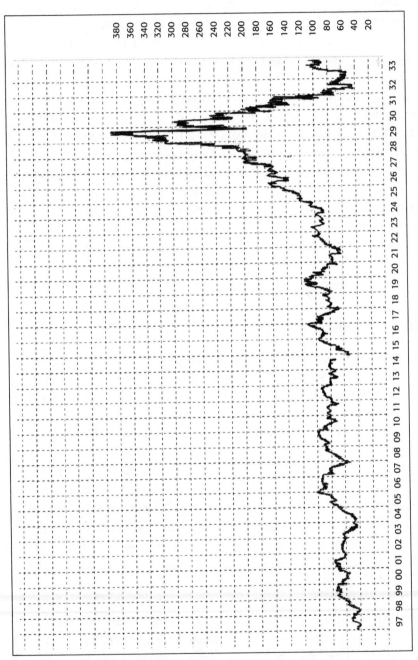

FIGURE 25-1 Monthly Chart for the Dow Jones Industrial Average from 1897 to 1934.

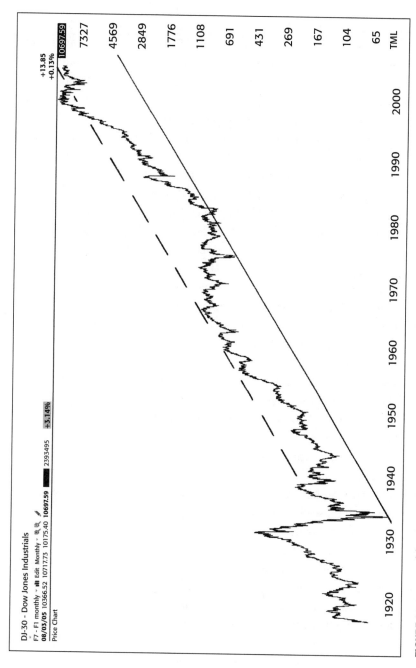

FIGURE 25-2 Monthly Chart for the Dow Jones Industrials, 1916–2005.

establish statistical reliability but they suggest a reasonable *prima facie* case for believing that historical precedent might recur. It took 25 years from 1929 until 1954 for the Dow to regain its 1929 peak. Then there was an extended period of sideways consolidation from 1960 to 1982, a period of 22 years, which was similar to the sideways market action between 1897 and 1925. Coming, as it did, at the end of a secular bull market from the low in 1932, the sideways market action during the 1960s and 1970s might well be a harbinger of what can be expected during the first two decades of the twenty-first century.

The chart for the Dow from 1916 to 2005 shows a broad upward channel from the low in 1932. There is some question as to where the trendline and the channel ought to be. The trendline is drawn here through the most prominent downward spike in 1974 despite the fact that it was to be penetrated briefly in 1980 and 1982. The result is to achieve a higher channel line that comes closer to containing the high in 2000, although of course it does not succeed in doing so. Similarly the assumed channel line would be slightly exceeded by the high in 1937. As discussed in chapter 11, trendlines and channel lines often require a *best fit* when points of contact are imperfect. Interpretation of this chart suggests a greater likelihood that the high in 2000 was aberrational in extending beyond the channel line rather than that it signified the likelihood of a further upward extension equal to the historic ampli-tude of the channel. When the Dow made its all-time high at 11,750, the long-term trendline below that bar was at 2,897. Add the difference of 8,853 to 11,750 and an upward extension according to channel breakout theory would set a target for the Dow of 20,603! On the other hand, trendline theory strongly suggests that the Dow and this uptrend line will eventually converge, whether by way of a severe decline, by sideways market action extending for a very long time, or by a combi-nation of these developments.

None of this pouring of cold water on bullish expectations for the overall market detracts from the certainty that there will be opportunities for profitable investment in specific stocks in specific sectors. During the 1960s and 1970s, for example, there was a roaring bull market in precious metals and their corresponding mining stocks, with many of them advancing by 10 times and more even as the overall market was going nowhere on balance. Since 2000 the beginnings of similar market action might have been emerging in energy-related stocks. In sum the twenty-first century is almost certain to provide superior opportunities for market-timers focusing on sectors and individual stocks where the action is, rather than in the broader market of traditional Dow stocks. Table 25-1 shows the major fluctuations in the Dow during the twentieth century.

This table shows two periods of essentially sideways market action within which there were big swings up and down, enough to constitute full-fledged bull and bear markets in their own right. The first was between 1897 and 1925, when the market broke upward at last. The second period of sideways action was between 1961 and 1983, when stocks began a roaring bull market similar to the one in the 1920s. The bear

TABLE 25-1   Dow Jones Industrial Average: Major Highs and Lows

Date	Low	% Change High to Low	Date	High	% Change Low to High
1897	40	—	1901	78	95
1903	42	46	1906	103	145
1907	53	49	1909	101	91
1914	53	48	1916	110	168
1917	66	40	1919	120	82
1921	64	47	1929	386	503
1929	195	49	1930	297	52
1932	41	89	1937	196	378
1938	97	51	1938	159	64
1942	93	42	1966	1001	976
1966	735	37	1968	994	35
1970	627	37	1972	1067	70
1974	570	47	1976	1026	80
1980	729	29	1987	2746	277
1987	1616	42	2000	11,750	627
2002	7149	39	2005	10,984*	54

*Using a March 2005 cutoff.

market to the June 1932 low went to 41.22, which was actually a point below the low in 1903, for a total decline from the top of 89 percent. As measured by the Dow Jones Industrials, all the gains of an entire generation were given back at that low. At its low, the bear market from 2000 to 2002 saw the technology-weighted NASDAQ 100 decline by a similar amount, by 84 percent, returning to a level last seen in 1997. Even after that immense decline, many NASDAQ stocks retained huge gains from the 1980s, with this index still more than five times what is was at the low in 1990.

The Risk of Buying at a Market Top

The opportunities for making money by buying stocks in a bull market are clear. Less obvious is the risk that depends on when you buy. This risk is considerably greater than you might think at first. You cannot assume that you will buy all or most of your stocks in the early stages of a bull market. On the contrary, the probabilities are high that you buy many stocks past the halfway mark or toward its end. You could theoretically invest all your money at or near the absolute high point for a bull market. The statistical probability of doing so is small. Nevertheless, the real risk of buying at or near the top far exceeds the statistical probability. Market tops occur when there is maximum enthusiasm. Then there is no fear, and people expect the bull market to continue to infinity. It is all too easy to be drawn into the collective enthusiasm near the top of the market when all about you are making, at least on paper, their collective fortune.

Table 25-2 shows how long it would have taken to get your money back if you had invested your capital at the top of some of the biggest bull markets.

The good news for buy-and-hold investors is that stocks, overall, always have come back eventually. Also, they have always gone on to make new highs far beyond previous highs. The bad news is every bit as bad as you might think because there is so much rotation among stocks during each recovery. Some stocks make new highs twice as quickly as the averages come back, and some take twice as long or never do, and as we have seen, the averages may or may not correspond to what happens to the stocks that you own even if you try to

TABLE 25-2 Dow Jones Industrial Average:
Markets, Peak to Peak

Market Peak	% Decline	Years to Recover
1890	64	15
1906	64	10
1916	56	3
1919	47	6
1929	89	26
1966	38	7
1973	45	10
1987	42	2
2000	38	?

replicate an index. There is an informal rule that the most popular stocks of the previous bull market, the ones you are most likely to own, are the least likely to be at the forefront of the next bull market. Market action since the top of the bull market in 2000 strongly reinforces this probability: It is extremely unlikely that the NASDAQ stock indexes will regain their highs for many years.

After a bear market, it can take many years, and sometimes decades, for an individual stock to regain a previous high at the top of the last bull market, if it ever does. It took Avon until 1998 to recover its peak price in nominal dollars at the 1973 high, a full 25 years later and despite the huge bull market going on around it. Some recovery stories are less encouraging than you might think. In 1972, IBM began a long downtrend, departing for a time from the Dow, after starting from a price-earnings ratio of 78! It was a very long road back and, even then, not to the preeminence that it once had. In inflation-adjusted terms, IBM recovered the purchasing power of what it was worth at its high in 1972 only at the end of 1998.

Table 25-3 shows how the inflation-adjusted record for the Dow Jones Industrials puts the risk of buying at a market top or a market bottom into better perspective than the index numbers alone.

TABLE 25-3 The Performance of $1,000 Invested in the Dow Jones Industrials in Nominal and CPI-Adjusted Dollars

	Nominal	CPI-Adjusted
From the 1974 low to the 2000 high	$25,440	$7,275
From the 1972 high to the 2000 high	12,720	3,091
From the 1972 high to the 2002 low	6,295	1,463

Fashions in the Stock Market Change

Every conspicuously profitable opportunity for investment attracts more capital investment. If the opportunity is highly attractive, it will attract so much investment that in due course everyone's investment becomes unprofitable. Then there has to be a period of cleansing, liquidations, bankruptcies, and obsolescence, all of which shrink the industry—often below the level needed for ongoing demand. Finally, the survivors start making money again, and if the industry has shrunk enough, then business will become very profitable. The swings in the price of shares in industries subject to these cyclic swings rise to unsustainable highs at the top and sink to lows at the bottom that suggest no possibility of recovery.

Hard as it may be to believe, almost every line of business has had its time in the sun. For much of the nineteenth century and into the early years of the twentieth, there were no more rewarding places to invest than in railroads, steel, and shipping. The sinking of the *Titanic* was caused by the quest for prestige in a profitable line of business. By contrast, for long periods during the twentieth century, rails, steel, and shipping were totally out of favor, and rightly so.

Then, at about the end of the 1990s and into the first years of the twenty-first century, these apparently rusted and busted industries made a dramatic comeback. Between March 2003 and March 2005, for example, the price of US Steel Corporation dramatically reversed the 10-year bear market that had been almost a mirror image of stocks generally. During these two years, US Steel went from the $10 level to the $60 level. Apart from the corporate reorganization that left pension obligations behind, burgeoning demand from China closed in on the world's steel-making capacity. Prices surged, and so did profits, and the shares of steel-makers.

Chinese demand for basic materials such as steel and chemicals and U.S. consumers' appetite for goods imported from China had a similar impact on the shares of previously beaten down railway and shipping companies. Newfound prosperity may be soundly based for transportation companies, but for steel, the outlook is questionable. During the period of apparently insatiable demand between 2000 and 2005, Chinese domestic steel capacity doubled, to a level where it represented 30 percent of total world steel-making capacity. It is unlikely that China can absorb what its own industry is capable of producing, let alone keep busy the global steel-makers that had been exporting to China so profitably. Should China become a significant exporter of steel, the worldwide industry would likely sink back, yet again, into depression.

Xerox Falls Off a Cliff

Xerox provides a prime example of corporate senescence that had been under way for some time. However, awareness of corporate decrepitude arrived suddenly in the stock market, as the monthly chart shows (Fig. 25-3). At one time, there was no more prominent leader in the general area of technological innovation than Xerox. In the 1940s, this company developed photocopying, as we now know it. However, its success was also its excuse for complacency. Its immense success and profitability enabled research engineers in its Palo Alto Research Center to produce many of the most important features of the computer age that we now take for granted. For the record, Xerox employees developed the laser printer, with which Hewlett-Packard came to dominate that industry; flat-panel displays; the mouse; ethernet connections; and the graphical user interface—the icon; and Xerox put it all together to produce the Alto, the first personal computer combining a mouse and a graphical user interface. Xerox labored but others reaped the fruits.

Profitability at Xerox kept on rolling for a very long time. The technology of photocopying didn't become obsolete, but Xerox very nearly did. At the depths in 2000, there was considerable question as to whether the company could survive. Able new management brought Xerox back from the brink, but it is improbable that the company will soon regain the preeminent position it once enjoyed.

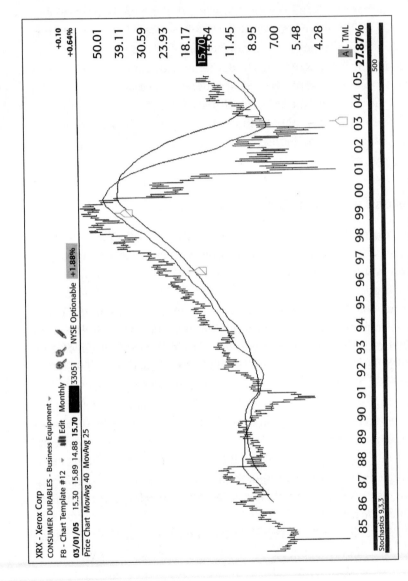

FIGURE 25-3 Xerox Monthly Bar Chart with 25- and 40-Month Moving Averages.

The Lesson of Market Fluctuations

If it is important to own rising stocks in a rising market, it is imperative to own few stocks or none in an established bear market. In a bull market, most boats rise, and even random selection of stocks is likely to make money. Many that lag eventually get moving. Even if you fail to pick big winners, it is unlikely that you will pick many serious losers. On the other hand, about 90 percent of all stocks go down in a general bear market.

The fundamental reasons for a bear market become apparent only after the event, generally in the form of higher interest rates or an economic contraction or both. Then profits decline, lowering the apparent value of all stocks, as well as their price. In a severe bear market, investors don't sell just poor stocks. Some stocks become unsalable at any price. Therefore, investors also sell what they can sell. Once this downward spiral becomes entrenched, you never know how far the bear market will go or how long it will last. If you park your money in Treasury bills or an equivalent safe haven during a bear market, you have that all-important cash with which to buy back stocks again at favorable prices.

It is remarkable how much more money you make and how much grief you avoid by avoiding bear markets and having money to buy stocks in the early stages of the next bull market. The difference in performance that results from avoiding even one bear market is huge. The cumulative difference resulting from missing several bear markets is staggering. Of course, avoiding bear markets is more difficult than looking at previous bear markets in hindsight might lead you to believe. It is all too easy to confuse a routine retracement, however severe, with a bear market. If you inadvertently do so, you must be prepared to buy back in. Bull markets truly die hard, and they seldom die without plenty of strong signals showing that the trend may be reversing.

You cannot, of course, both ride stocks to the bottom of a bear market and also have the money they once represented with which to buy low. The standard alternative to using timing techniques, staying fully invested all the time, cannot reconcile this conflict.

Where Mutual Funds Fail: The Case for Doing the Job Yourself

The Record in a Bear Market

Mutual fund managers are supposed to be experts—Right? Logically, mutual funds should do the following:

1. Make more money for you than you could do for yourself

2. Lower the risk of major fluctuations in your investment portfolio

Table 26-1 shows the record during the 2000–2002 bear market for various stock indexes and the total performance of all stock mutual funds in billions of dollars, 20-year U.S. Treasury bonds, and a few selected major stocks, of which two are components of the Dow. The performance for stock fund assets is even worse than the table suggests because, unlike the other investments in the list, fund assets include reinvestment of dividends. In the case of Treasury bonds, the interest was significant over the two-year period, adding approximately 10 percentage points before tax. It has to be said, of course, that it would have required good management to find and hold stocks during that period that held their own or ones that went up, such as Lennar Corp. and other home builders. The majority of stocks went down.

Table 26-1 shows the comparative performance of the Dow Jones Industrial Average, the Russell 500 Small Capitalization Index, the actual performance of net assets in all stock mutual funds, and the Nasdaq 100 technology index. Since, by definition, averaging evens out

TABLE 26-1   Performance of Indexes, Stock Fund Assets, and Selected Stocks in the Bear Market

	12/31/99	12/31/02	% Change
Dow Industrials	11,497	8,902	−23%
Russell 500	505	383	−24%
Stock Fund Assets*	4,355	2,667	−34%
Nasdaq 100	3,707	984	−73%
3M	48.94	61.65	+26%
Canadian National	17.68	27.72	+57%
Johnson & Johnson	46.63	53.71	+15%
Lennar Corp.	7.39	23.48	+218%

Source: Investment Company Institute. Starting assets include 1999 year-end total plus net additions to end 2002.

the good, the bad, and the indifferent (the average), and since there were some stock mutual funds that made money during the bear market, it follows that some must have done abysmally.

The Problem with Financial Planners

The ordinary investor has to beware of the so-called financial planner, advisor, or consultant who is really engaged, no more and no less, in selling mutual funds and sometimes also life insurance. If this statement seems harsh, go and find such books as *Where Are the Customers' Yachts?* by Fred Schwed, Jr., first published in 1940, or *Take on the Street: What Wall Street and Corporate America Don't Want You to Know, What You Can Do to Fight Back,* by Arthur Levitt, former chairman of the Securities and Exchange Commission, or *The Naked Investor: Why Almost Everyone but You Gets Rich on Your Retirement Savings Plan,* by John L. Reynolds.

There is an iron-clad rule in the investment industry: *Know your client!* Those selling investments, including mutual funds, represent themselves as having superior knowledge that matches what they are selling, especially with respect to risk, to what is appropriate for the buyer. This may sound obvious, but it's not the way it happens. To start with, financial planners may say that they are independent, but this may mean no more than that they have some kind of agency in a separate office that gets paid by sales commissions and not with an ordinary paycheck. It doesn't mean that they work independently for you. Regardless of apparent sincerity, their income almost certainly depends on selling you what pays them the best. Why sell a mutual fund that kicks back $1,000 in commissions when you can sell one that kicks back $3,000? The average buyer will never know the difference. Even if the fees are disclosed, as the regulators require, this doesn't mean that comparative choices will be offered between low-fee and high-fee funds or between funds with a good record and ones with a poor one or, indeed, choices other than buying funds at all.

Most people need the kind of financial plan that considers all aspects of their situation and all the available investment choices, including ones other than mutual funds and life insurance and even beyond stocks and bonds. Under certain circumstances, for example, someone looking for a secure above-average income might want to invest in well-secured second mortgages, which can be found through mortgage brokers. There is a reasonable chance of getting truly independent financial advice from someone engaged in direct portfolio management. And there is an even better chance of getting independent advice from someone who charges on the basis of time rather than commissions—as you normally pay a lawyer or an accountant. You can never entirely avoid the risk of getting into the hands of a larcenous or simply an incompetent agent. However, you can help yourself by asking around for references and by asking plenty of questions.

When you are dealing with any amount of money greater than, say, $100,000, you should get a complete plan in writing. It is amazing how many financial disasters would have been avoided or at least mitigated if a financial planner had been required to put a plan in writing and therefore making it available for comparison with the result. Of course, it is always the most seemingly plausible salesperson who gets away with the murder. If it's too good to be true, it probably is. Hear this clearly: *Too good to be true is not true.*

The Mandate of a Mutual Fund

As discussed in Chapter 13, when there is too much enthusiasm for stocks and mutual funds hold minimal cash balances, it may be a sign of an impending market top. Mutual fund managers interpret their mandate as having to invest all their money (except for a working cash balance), all the time, even in a bear market. It could readily be seen in the fall of 2000 that there was scarcely a single stock in the general area of technology that represented fair value by any generally accepted standard, or that had an acceptable chart pattern such as to justify retaining the stock. All that the marketplace offered was a choice of falling rocks. Logically, if fund managers had the expertise they claimed when they took in money from investors, they should have sold all stocks by the end of 2000 and stayed out of the market so as to have cash with which to buy those stocks some time after this sector made its low in the second half of 2002. Needless to say, this did not happen.

Typically, a mutual fund has to invest in accordance with inflows and outflows. If investors get carried away with excess enthusiasm and therefore provide high inflows at market tops, then the funds buy at market tops. When inflows dry up or reverse at market bottoms, then stocks are sold or at least not bought—the exact opposite of what funds ought to do. The problem with owning mutual funds in a bear market is exacerbated by the fact that declining prices lead to redemptions. Redemptions force funds to sell. Fund selling further depresses prices, so there are more redemptions, and so on.

The structural problem of funds having to put money to work was far less serious during the recent bear market for those funds having a mandate to take a broader view of investment opportunities. One example among a relatively small number that made good money between 2000 and 2004 was the T. Rowe Price Appreciation Fund. Overall, however, the experience of owning mutual funds between 2000 and 2004 was dismal.

Buying Mutual Funds Is Buying Retail

For almost everyone except those saving perhaps a hundred bucks a month, buying mutual funds is an exercise in buying retail when you are a big enough fish to have access to wholesale: There's an extra person in the middle more than you need and who makes a living on the turn—and a very good one too. This is not to say that there is no place for mutual funds, but there are serious pitfalls. You pay a premium for little or no added value compared with doing the job yourself or with other ways to go, and you get subtracted value if the funds you buy lose money. Unlike the one-time premium for buying tickets to a big hockey game from a scalper, when you buy a fund, you keep on paying, paying, and paying for as long as you own those funds. The mutual-fund scalper—the salesperson and the fund manager—keeps on clipping your coupons regardless of whether or not they make you any money.

What a Mutual Fund Really Is

A mutual fund is really no more than another stock, a conglomerate comprising a basket of other stocks. Except for a closed-end market-listed fund, you merely buy and sell it differently. As with any public stock offering for a mining company or any other business, the first objective is to make money for the promoters, who say that they can make money for investors after paying themselves. There's nothing wrong with that. It's how all capital is raised. As with any promotion, however, and without being able to guarantee that they really can make money, let alone deliver a superior performance, fund managers make sure that they get paid first regardless of what happens to your money. In the final analysis, a mutual fund is as good or as bad as its investment managers. The quality of management of the companies in which those managers may or may not invest, whenever they actually own the shares in those underlying companies, is something quite different.

When a Mutual Fund *Is* the Market

When a mutual fund gets to a certain size, it starts competing against itself in the marketplace. Therefore, it is very difficult for a mutual fund to do better than the general market or better than its niche-specific benchmark. When you are dealing with a mutual fund comprising tens of billions of dollars worth of stocks, that fund is, in effect, the market itself. This is how it works.

If Superfund wants to build a big position in U.S. Widgets (USW), it cannot buy without competing against itself. When the fund starts to buy at, say, $20, there may be only half a million shares available to buy around that price. Superfund takes them all. The next offers permit the purchase of a further half million shares at prices up to $21, with lots offered at successively higher increments of a few pennies here and there. Even with patience, it may not be possible to build a position of 10 million shares without pushing the price up to $25. Those already owning the stock, including the specialists and market-makers, observe the emerging demand and hold out for higher prices. On the way, other investors see the price going up, so they get on the bandwagon, picking off what sellers are offering. Accordingly, USW shares go up, and especially if the underlying fundamentals are respectable, the price stays up if the shares have moved into strong hands. Even if the price gets ahead of a level that might seem warranted by those underlying fundamentals, in due course, as profits grow, the price will grow into its new and higher valuation. However, the price level is still one that has been created for the most part by Superfund itself.

You can see how Superfund has become the market if its managers want to reverse the process. Then they have to find takers all the way down as it unloads the 10 million shares acquired at prices between $20 and $25, and they may well be unable to recover what they paid to get in. Instead of having to buy at successively higher prices, they will be selling at progressively lower prices. If there has been an unfavorable corporate announcement in the meantime, the price may be down to $15 before the entire 10 million shares has gone back out. As you can see, there are special challenges when a large mutual funds tries to beat the market, even when the general market is rising.

In a bear market, it is even more difficult for Superfund to get ahead of what others are doing. Say that a big mutual fund owned a large block of Nortel in 2000. With the fundamentals deteriorating rapidly and the knowledge of that deterioration becoming well known, it would have been exceptionally difficult for a huge mutual fund to get out of a position at a good price if it owned several percentage points worth of the entire company.

This challenge is illustrated by Berkshire Hathaway's huge position in Coca-Cola. Warren Buffett said that with the wisdom of hindsight, he should have sold some or all of the stock when the price was approaching the $90 level in 1998 and 1999. Over the years, however, he had built a position in the company that comprised more shares than those held by all mutual fund companies put together. During that time, of course, his reputation had grown, and he had become a director of Coca-Cola, and people paid attention to what he was buying and selling. It is inconceivable that Berkshire Hathaway could have sold all or most of its holding without people saying, "Well, if he wants to sell, and especially if he wants to sell, then maybe I should sell too." As far as Coca-Cola was concerned, Berkshire Hathaway had become the market.

Slightly but by no means entirely different is the way that the great John Templeton's funds were accustomed to operate. He said that he liked bear markets because they gave him the opportunity to buy shares at a good price. Here again, though, he made the market, and in some stocks he became the market. At one point he started buying shares in Ford at $40. He had great confidence in the company for the long term, and he went on supporting the price on its way down until the shares reached a low at $16. In due course, the shares went up again, and the holding made good money for his fundholders.

Over time, this kind of staying power served Mr. Templeton very well. One might note, however, that he was operating during times when share values overall were generally quite moderate by historical standards, and the major direction was upward. It is not clear whether such staying power will be rewarded in the first decades of the twenty-first century given that, by historical standards, starting values for the general market are very high.

Obviously, this problem of dealing in what is called *size* is not one with which the small investor is normally concerned, or even a money manager looking after any but the very largest private fortunes.

Major Corporations Do the Same Job

Banks invest predominantly in a loan portfolio and insurance companies in a policy portfolio. A major corporation such as General Electric or Johnson & Johnson resembles a mutual fund because it has a wide range of products, and its operations are diversified across a broad customer base, with both production and sales widely diversified geographically. They have divisions that operate as autonomous entities that happen to be under the same umbrella of corporate ownership. Warren Buffett's Berkshire Hathaway is not by any means unique in having a spread between ownership of operating companies, notably in insurance, and ownership of a portfolio of passive investments.

In effect, you can create your own mutual fund that holds just the three stocks, say, General Electric, Johnson & Johnson, and Berkshire Hathaway. You achieve more diversification than you might expect and, in fact, better diversification than you get from investing in most sector-specific mutual funds. Expand the portfolio further to include, say, a major gold mining company such as Placer Dome and some Treasury bonds, and these five holdings alone achieve a very substantial measure of diversification. Make sure that what you buy maintains an acceptable chart pattern, and you will likely stay ahead of what you might make in most mutual funds.

Proven Management versus Unproven

By investing directly in a few major corporations, you get proven management that has breadth, depth, and decades of experience. This is more than you can say of some mutual fund companies, where managers change with the seasons. A few fund managers—very few—are, of course, extremely good, but many are extremely bad. The *Hulbert Financial Digest* tracks the performance of mutual funds. You may have thought that you should buy the best "five star" funds when they first emerge and redeem them when they lose their top rating. Surprisingly, according to John C. Bogle, founder of the Vanguard Group of funds, this approach produces below-average returns with above-average risk.[1] Look for success, if you will, but over the long term, slow and steady professionalism beats the performance of stars that soon burn out or simply move on to manage another fund.

Limits to Diversification

Contrary to what mutual funds say, there is a limit to the benefits of diversification. A substantial level of diversification can be achieved across as few as a half dozen companies such as 3M, General Electric, and Berkshire Hathaway, and once you get more than about 30 stocks altogether, the benefits of diversification tend to be counterproductive: Further diversification leads to a lowering of quality and a dilution of the profits on successful investments.

Some mutual fund management companies have set up funds that consist of other funds so as to achieve better diversification beyond

[1]John C. Bogle, *Common Sense on Mutual Funds: New Imperatives for the Intelligent Investor*. New York: Wiley, 1999, pp. 98–99.

any reasonable point. This is like the old saying about fleas: Big fleas have little fleas on their backs to bite 'em. And so *ad infinitum*. All such an approach really does is to establish a further excuse for charging fees.

In practice, you can set up a reasonably diversified portfolio with little as $10,000 or so divided among three or four stocks in major blue-chip companies.

Invest for the Long Term versus Churning

Most mutual funds tell you to invest for the long term. When you look at the long-term chart for a company such as Johnson & Johnson, you can see that there are indeed stocks that have done well year in and year out for many, many years. In all likelihood, such companies will continue to prosper, and their shares will continue to increase in value over the long term. It is not rocket science to find these stocks, and you don't need to own more than a handful of them to offset poor performance and losses from shares bought mistakenly.

Almost amazingly, the majority of fund managers totally fail to practice what they preach. Ironically, one of the buzzwords used to demonstrate prowess is that a fund is *actively traded*. In practice, this means that if the fund isn't changing its investments, its managers don't think that they are really working.

The industry-wide turnover for the U.S. mutual fund industry since 1997 is running at around 100 percent, up from 30 percent in 1977. This means that, on average, every fund turned over its entire portfolio every year. Looking at it another way, mutual funds themselves seldom hold any stock for longer than a year, whereas many stocks are bought and sold within a much shorter time. Since some funds—generally the better performing ones—hold stocks for many years, it follows that there are others that rotate their holdings constantly. Their managers are traders, not investors.

You can tell from a mutual fund's reports whether its turnover is high by seeing what the shareholding's cost is compared with its latest market value. Where there is a substantially lower book cost relative to the current market value, you can assume that the majority of the shares were bought some time ago at a good time and at a good price. When the recent price is about the same as cost, most likely the shares were bought recently—unless it is a share that has been stagnating for a long time, and then you don't know. Where there is a substantial loss relative to book value, as can happen, you can assume that the manager fails to live by the axiom recommended in this book—of letting profits run and cutting losses short.

Mutual Fund Management Fees

It is a real minefield trying to figure out what mutual funds really charge in the way of fees because the loads, management expense ratios, trailer fees, and exit fees come in such a complexity of combinations and flavors. One thing, however, is clear: One reason why funds generally have difficulty in even matching the performance of stock indexes is that their managers take so much off the top.

There are fund companies that charge very reasonable fees, and some of them have a reasonable record of performance. Notable is T. Rowe Price's Capital Appreciation Fund, already mentioned for its good performance during the bear market. Its returns to the end of 2004 have been 12.62 percent for 1 year, 12.35 percent for 3 years, 16.10 percent for 5 years, 13.59 percent for 10 years, and 13.08 percent from inception in 1986. Management fees run at a very moderate 0.62 percent plus other expenses of 0.21 percent, for a total of 0.83 percent. It is particularly notable that the Capital Appreciation Fund continued to make good money over the five years since the top of the bull market.

In addition, deserving mention is the market leader in low fund fees, the Vanguard Group. Few of its funds have had outstandingly good performance, but the results show good solid professional plodding over the long term. Vanguard's bond funds have really done quite well, charging management fees as low as 0.14 percent of assets! As the founder of Vanguard so rightly says, everything you pay in fees has to come out of what the investors make in the long term. Compound interest works against you, very markedly, when high fees chip away at the value of your investments.

Vanguard, Low Fees—
Axa's Alliance Capital, High Fees

According to data compiled by the Bloomberg news service, the Axa insurance company's Alliance Capital subsidiary charges among the highest stock fund fees in the industry, averaging about $20 annually per $1,000 invested. Many investors should be concerned about this disparity because Alliance is the world's third largest mutual fund company and Axa's annual reports say that they are aiming to be the world leader in money management. Vanguard Group's average annual fees, by contrast, are about $2.55. The industry average is $14. No, the decimal point is not in the wrong place—Alliance charges approximately eight times what Vanguard does! (The Securities and Exchange Commission and New York Attorney General Eliot Spitzer made Alliance pay the largest penalties ever imposed on a mutual fund company for defrauding investors—$250 million plus $350 million to rebate fees to fundholders, making a total of $600 million.) You might expect superior performance to account for higher fees, but tables published in *Barron's* show Alliance Capital a long way down the list of fund families in terms of overall performance.

Using the assumption in their prospectus, of 5 percent annual gains for a fund run by Alliance's parent company, the Axa Enterprise Multi-Manager Technology Fund expects to make $6,289 for the fundholder over 10 years. (It takes three different firms of advisors to do the cooking, and hence the *multi-manager!*) The company says that, on the basis of those 5 percent annual returns (which the company doesn't calculate for you), it expects to charge $6,762 in fees and expenses. Thus fees and expenses, on the company's own admission, are expected to exceed what the fundholder makes. This compares with 20 percent of net new profits (above each successively higher level and nothing for losses) that is the standard basis for paying hedge fund managers. Worse, the record shows that in 2002 the value of fund units declined by more than 40 percent, including the fees paid out for losing money. And in 2004 there was a 172 percent turnover of investments in the fund.

Entry and Exit Fees

A further problem with mutual funds is what you pay in entry or exit fees. Some funds are permitted to charge as much as 8.5 percent that is taken right off the top when you buy in. This means that for every dollar you invest, only 91.5 cents goes to work for you. In practice, few people pay that much of a sales commission, but a 5 percent deduction right off the top is relatively standard.

You may think that a no-load feature gets around the problem of the high entry fee. Not so! They take it off you in one of two ways or a combination of the two. A no-load fund almost always has higher management fees and expenses, partly to compensate for there being no front-end load. The second way they get it from you is with exit fees.

In practice, you generally pay appreciably less altogether if you gulp and pay the higher front-end commission.

The person who sells you a mutual fund is supposed to tell you what he or she gets paid for making the sale, but this is sometimes glossed over. At 5 percent on $200,000, the sales commission is, of course, $10,000. This puts the scale of commissions in the same league as what you pay in the United States for buying a house but for significantly less actual work. Over and above this, the seller may well get what is called a *trailer fee*. As long as you own the fund, there is a kickback each year paid to the selling agent.

The Need for Liquidity

Many mutual fund managers would have you believe that the great Benjamin Graham and David Dodd established the criteria that they and all investors should heed. Quite right, too! But they don't tell you that one of Graham and Dodd's foremost requirements for an investment is liquidity. You must be able to buy and sell and to do so at a reasonable cost—the very thing that mutual funds make difficult and sometimes also expensive.

However much it may be your intention to make a long-term investment, you take a risk when locking yourself into almost all mutual funds because of their onerous entry and exit fees. Even people with the most solidly based financial position can never know when some completely unexpected call for money can come out of the blue. However, most mutual funds don't come with an easy and economical exit. On the contrary, the fee structure is intentionally established so as to make it unattractive to get out. Many no-load funds have an exit fee that declines over a number of years, but you still have paid dearly over that duration. If you have paid an entry fee to get in, it is unlikely that you will be able to get back what you paid until some appreciable time later. As a best scenario, it will take a year's worth of 5 percent gain just to recover a 5 percent sales commission.

In theory, you can sell mutual funds almost immediately. However, a fund representative is almost certain to argue with you and try to talk you into staying the course for the long term. A mutual fund redeemed is almost certainly a trailer fee lost—in effect and as noted above, a delayed sales commission that is charged to the fund each year and constitutes the financial planner's pension.

In sum, if you want to get out after owning a mutual fund for a short time, there is a high probability that you will not be able to get out what you put in unless the fund has done very well indeed with the underlying investments. This, as already seen, is not something that you can count on.

Index Funds

Fund management companies have addressed the challenge of their collective failure to keep up with benchmark indexes by promoting funds that replicate those indexes. In doing so, they have been able to do away with research and have simply set about buying index stocks robotically. This approach has made it possible to reduce fees and expenses, which in some cases has been done substantially and in others only rather grudgingly.

There are several reasons for being cautious about index funds. You still have a structural problem with the cost of doing business. More serious, however, is that you are still wedded to the market whether you want to be or not when the indexes decline. Yes, it is true that in the long term the overall direction is upward. As we have seen in chapter 25, however, the indexes can go sideways for a very long time indeed—even for decades. If you buy at a bad time near a market high, the experience of owning an index fund is likely to be a prolonged agony.

A further problem with replication of an index is that, by definition, you are locked into the good, the bad, and the indifferent. In recent times, it should have been obvious that you would have not wanted to own such stocks as General Motors (GM), Eastman Kodak, and AT&T. GM is still in the Dow Jones Industrial Index, whereas Kodak and AT&T have, at last, been dropped. However, it was obvious before their departure that these stocks were extremely unattractive to own and that ownership of a Dow Jones Industrial Index fund would to that extent be an exercise in owning stocks that ranged between good and conspicuously bad.

Taxes on Mutual Funds

When you buy stocks for yourself, you are in control of your tax bill. Sell a stock that has made money, and you are responsible for paying any capital gains taxes that may apply. When you own a mutual fund, however, you may find yourself responsible for paying taxes on gains made within the mutual fund that you have never seen. Buy a fund toward the end of the year, and you join in paying tax on the gains made by other people. The industry has been taking steps to get around this cost and corresponding annoyance, but it is a problem that has not gone away. It is also a problem that you may well not be told about when you invest. The used car seller makes no special effort to point out the rust under the floor.

Choices Other Than Mutual Funds

The foremost thrust of this book is to show how an individual or a money manager can find and hold great stocks. If, as an individual and for whatever reasons, you don't want to do the job for yourself, there is another way to go if you have more than about $100,000 to invest and certainly if you have more than half a million. Go to a private portfolio manager who will construct a portfolio for your specific needs. There are many very good ones, and it is not unduly difficult to find them. For those having higher net worth, the major banks and brokerage houses have wealth management departments, although you may be better off with an independent firm that does nothing else than manage money. Just make sure that the person billed as a so-called financial advisor does more than sell mutual funds! You may not like the idea of parting with money the way you do when you pay your lawyer, but that is exactly what you need: fee for service. It comes cheap at the price compared with all the costs buried in most mutual funds.

Before you commit yourself, make sure that you get the track record at least from 2000. This should give you some idea of what to expect, and it is important to know how the advisor did during the general bear market.

If you have less than $100,000 and want help that is responsible and generally competent, you may want to find the nearest branch of the storefront broker Edward Jones. The only problem, which for most people should not be serious, is that this broker may forbid you to buy smaller, more speculative stocks if you get the notion to do so. From experience, this broker has found that this is simply not its business. If you want to buy more speculative stocks, you may have to open you own discount brokerage account and handle your account for yourself anyway.

What to Do If You Own Funds

If you own mutual funds, review what you have in terms of their past performance, their fees, and your own investment objectives. Some—just a few—really do earn their keep! However, it almost always pays to bite the bullet to get out of an underperforming high-fee mutual fund and to start again. The longer you keep a poor high-fee fund, the longer compound interest is working against you as compared with alternative investments carrying less dead weight. As a worst case, there are mutual funds that charge as much as 1.5 percent of assets (or more) to run a bond fund. If a pretax return on a high-quality bond is about 6 percent, this means that a quarter of the income goes to the fund manager. Imagine having a million dollars in a bond fund that is bringing $50,000 in income, but you are paying someone $12,500 to manage it. You won't get any useful advice from a fund manager as to whether you ought to own bonds at all, but assuming that you do, you can go to any reputable broker and buy them direct for a one-time cost of perhaps $1,000. Or buy Treasury bonds direct for no fee at all.

Closed-End Funds: The Best of All Worlds

As something of a footnote to the fund business, there is one area where you can come close to having your bread buttered on both sides, and that is with closed-end funds. You might think of them as existing in a specialized area off the beaten track, but their apparent lack of visibility does not detract from their merits.

A closed-end fund is like a mutual fund in that it is strictly an investment company whose business is to find and hold stocks or bonds, generally in some specialized area. They are listed separately in *Barron's,* where you can see the latest price as well as the current net asset value. There can be enormous swings in price between their having a substantial premium over net asset value and a substantial discount under net asset value. It seldom pays to buy when the premium is much more than about 10 percent and, in addition, the charts show an over-bought condition. However, a discount of 15 or 20 percent may offer some protection on the downside when the price is down, as well as offering the potential for the double benefit of an increase in the underlying asset value and elimination of the discount. As with most investments, there can be big fluctuations either side of the mean, which is parity with net asset value, and although discounts can last for a long time, they are seldom more than 10 percent for long.

Closed-end funds are particularly attractive for investing in overseas markets when the charts and the overall economic and financial situation are attractive, as they often are for quite long periods of time. The ordinary investor can seldom learn much about individual prospective investments in Brazil or India, say, but the managers of these funds generally know their stuff and put together a good portfolio. What may be taken out of the fund in moderately higher management fees may be well worth it if you buy when the charts are good and there is a good prospect of the stocks taking off. Sometimes these stocks can make some huge moves quite quickly. You buy and sell them through a broker in the ordinary way, and you use the buy and sell indicators described in this book. There is generally no problem getting in and out right away at a fair price.

Closed-end funds also exist for specialized areas such as biotech and corporate, municipal, and federal government bonds. Here too, what you may spend on management fees may well be worth it because you are committed to paying their management costs only for as long as you own the funds.

Heave a big sigh of relief that you are not locked in, by moral or financial pressure, through the bad times as well as the good!

How to Use Options

What an Option Is

Options are a specialized area of market operations and are suitable for relatively few people having the temperament and the capital to engage in this business. The nature of the business is generally oriented to the short term, which is contrary to what this book recommends as a normal approach to investment. Nevertheless, even for the most conservative investor, there can be a place for options occasionally, and it is useful to know how they work and what people do with them.

First, for those unfamiliar with options, this is what they do. A *call option* allows you to buy a stock at a fixed price some time in the future. Every optionable stock has a series of strike prices and expiry dates. Assume that it is January 1 and that you expect U.S. Widgets (USW), now trading at $95, to go to $130 by May. For $10, you can buy an option to buy USW at $100 any time up to the third Friday in May. If you expect to be receiving money in the future but don't have it in hand now, but you expect you want to own USW, you can buy a call option so that the price doesn't run away on you before your money arrives to pay for it. You pay more than you would have to pay if you bought now, but your money is not at risk, and you can change your mind if you want. The person who sold you the option carries the risk of the stock not going up, such as when an insurance company under-writes a policy, and your buying price is guaranteed if it does.

Options for Speculation

A call option may be used for speculation if you have no intention of buying the stock. If you buy a call option in USW and the stock goes up as expected, you can pocket the difference. In this example, if the stock does go to $130 by May, you make the difference between $100 and $130, or $30, minus the $10 you paid for the option and minus the two commissions. Your net profit, in round numbers, is $20 per share, or twice what you paid for the option.

An obvious problem with buying a call option on USW is that the stock has to go up by May. Options start losing value the moment you buy them, since the clock starts running against the expiry date. For the option buyer, being wrong on the timing is just as bad as being wrong on the stock. Either way, you lose money. An option seller who owns the stock merely has to sit back and hope that the stock does not fall in the meantime below the $85 breakeven level—the $95 price when the deal is done minus the $10 received for the option that is put in the bank.

Similarly, a *put option* allows you to sell a stock at the designated strike price. If you own a stock you know you want to continue to hold but you fear it may go down, you may buy a put option to protect your position. You might pay $5 for a put option having a strike price at the current price of $95—an *at-the-money* option. If nothing happens or the stock goes up, you lose the $5. If the stock goes down to $85, you can deliver the stock and collect $95 per share—the *strike price*—minus the $5 that you paid for the option. The result is the same as a sale at $90. Really useful protection kicks in if the stock goes down to $75. In this case, you can still sell the stock for $95, but you got $15 per share of real protection from the decline.

As with call options, a speculator can make money by buying put options if the price goes down. In the example earlier with USW, a put option with a $95 strike price bought for $5 makes four times what it cost if the stock goes down to $75, of which, of course, $5 is simply getting back the money you paid for the option.

Many speculators regard options as a means of making a lot of money quickly. A call option on USW makes a huge profit if the stock skyrockets from $95 to $130 or more. You make an immense profit if USW not only goes to $130 but keeps on going to $200. Then you make

10 times your money. You also make a huge profit by buying a put option if the stock plummets. However, these home runs happen relatively seldom, and in any case, the price of options on a volatile stock is high, just as insurance premiums are high on a high-risk policy.

Professionals and Conservative Investors Sell (Write) Options

It is mostly professionals and institutions such as pension funds that sell (or *write*) options. A mostly unwary and amateurish public buys them. It pays to be on the side of the professionals, the smart money, not the amateurs. (The exception is when someone in the know buys call options ahead of a takeover or the announcement of positive corporate news or buys a put option ahead of bad news. This is not supposed to be legal, but it happens. In any case, it is impossible to keep news of all corporate developments secret. Sometimes people close to a company can simply make an educated guess and be right.)

Large investors, institutions, and also conservative smaller investors may sell call options, knowing that they want to own the stock but, unlike the buyer, doubting that it will go up substantially over the near or intermediate term. If the stock stays around the same price and does not exceed the strike price at maturity, the seller just pockets the premium like an extra dividend. Then the seller can repeat the process. If the stock goes above the strike price, the buyer of the option may call for the shares and pay for them at the strike price. Using our example of USW, the stock that was selling at $95 when the call option was sold now has to be sold at $100. The option seller also keeps the money received for the sale of the option, so the effective selling price for the shares is $110, or $15 more than the market price when the option was sold.

For those in the business of writing call options, it's a business of sometimes having the stock called away and sometimes not. It's a steady bread-and-butter business that makes good money over time, particularly in a market trading sideways or with a slight upward tendency. In a roaring bull market or when a stock unexpectedly soars, the option writer forgoes a substantial profit. Then, however, the premium for selling the option in the first place was higher than it might otherwise have been. Options are priced on a supply-and-demand basis to reflect the expected volatility and the risk of forgoing the superior profit that the option buyer hopes to make.

A seller of covered calls runs the risk of forgoing a good profit if the stock goes strongly higher. It is relatively unlikely that an investor using market-timing techniques would want to sell options: you don't own a share unless you are expecting it to go up—if not, you don't own it. You can lose money if the stock goes down sharply and you don't sell it in good time. Pocketing a $10 premium provides protection against a decline to the breakeven level of $85, but the operation loses $10 per share if the stock goes down to $75.

Professionals Also Sell Put Options

Many money managers have a steady inflow of money to invest. They also have a list of stocks that they want to buy, and often a list of ones they want to buy cheaper than the current market price. A money manager may want to buy USW if it goes to $85 but not at the current price of $95. Selling a $90 strike-price put option for $5 brings the stock halfway to the desired buying price. If the stock stays above $90, the option seller simply keeps the $5. If the price goes to $90 and the option buyer puts or delivers the stock for payment, the effective cost is $85, represented by the $90 strike minus the $5 proceeds from the sale of the put option. The operation loses money if the stock goes below $85, in which case the stock could be bought cheaper still.

The Importance of Timing

In practice, few speculators make money on balance by buying options, but most professionals profit well by selling them. Emotion carries many speculators away so that they buy call options when a stock, or the general market, makes an upward surge, and they buy put options when there is a downward plunge. In the real world of stock market fluctuations, there are almost always rebounds from temporarily stretched swings up or down. Emotional money chases a stock and then runs out of firepower. Professionals are prepared to let them have what they want and then buy back at their leisure when the emotion-driven buying power dries up.

During a plunge, investors sell who feel a need to do so urgently. Then emotional selling ends, and a relatively small amount of buying permits the stock to bounce back. Some of the rebound may be fueled by those who sold the stock short at a higher price, expecting to be able to buy back at a lower price on just such a plunge and now succeeding in doing so. This is what the expression *short-covering* means.

The Contrary Opinion Approach

If the biggest risk in trading options is to pull the trigger at an extremity of enthusiasm when buying calls and at an extremity of pessimism when buying puts, it also follows that the biggest potential reward comes from doing the opposite of what seems, emotionally, to be what you want to do. This is where the approaches recommended in this book kick in. When there is a significant decline in a bull market and price does not violate a bull market designation, the selling will probably run its course, and the price will start going up again. In this case, there might then be a good opportunity to buy a call option.

Similarly, as discussed in Chapter 13, in October two years before the next presidential election, there may a prime opportunity to buy call options, especially if the monthly or weekly stochastics have reached a very low level, and the market is technically washed out. On balance, however, it may be better to wait to see whether the market or the individual stock shows at least tentative signs that it can stop going down. Otherwise, the washing out may have much farther to go, and the price that seemed cheap at the time turns out not to be nearly as cheap as it eventually gets. Obviously, the potential reward versus the outlay may be superb at such major turning points, and timing signals may enable you to catch some of them. There is the additional advantage that call options are usually quite cheap when everyone is rushing to sell or when investors are very pessimistic.

When attempting to catch the crest of a more long-lasting top, as at the top of the presidential cycle, it's foolhardy to try to catch the absolute top. Cresting action at a second or third top at a lower level than the one before, and ideally on lower volume, is much more likely to lead to a worthwhile decline within the life of the put option. Although it may seem as if the potential gain has gone out of the trade, there may be plenty left when buying a put option at the crest of a rally in an established bear market—as we saw with the opportunity to sell General Motors short that was illustrated in Chapter 21.

Sell Naked Options Against the Trend

There is another approach that gives the speculator a chance of beating the odds: Sell call options without owning the stock, the procedure called *selling naked options*. As when writing covered options, the returns are smaller than the home runs you can make by buying options that make big gains. However, the likelihood of making money consistently is more important than hitting home runs.

Sell naked call options on stocks that you expect to go sideways or down. When you expect a stock to go sideways or higher, sell naked put options. Make sure that you get this concept the right way around. Do not, ever under any circumstances, sell naked call options on a stock in a strong uptrend. This is a bet asking for trouble, an exercise in inviting financial suicide. As when selling a stock short, the probabilities are extremely unfavorable that you will ever catch the top of a market. Yes, you might be lucky and do it once or even a few times, but this still doesn't mean that the probabilities are on your side. Similarly, do not ever sell a put option on a stock in a strong downtrend.

To illustrate, you do not own any USW, now trading at $95. You expect the stock to continue going higher. Instead of buying a call option, you sell a put. You sell the $95 strike-price put option for $5 and put the money in your account. If the stock goes down instead of going higher, as you expected, and the buyer exercises the option, you have to buy the stock for $95. However, you already have $5 protection from the money you sold the option for. You lose money only if the stock goes below $90. If the stock stays above $95 by the option expiry date, the $5 stays in your account, and there is no more exposure to risk either.

Similarly, when USW is going sideways or down and trading at $95, sell a call option for $5 at the May $100 strike price. Here you lose money only if the stock goes above $105. If the stock does not exceed $100, you keep the $5, and after expiry, there is no more exposure to risk.

There are various strategies for protecting yourself from ruinous losses when selling naked options. If all you do is to sell a call option on USW for $10 with a strike price of $100, you can lose your shirt if the stock soars. You can protect yourself against disaster by *buying* a call option at a higher strike price, say, at $120. The $120 call option might cost you only $2. If the stock goes to exactly $120, you lose $10 on the difference in the stock price plus what you paid for the higher strike-price option, or a total of $12 per share. For every additional dollar the price rises above $120, you start making money on the call option that you bought for disaster insurance. Breakeven is at $132 for the stock, and you actually make money on further gains above that price.

In practice, there are two different approaches that work when selling naked options. If you have confidence in the trend, you can sell options that are close to the strike price and have a longer time to run. This approach ties in with market-timing techniques for buying stocks or selling them short. Then you can sell the naked options at a very good price, maximizing the amount of premiums coming into your account.

An alternative approach, more for short-term scalping but still with a reasonable prospect of success in the long run, is to sell naked options that have a strike price far out of the money and also have a short time to expiry. For example, it is May 1 and USW is selling at $95. With three weeks to run, you might sell the $110 call option for $2. The chance of the stock going past $110 is small. The reward may seem small too, but time is on your side, and the probabilities are favorable for simply keeping the option premium. It takes a major corporate development to move the stock so far in such a short time.

Responsible capital management is essential when writing naked options. It generally pays to budget for potential losses of about two to three times what you receive in premium. It also pays over the long term to accept smaller but more reliable returns than to risk more in the hope of making superior gains.

Because of the risk of a market accident, diversification is more important when writing options than it is when buying stocks. It is also important to deploy only a small proportion of your capital to this area of operations, if indeed you decide to do it at all. As with any investment approach, there are certain to be losses as well as gains. Occasionally, a stock may lunge against you on some completely unforeseeable corporate development. The option writer is in a position somewhat similar to an insurance company. You pocket premiums but you also have to pay off claims. Options writing, like writing insurance, can be a very good business in its own right. As with anything else, though, you have to know what you are doing, and this chapter gives only a few introductory insights into the use of options.

Market Myths

The Savings Myth

The investment industry spreads with indecent urgency the proposition on which its income and well-being depend, not yours. It is that you must save and save and start saving early. Only then can you expect to reap the benefits of compound interest and build a fortune. By saving regularly, you can make your dreams come true.

Saving is good, of course, and financial planning is essential. However, saving should not dominate your lifestyle, particularly when the first priority may be to provide for a young family. It is true that you need some money to invest. It is not true that you need a large amount to start. Far more important than how much you save is what you do with what you have.

There are almost always superior opportunities somewhere if you are patient and know what to look for—such as eBay and Johnson & Johnson. On the other hand, a dollar saved and invested badly can easily become a dollar lost.

The Myth of Corporate Profits

Contrary to popular belief, the real underlying rate of increase in corporate earnings has almost certainly not been what it seemed. Although it may seem that profits rebounded smartly in 2003–2004 after a brief recession, and furthermore to near-record levels, the problem remains for the future that profits in many industries may not be anywhere near as robust as they seem.

Much of the increase in corporate profits during the 1980s and 1990s occurred as a result of nonrecurring shifts. These included declining interest rates and lower corporate taxes. Corporations starting the 1980s with high-interest bank loans outstanding gained considerably from declining interest rates, with the benefit flowing immediately to profits. Savings from the extensive introduction of a new generation of cost-saving computer technology are not likely to continue their rapid enhancement of corporate profits in such industries as banking and telecommunications. There were substantial but nonrecurring savings from laying off personnel and rehiring on contract, often at a lower rate of pay and without the staggering cost of employment benefits.

A study in *Grant's Interest Rate Observer* (August 15, 1997) set out assumed true results for the 30 Dow stocks and several other major stocks, as opposed to their reported earnings. *Grant's* used operating income before taxes less any net interest expense and backed out non-recurring gains and losses. To neutralize the effect of share repurchases, the study used total dollars, not per-share results. On this basis, Kellogg delivered a 4.3 percent decline in sales and a 4.6 percent decline in earnings, not, as reported, a huge increase in sales and earnings. Coca-Cola, popularly thought to have an annual growth rate above 15 percent, had true sales growth of 0.4 percent and a decline of 3.7 percent in net earnings. The story was repeated almost across the board.

The average reported growth rate for corporate profits during the 1990s was 16 percent. This reported and to a significant extent mythical rate of gain in profits occurred in conjunction with a growth rate in sales of only 4 percent. It is mathematically impossible to sustain this divergence between the rate of gain in profits and that for sales. Profits can never reach 100 percent of sales.

Most real and substantial growth during the 1980s and 1990s was attributable to a very small percentage of the total corporate universe, and it was mostly concentrated in such areas as computer technology and pharmaceuticals. Even within apparent growth sectors, there were many companies that were stagnant or losing money. Since 2002, much of the apparent growth in corporate profits occurred in the energy sector. It also occurred in the banking industry where, however, profits may have been overstated because of seriously insufficient provision for loan losses.

No doubt the information technology business generally will continue to grow exponentially. However, there is no sector under more pressure to keep reinventing itself in order to stay alive and never mind to move forward. The surge in Apple Computer's fortunes that began in 2003 may be only as durable as the next successful business development. The same principle applies across the board, even for such titans as Microsoft. Some sectors in technology, such as chip-making, have become a commodity business like running buses.

In sum, one is entitled to be optimistic about human progress and the spread of a good life to more and more people. However, as with all human and industrial development, progress has tended to come in surges, and progress in the future is likely to be lumpy.

The Myth of Pension Profits

As suggested in the first edition of this book, during the 1990s, profits for many major corporations were overstated by booking gains on investments in pension funds. When a pension fund is already fully funded, it does not need those further contributions. Therefore, money that would otherwise have gone into the pension fund was booked as profit. When, however, there is a deficit, supplementary payments into the pension fund have to come out of profits.

Pensions are generally paid at a predetermined rate. There is seldom provision for major increases in benefits in the event that the pension fund achieves conspicuously good returns on the fund's investments. Nor are pensions normally reduced after a period of conspicuously bad returns. The company reaps the benefit if the fund is actuarially overfunded. It has the obligation to make up the difference if the pension plan is underfunded.

During the great bull market, many pension funds were invested successfully enough to achieve big surpluses. Since its plan was fully funded, General Electric (GE), for example, was able to stop making contributions to its corporate plan after 1987. At the end of 1997, GE's pension fund had a market value of $38.7 billion, after achieving a return on its investments that year of almost 20 percent. The result was that GE could book $743 million as income that otherwise might have had to be paid into the pension fund and charged against profits accordingly. This gain boosted GE's profits by 6.7 percent. For the first half of 1998, Northrop Grumman reported net pension credits equal to 29 percent of operating income. With numbers like this, investors have to be concerned about the true source of profits and whether they come from operations or from pension fund investments.

Most companies project pension fund returns of between 8 and 10 percent, or about the long-term historic norm for the return on stocks. When portfolios were increasing at 15 or 20 percent each year during the great bull market, those projections looked conservative. However, returns for some pension funds turned negative after 2000, and even with the recovery into 2005, rates of return had fallen sharply. In the future, a return over the long term closer to 5 percent may be all that pension fund managers can count on.

General Motors (GM) provides a prime example of the impact of declining pension fund returns. Its large cohort of retired workers, its pension fund obligations, and especially also its health fund obligations are so immense as to jeopardize the future of the company. Some major corporations such as Bethlehem Steel (once a Dow stock) went through a bankruptcy that shed its pension obligations and permitted a return to apparent prosperity. The Pension Benefit Guaranty Corporation (PBGC) picked up responsibility for pensions for the company's 95,000 workers. Fine for them, but there are only so many Bethlehems that PBGC can bail out before running out of money, and so many is not many. Bethlehem's pension fund was 45 percent underfunded, and this company alone needed $3.5 billion to keep it afloat.

The pension fund challenge is much more serious for long-established corporations such as GM than it is for relative newcomers such as the U.S. operations of Toyota or for information technology companies. With a different pension fund structure and having few retired workers to support, they enjoy a major competitive advantage—for a time.

The Myth of Corporate Buybacks

There is a myth that a corporate stock buyback is always good for shareholders. In a bull market, the initial reaction to the announcement of a stock buyback is almost always positive. But what does a buyback really mean?

In the short run, a buyback means that fewer stockholders own the same company, so there is more value in the stock. Or is there? A buyback means that fewer stockholders own a smaller company. The value of corporate assets is reduced by an amount exactly equal to what is spent on buying back stock, as it is when a dividend is paid. When a company buys back its own shares, there will normally be an increase in earnings per share for the remaining shareholders, assuming that the company is earning more on its shareholders' equity than it earns on surplus cash. This may be a good thing if the cash is really surplus to requirements for the operations of the business, and in addition there continues to be the same or a higher level of earnings in the future. Nevertheless, buying back shares reduces the margin of safety comprised in the company's balance sheet. It also has the obvious effect of reducing the value of the company as a takeover target for any company looking to buy it for its balance sheet as much as for its earnings.

There is a case for a company to buy stock back if that is an inherently profitable thing to do. If it buys stock at a price below the replacement value of the underlying assets, that should be good for stockholders. It should also be a good deal if the company can buy back its stock so as to earn 15 percent or more on corporate equity. In most cases, companies buying back stock at an earnings multiple greater than about eight are playing with smoke and mirrors. Dividends alone provide the proof that a company is really earning its keep over the long term. A sustained and, ideally, rising rate of dividend payout provides a wonderful, if only partial, support for the stock price in a general bear market.

Corporate stock buybacks occur when business conditions are good and stock prices are high. But what happens if there is a recession, profits are declining instead of rising, and the stock price falls? Many a company buys back stock only to find that it needs the money after all. The case of IBM in the early 1980s is typical. Having parted with its cash to buy back stock, it had to sell bonds at an exorbitant rate of interest when it needed money. For a time, there was no return at all on the money invested in the stock bought back.

A stock buyback weakens a company unless the return on the investment is both immediate and high. If these conditions are not met by a company whose stock you own, review whether you want to continue owning the stock in a weaker company. Any rise in the stock price spurred by the buyback program could well provide a prime opportunity to sell stock. On the other hand, a buyback at four or five times earnings should in due course strengthen the company and lead to a higher stock price. It's almost certain to be a good buy when, in addition, price action is favorable.

The rise in price on the announcement of a stock buyback may be outright damaging to shareholders. When, in the 1990s, IBM announced a buyback of $850 million of its own stock, the share price went from the $120 level to the $160 level, increasing the market value of the company by—yes, that's right—$850 million. The announcement of the intended buyback had the effect of raising the price in a bidding war against itself.

If a buyback program pushes the price of a stock higher only temporarily and then it falls back, clearly stockholders are worse off. It is the same as if you yourself bought the stock high and then saw the price fall. You as a shareholder and the company that you own as shareholder have an exactly interchangeable interest in the price paid for stock.

The Myth of Cost-Free Stock Options

Although progress is happening with the expensing of stock options, the overstatement of profits still seemed to be a problem in 2005. Reported corporate profits may be mythical to the extent that employees are paid with stock options instead of money when their true cost is not charged against profits. The cost of paying employees with stock options comes at a cost to shareholders that is insufficiently recognized and in some cases is huge. At first sight, there is no cost to existing shareholders when employees are granted stock options. There is no charge against profits for the options' value as there is with a paycheck. The cost to shareholders, however, is real. It comes directly at their expense by diluting their interest in the company by an amount exactly equal to the value of the option granted.

The stock market generally pays no heed to the grant of a stock option because the granting of individual options is generally imper- ceptible. Collectively, however, stock options can amount to real money over time. The shareholder has a smaller investment in the company as surely as when a dividend is paid out of the corporate treasury. In recent years, it has been estimated that reported profits for the stocks in the Standard & Poor's (S&P) 500 Index really should be adjusted downward by 10 percent to provide for employees receiving stocks, and for some companies such as the immensely successful Adobe Systems, this is long overdue. Adobe's business is wonderful, but too much profit flows surreptitiously to employees and not enough to shareholders.

The Myth of Defensive Stocks

Contrary to popular belief, for all practical purposes, there are few stocks, or none, to own when the general direction of the market is down, and it generally pays, as it did in 2000, to sell everything or almost everything until it can be seen whether there really are any special situations. As a general principle, the odds are against finding stocks on the general list that will fight the trend in a general bear market. The reason for selling all stocks at an obvious top such as the one in 2000 is that when investors have to sell stocks, they sell all the stocks they can because some stocks become unsalable at any price.

This is generally the case, in a bear market, and as it was after the crash in 1929. Between 2000 and 2003 was a great time to own top-quality bonds, meaning for the most part Treasury bonds, until it was clear that the entire economy was not going into depression.

The Market Fuel Myth

There is a popular myth that savings drive the market. Curiously, this appears to be wrong. It is more accurate to say that during the 1990s, stocks went up because stocks went up. Rising stock markets did people's saving for them. The imbalance that tips toward the buy side mostly occurs as a result of buying fueled by credit, not by new saving, and credit comes, of course, from the Fed. Insofar as accurate numbers exist (which is a problem), in 1997, the U.S. savings rate was 3.85 percent of disposable income, the lowest in 58 years. By 2004, the savings rate had appeared to decline almost to zero. In boom times, people do not save; they spend. This spending makes the boom that makes the pony go.

As discussed in Chapter 23, the big worry about a huge spending boom in parallel with a huge asset inflation is what happens in recessions and depressions. Then people save. The harder the times, the more they save. They believe that they have to, and generally, they are right.

The Winning Attitude

The Psychological Challenge of Success

Success is as much a psychological challenge as it is a practical one. For a winning attitude, it is not enough to say that you want to be successful. Everyone wants to be successful. The question is whether you are prepared to do the things to be successful. To achieve success, you have to ask yourself some questions:

- Am I prepared to learn thoroughly the techniques proven to make money in the stock market?

- Am I prepared to follow signals and to respond to them as readily as I respond to traffic lights when driving a car?

- Will I manage my capital responsibly and not expose it to undue risk, or will I cheat and overload the wagon when an opportunity appears to offer all the chance of gain and none of loss?

- Will I do the homework regularly to keep on top of my investments and the technical action in the market?

Few people can be expected to give a totally unhedged answer to all these questions. Fortunately, perfection is by no means necessary for success. However, success is likely to be, at least to some extent, proportional to the quality of the work done to that end. One way of preparing yourself psychologically for the challenge of successful investing is to guard against the following seven deadly sins of investment.

Sins to Avoid

1. Impatience

Impatience afflicts most people some of the time and some people all the time. You see what looks like a great stock to buy shaping up, and you are tempted to jump the gun on a signal. You hope to get in at a good price, only to see the price get "better" by going lower or to see the stock going sideways interminably. Many people have bought General Motors or Homestake at a good price over a period of several decades.

It is all too easy to be impatient about banking a good profit and doing so prematurely. Great stocks often go far higher than ever seemed possible at the beginning. However, you have only to look at a chart for Microsoft to see the merits of patience. There have been times when the stock did nothing for many months on end, sometimes even for a couple of years or more. Investing for the long term is the right thing to do when a stock and the underlying company represented by the stock continue to perform well. One partial cure for impatience is to look at the rate at which a long-term moving average or a long-term trendline is going up. Then you can make a tentative extrapolation of how patience—and holding a stock—will pay off in the long term.

It is human nature to want to bank a profit "while it is there." Many, many investors are neurotic when making money. They feel constantly challenged by the need to make a decision about whether to take their profit in case what went up comes back down. For a pastime, brokers like to call their clients and invite them to bank profits, or at least to bank half. Unfortunately, this is often the worst thing to do. Time and again the profitable stock that you sell is the one that goes on to make huge profits. Then you have to start all over again, looking for the next stock in which to invest the proceeds. Not only should you be wary of selling, but the best place for new money may be the stock you already own.

2. Fear

Many investors are afraid to buy the strongest stocks and to act on strong signals. It is hard to believe at the time that the stock that moves most strongly out of a consolidation is the one least likely to look back.

However, what goes up does not necessarily come back down. The likelihood of it coming back down is actually in inverse proportion to the strength of the launch.

The remedy for the fear of taking a strong signal is not to miss buying the stock. It is to buy only as much of the stock as you can sensibly afford to buy if you get stopped out at the initial protective stop.

When deciding whether the risk is manageable, remember that there will always be other opportunities, and remember too the futures trader's saying: *Never trade scared money!* This does not mean that you should refrain from taking calculated risks but that you should truly make the calculations in relation to your emotional and financial capital. For many people, it really is psychologically difficult to set aside emotions and to be objective. You should be able to treat real money like Monopoly money. If you let the importance of money trouble you, it becomes very difficult to make good decisions. Inevitably, the psychological pressure to succeed leads to poor decisions. The remedy for psychological challenges is to sell down to your sleeping level. If either a bad loss or a big profit affects your emotions, you probably have too much money in the market.

There is a saying about fear that may be helpful. Let's say that you find yourself deciding whether to buy a stock that has just delivered a conspicuously powerful signal. You previously sold out the stock at a much lower price. You now fear that the new signal may be an exhaustion move rather than the start of a major new leg up. Remember the saying: *Fear can be overcome effectively by the repetition of acts of courage!*

3. Greed

Many investors buy more stock than they can afford, either with their financial or their emotional capital. They set aside fear and reasonable caution and go in deeper than they should. The surefire stock often turns out to be no such thing. Joe Granville has a saying worth remembering: "If it's obvious, it's obviously wrong." What this often means is that if an opportunity is obvious, then everyone wanting to exploit the apparent opportunity may already have done so.

Greed leads many people to buy more stocks on margin than they can carry through routine market fluctuations. It is all too easy to buy at highs using all the available margin. On a retracement, you get a margin call that necessitates selling some or all of the stock bought high. However, this is likely where you should be buying more, not selling out. Greedy use of margin can double losses instead of doubling profits.

Greed also leads many people to stay with a stock that has run its course. You look at what you might once have sold a stock for, one such as Nortel. You say to yourself, "I can't sell it at only $60. I'll wait for it to go back to $80 again. Then I'll sell it." The problem is that instead of going back to $80, it goes down to $30, and then $15, and then $5.

Ideally, a great stock should be forever. Many people agree about this. Forever, however, practically never happens. You must have the discipline to accept that every move in a stock has a beginning, a middle, and an end. All that you can expect is to take a piece out of the middle. When you score a bull's-eye like Microsoft, it is all middle, and the beginning and the end are barely perceptible.

One of the surest ways of being successful in the stock market, and in any business, is to keep aside capital for a rainy day or for new opportunities. This is the opposite of buying all the stocks you can on margin. The main thing is to remember how much money you can make when you are right.

4. Hope

Investors fall back on hope when the technical case turns against a stock. Hope is an abdication of control, and it seldom works. It is easier to wait for tomorrow than to make a decision today. However, the delay can cost you money. The longer you wait with a market going against you, the more likely it is that hope will prove ruinously costly. When a stock goes up, a trend in force is likely to remain in force. The same applies when a stock turns down.

You sometimes hear it said of a stock that it's too late to sell, too early to buy, but not too late to pray. If you find yourself even thinking of praying about a stock, the chances are that you should not own it.

Reliance on hope is like reliance on luck. There will always be unforeseeable events that can be attributed to good or bad luck. In the long run, however, good luck comes to people already doing the right things.

5. Pride

Pride assails investors who believe that their intelligence and personality are superior to the market or to a systematic approach to buying and selling stocks. Many otherwise successful people bring to the stock market the attitude of the conquering hero. Successful experience in wrestling with knotty problems can lead to false conclusions about markets. There is no point in perceiving value if the market disagrees and sellers dominate. There is no point in arguing with the ludicrously high price of a stock by selling short if other investors keep on buying it.

The power of the mind over markets is no contest when there is a conflict. Markets always win.

6. Carelessness

After a big success or a big loss, depending on your personality, it is easy to get sloppy about doing your homework. Monitor your actions carefully after both a big win and a big loss. You may find that what looked easy last time just does not work the next time or the time after. Carelessness may lead to failure to do homework thoroughly or cause you to overlook new variables. Yes, luck is a factor, but it is no substitute for thoroughness.

Sometimes people seem to have runs when they do very well or very badly. Often these runs are an expression of underlying optimism or negativity. It is much easier to take a strong signal when confidence is up after recently making money. It is much harder to take a strong signal when you just took a bath in a stock that collapsed.

7. Gambling

Some people regard the stock market as a substitute for Las Vegas. These people buy into the myth of the high roller, those hugely successful investors whose names are household words. Almost all famous investors become famous by venturing money when the probabilities are overwhelmingly favorable. They refrain from doing so when the probabilities are not with them. Speculation in the true sense of the word means looking ahead. It does not mean gambling. Gambling means taking chances when the probabilities are not in your favor.

The other side of the challenge of staying with winners is what to do about losers. Staying with losers is generally an exercise in gambling. The probabilities most likely have turned against your stock, and responsibility has passed from you to the whims of the market.

Remarkable as it may seem, some people are comfortable only when losing money, whether in Las Vegas or in the market. Getting ahead feeds on a neurosis, the fear of letting the profit slip. There is a constant nagging requirement to confront the decision of whether or not to sell, to take a profit "while it is there." For many people, decision making is a process more painful than losing money. If you are in the market "for the long term," holding a losing stock means that there is no requirement to make a decision.

No doubt you have met people who deny their losses totally. Their loss is a loss only when they sell. Assume that you bought Nortel at $80 and that it is now trading at $3. You had better believe that you lost money! No doubt, too, you have found that the same people who deny their losses are not similarly slow to bank their profits. They run their losses and cut their profits off at the knees, the opposite of what is required for success.

There is one even more devastating gambler's loser play than the inability to make the decision to stay with winners and to heave out losers. It is the siren song of the mutual fund salesperson who says that you should "average down." Buy more in a declining market, and you lower your average cost. Then you make twice as much money when the market goes back up. The logical outcome of many an addition to losing stocks is that you lose twice as much money if the market continues to fall. If you are ever tempted to average down, remember the futures trader's imperative: *Never add to a losing position!*

Adding to a losing position gets you two ways. First, it truly increases the probability of adding to a loss. The second way that adding to a losing position gets you into trouble is that it doubles the psychological difficulty of facing up to the loss and of doing something about it by getting out.

Capital Should Be Forever

Make Money and Also Keep It

Capital once made should be for generations. Some fortunes have remained intact for centuries, but not many, and many of those have remained intact by investing, through thick and thin, in real estate, which is the one area that has always come back, except where it has been taken over by the state. Sometimes the money has simply been spent or gambled away. Nevertheless, many great fortunes have gone down the drain because of poor investment management and disasters that should have been avoided. This book is about making money by investing in the stock market. Equally important, as the recent bear market has shown, this book shows how to keep it by getting out of investments that have run their course.

Without using a proven methodology both for buying stocks and for selling them, it is more difficult than is generally believed to keep a fortune intact with stock market investments.

A buy-and-hold strategy is likely to fail if you invest in almost any area long enough. It used to be that you could invest in British government bonds forever. Forever lasted from 1660 to 1946, which is almost three centuries. Then they became almost worthless. In recent times it was hard to beat the apparent blue-chip quality of such stocks as Enron, Montana Power, and Nortel. Nortel staggers on as a shadow of its former glory, whereas the others were reduced to wallpaper. The number of companies that have been in existence and that also have prospered for more than a century is miniscule. Even some companies that have been around for a long time may not necessarily have stocks that are worth buying. The Hudson's Bay Company, chartered in 1670, has been a three-hundred-year recovery story that never really worked, and it fumbles along as a potential takeover target.

The price of financial freedom, like that of personal liberty, is eternal vigilance.

His publishers told Gerald Loeb that they did not like his proposed title, *The Battle for Investment Survival.* They said it was too negative for the book to sell. Loeb insisted that investing in the stock market, let alone making and keeping money over the long term, really is a battle for survival. The public should not be misled into thinking otherwise. Loeb's title was accepted. Published in 1936, his book was written with the wisdom of looking back over the best of times as well as the worst of times. Loeb knew well from recent personal observation and participation that a bull market leads to a bear market. Then a bear market leads to the next bull market, and so on, ad infinitum: Slump follows boom as night follows day, and as the earth goes around the sun, so the cycle rotates. The title of Loeb's book, like the book itself, stands the test of time.

There Are Times to Stand Aside

One of the hardest things for many investors and money managers to accept is the wisdom of the saying: You don't have to be in the market all the time! Money burns a hole in the pockets of most people. The question is automatic: Where should I invest my money? Ask most people this question in the 1990s, especially stockbrokers and fund managers, and the only answer was, "Put it into stocks!" or "Buy mutual funds!"

It is worth recalling that this was not the standard answer in the late 1970s and early 1980s. Almost no one then was saying you should buy stocks (when the Dow sold at seven or eight times depressed earnings). They did not say to buy bonds (when long-term Treasuries sold on a yield basis of 14 percent). There were, of course, a few wise stockbrokers and advisors, but it took years for the general public to wade into stocks up to their armpits and in some cases over their heads.

Gerald Loeb was one of the most successful investors of all time because he recognized that he had to keep cash reserves, however wonderful the opportunities in the market. He knew that there would always be new opportunities and probably better ones. He knew that he could profit from those new opportunities only with cash on hand. When fully invested, let alone when heavily committed on margin with borrowed money, you do not have cash on hand.

The Paradox of Cash

Cash is most valuable when you most want to part with it, and when you most want to part with it, the risk is high that you will be doing so foolishly. Cash never seemed to be more valuable than in the early 1980s, when you could get 20 percent from Treasury bills. That, of course, was the prime time to buy stocks and bonds and to part with cash. The immediate yield was half or less what you could get on 90-day money. However, very high interest rates could not be expected to last, and they did not. Investment in stocks and bonds, although offering a much lower immediate return at the time, delivered long-term gains. Stocks, with the expectation of increasing dividends over time, could be expected to pay more income in due course. The return on money market and Treasury bills or, worse, mortgages and investment certificates could only go down, and it did, with lower rates paid on each renewal.

In 1999, the last thing most people wanted was cash—they wanted stocks. In some cases, they wanted stocks and stock mutual funds so much that they borrowed, and even mortgaged their houses, to buy more stocks than they could pay for.

When the bear market got under way, cash became increasingly attractive as compared with stocks, but it was difficult to sell stocks that were underwater. "They must come back if I hang on" were words often heard. Of course, what stocks *must* do and what many actually did were by no means the same thing. When interest rates finally declined to their low at 1 percent, it was fantastic to own cash even though the return was close to zero. With that cash, you could then buy stock again at bargain-basement prices.

The Best Decisions Are Often Difficult

Another paradox of investing is that the hardest thing to do psychologically is often the most necessary thing to do. Even with the best methodology in the world for buying or selling, it is still a psychological challenge to pull the trigger. It is genuinely hard to buy into a runaway market and to stay in for as long as it lasts. It is also hard to keep a cash reserve when all about you are proclaiming the wonders of a "new era" or a "paradigm shift." It is equally hard to believe that stocks have a future when all is gloom and doom. It was hard to sell stocks in January 2000 but all too easy to sell them at the bottom in October 2002.

There is always a trade-off between following a trend and going against collective wisdom. Both are right some of the time. However, you must always be aware of the potential for disaster when no one considers disaster possible. Charles Mackay summed up the challenge succinctly in 1841 in his book, *Extraordinary Popular Delusions and the Madness of Crowds:* "Men, it has been well said, think in herds; it will be seen that they go mad in herds, while they only recover their senses slowly, and one by one."

Buy the Strong, Sell the Weak

Always buy the strongest stock in the strongest group when there are signals to do so, and sell the weakest stock in the weakest group. Buy Dell, not Hewlett-Packard, let alone Gateway.

Think of stocks as a car dealer thinks of inventory. When black cars are selling well and yellow ones are not, the dealer does not buy more yellow ones. Price is irrelevant. If the public does not want yellow cars, there is no point in arguing with the market, even if you can buy yellow cars at a discount. Yellow cars cost money waiting for buyers. It is best to get rid of them as soon as possible and at any price you can. Holding a stock and waiting for other investors to show an interest by buying amounts to the same thing.

There is always a trade-off between giving a stock room to move and getting out quickly to bank a small profit or keep a small loss small. Keeping losses small is important, of course, but you have to give some latitude to a stock with strong confirming signals for the big picture. There is almost never a case for taking a profit prematurely. A trend in force is likely to remain in force. Stock market trends can go on so far beyond what seems remotely imaginable that they should not be abandoned lightly, especially not in the absence of signals. Unavoidably, market timing techniques will sometimes get you out of a stock too early or into a stock too late. This is not the point. The point is that you are working with probabilities. You have only to be successful in finding a few great stocks among the ones you buy. Under the best of circumstances, you can hold a great stock for several years. Then those that make huge gains should make far, far more than the losers lose.

Attempting to buy near absolute bottoms and to sell near absolute tops is one of the worst loser plays. You can do it successfully so seldom that the effort of trying to do it is certain to be counterproductive. It is enough to take a piece from a middle that starts with an entry signal and ends with an exit signal or an exit with the stop.

Taking Losses

One of the hardest things of all for many investors is to take a loss when it is timely to do so. In the abstract, it is easy to see the car dealer selling off yellow cars at a discount. However, it can be very difficult for some people, even for most people, to admit a mistake when it comes to selling out a losing stock. There is always the temptation to hang on in the expectation that in due course it will come back. This is the all-time worst-of-all loser play. Count on a loss getting worse. Sometimes it goes on getting worse until the last possible moment when you and many others throw in the towel at the extremity of the move. This is how climactic market bottoms are made. However, not all stocks come back.

In his book, *The Education of a Speculator*, Victor Niederhoffer recalls how the beneficiary of a legacy in the 1930s handled an inheritance of stocks. All those selling above their cost price were sold. All those selling below their cost price were retained. As might have been predicted by a streetsmart investor, all the stocks that were sold subsequently went up, sometimes by many times. None of the ones retained went up, and most of them became worthless.

Heed the saying: *Remember how much money you can make when you are right!* Put the loss in this perspective and take it when it is manageable. You are unlikely to go broke by taking a loss—when you can afford to take it.

In the final analysis, successful investment comprises the art of being wrong. If you master the art of being wrong, of admitting mistakes and taking remedial action, success is not difficult to achieve.

Use Stops

Stops are an essential tool for implementing the art of being wrong. They are an invaluable defense against unexpected market action and a means of enforcing the discipline required to conserve capital.

There is never any excuse for failing to place a stop somewhere, if only for disaster insurance. Stops do not diminish the need for the discipline of reviewing stocks regularly, of selling underperforming stocks, and of upgrading the portfolio. Nevertheless, it is better to rely on stops as the only means of getting out than it is to stay in a stock forever, without regard to what it is doing.

Sometimes You Have to Pay Taxes!

One reason for the immensity of the bull market of the 1990s was the reluctance of investors to pay capital gains tax as a result of selling stocks in which they had big profits. This reasoning appears to have contributed to the extremely high price of stocks expected to do well for eternity.

For some people, it is, of course, difficult to sell a great stock that has multiplied by many times. It may continue to multiply by many times more. If you sell, you may suffer three times over. You may get left behind as the stock continues rising. A big chunk disappears while the technicals are developing to tell you that it should be sold. In addition, a big chunk of capital disappears into the maw of the tax collector.

These concerns are legitimate. However, their legitimacy is not so complete that they should overrule prudent investment timing. There is a serious risk that the excess on the upside caused by tax considerations may have an equal and opposite effect when the bull market finally unravels.

The best attitude toward taxes is to be pleased to have the good fortune that necessitates paying them. The widespread paranoia about avoiding taxes can be counterproductive when there are secular changes in market psychology.

The Foremost Rule: Preserve Capital!

There is nothing more important than conserving your capital. Money not made is but an opportunity cost, but losses lose real money. As long as you have money, you always can find opportunities. Without money, opportunity is worthless.

The remedy for conserving capital value overall is not to avoid putting money at risk in stocks. On the contrary, failure to put money at risk in stocks when it is timely to do so may be a greater risk than not investing at all. However, it is essential to keep a substantial reserve to allow for things that go wrong and for new opportunities or unforeseen requirements. You should be able to sleep equally soundly whether you have a spectacular success in the market or an unwelcome large loss.

Contrary to most popular wisdom in the investment business, there is less merit in widespread diversification than is commonly believed. Some of the biggest and most successful investors trade as few as a half dozen stocks—but what stocks they are when they do trade!

Take time, be patient, and remember the saying: "A fool and his money are soon parted." With any reasonable measure of luck, this book should help to impart some wisdom and to dispel some folly. However, remember also these words of caution: *Good luck comes to those already doing the right things!*

Index

About the Author

Colin Alexander retired in 2000 after 10 years of publishing *The Five Star Bulletin,* a popular advisory service for futures traders. This service was consistently rated in the top 10 by *Commodity Traders Consumers Report.* In 1998, he launched the successful stockscom.com advisory service for buying stocks and selling stocks short. He sold the service at the end of 2000, soon after telling subscribers to sell all stocks except the oils in September and telling them repeatedly for the rest of the year, "It's not too late to sell!" Mr. Alexander is author of several trading books, including *Capturing Full-Trend Profits in the Commodity Futures Market* and the widely acclaimed *Five Star Futures Trades.*